The One Show 1983

Hawley & Matthews Inc.
MARKETING/ADVERTISING/PUBLIC RELATIONS

The One Show

Judged To Be Advertising's Best
Print, Radio, TV

Volume 5

A Presentation of
The One Club for Art and Copy

Published by
American Showcase, Inc.
New York

The One Club
For Art and Copy

Len Sirowitz
PRESIDENT

Bill Weinstein
CHAIRMAN, PUBLICATIONS COMMITTEE

Beverley Daniels
DIRECTOR

Pat Reilly
DIRECTOR'S ASSISTANT

American Showcase

Ira Shapiro
PRESIDENT AND PUBLISHER

Christopher Curtis
DIRECTOR OF MARKETING
AND NEW PROJECTS

Fiona L'Estrange
PRODUCTION MANAGER

Chuck Novotny
BOOK SALES MANAGER

Seymour Chwast and Michael Aron
Pushpin Lubalin Peckolick Inc., New York
DESIGNERS

Terry Berkowitz, New York
LAYOUT AND PRODUCTION

Elise Sachs
EDITORIAL COORDINATION AND INDEX

Sunlight Graphics, New York
TYPESETTING

Dai Nippon Printing Co., Ltd., Tokyo, Japan
COLOR SEPARATIONS, PRINTING AND BINDING

PUBLISHED BY
American Showcase, Inc.
724 Fifth Avenue, 10th Floor
New York, New York 10019
(212) 245-0981

IN ASSOCIATION WITH
The One Club for Art and Copy, Inc.
251 East 50th Street
New York, New York 10022
(212) 935-0121

U.S. BOOK DISTRIBUTION:
Robert Silver Associates
95 Madison Avenue
New York, New York 10016
(212) 686-5630

OVERSEAS BOOK DISTRIBUTION:
American Showcase, Inc.
724 Fifth Avenue, 10th Floor
New York, New York 10019
(212) 245-0981

First Printing.
ISBN 0-960-2628-5-7
ISSN 0 273-2033

Contents

The Board
of Directors

President's Message

I can say with great pride that the One Show Annual is rapidly becoming *the* definitive text on creativity in advertising. It's no longer just found on art directors' and copywriters' bookshelves. It is cropping up in the libraries of art colleges and in the advertising class-rooms at universities around the country.

The reason is quite obvious. The Annual is a permanent record of our One Show. And our One Show is considered more and more to be the most prestigious awards show in the advertising industry. The reason? Simply, because of the One Show's high standards in the selection of the winners. That selectivity is accomplished by the quality of the judges themselves. It is our firm belief that the most demanding judges of advertising are those who create it well themselves. So the One Show is judged only by creative leaders in our business. Those talented art directors and copy-writers who have walked off with their own fair share of awards throughout their careers.

That's why winning a One Show Award is a truly important achievement. One in which the winners can take great personal pride. And for those whose efforts have not yet been recognized, may this book serve as an inspiration and a challenge "to knock our socks off!" next year.

My enthusiastic congratulations to all the winners whose work is honored on the following pages and recorded for posterity in this year's "better than ever" One Show Annual.

Len Sirowitz

Judges Panel

Jim Aaby
Wells, Rich, Greene

Hy Abady
Calet, Hirsch, Kurnit & Spector

Dominic Algieri
Albert Frank Guenther Law

David R. Altman
Altman, Stoller, Weiss

Hal Altman
Avrett, Free & Ginsberg

David Altschiller
Altschiller, Reitzfeld, Solin/NCK

Larry Anderson
Cunningham & Walsh

Anthony Angotti
Ammirati & Puris

Raymond Arrone
Venet Advertising

John G. Avrett
Avrett, Free & Ginsberg

Ellen Azorin
Geers Gross

Allan Beaver
Levine, Huntley, Schmidt & Beaver

Stanley Becker
Dancer Fitzgerald Sample

Norman Berry
Ogilvy & Mather

Stan Block
Della Femina, Travisano & Partners

Jack Bloom
Freelance Designer

Burt Blum
Rosenfeld, Sirowitz & Lawson

Francesca Blumenthal
Waring & LaRosa

John Blumenthal
Benton & Bowles

Ernie Bragin
Creamer

Walter Burek
N W Ayer

Barbara Burr
Cunningham & Walsh

Larry Cadman
Scali, McCabe, Sloves

Ed Caffrey
Benton & Bowles

Neil Calet
Calet, Hirsch, Kurnit & Spector

Rocco Campanelli
David Deutsch Associates

Mike Caplan
Shaller Rubin Associates

Elaine Charney
Cunningham & Walsh

Jay Chiat
Chiat/Day

David E. Clark
Backer & Spielvogel

Mary Jo Clayton
Benton & Bowles

Carole Cohn
Wells, Rich, Greene

Bob Cole
Laurence, Charles & Free

Diane Cooney
Sudler & Hennessey

Neil Costa
Campbell-Ewald

Dean C. Crebbin
Cunningham & Walsh

John Cross
Compton Advertising

Patrick J. Cunningham
N W Ayer

David Curtis
Leber Katz Partners

Ed Davitian
Bozell & Jacobs

Frank DeFilipo
N W Ayer

Chuck Dickinson
Cunningham & Walsh

Frank DiGiacomo
Della Femina, Travisano & Partners

Bob Dion
Chiat/Day

John Doern
Compton Advertising

Neil Drossman
Drossman Yustein Clowes

Dick Earle
Compton Advertising

Bernie Eckstein
Paula Green

Arthur Einstein
Lord, Geller, Federico, Einstein

Malcom End
Ogilvy & Mather

Sanford Evans
Bozell & Jacobs

Charlie Ewell
Ally & Gargano

Gene Federico
Lord, Geller, Federico, Einstein

Carol Anne Fine
TBWA

Maryellen Flynn
Grey Advertising

Paul Frahn
Needham, Harper & Steers

Marcella Free
Avrett, Free & Ginsberg

Gary Geyer
The Marschalk Company

Bill Giles
Grey Advertising

Jack Goldenberg
Richards & Edwards

Peter Greeman
BBDO

Herb Green
McCann-Erickson

Paula Green
Paula Green

Warren Greene
Cadwell Davis Partners

Lyle Greenfield
Compton Advertising

Anthony Gregory
Lockhart & Pettus

Graham Griffiths
Benton & Bowles

Ray Groff
Needham, Harper & Steers

Charles Guarino
Warwick Advertising

William Hamilton
Rumrill-Hoyt

Robert Hildt
Geers Gross
Advertising

Carolyn Hirschklau
SSC&B

Barry Hoffman
Lord, Geller, Federico, Einstein

Alan Honig
Grey Advertising

Steven Hunter
Ketchum Advertising

George E. Jaccoma
J. Walter Thompson

Murray Jacobs
Doyle Dane Bernbach

Caroline Jones
Mingo-Jones Advertising

Robert Joseph
Laurence, Charles & Free

Alan Judelson
Ted Bates Advertising

Valerie Kandel
Lord, Geller, Federico, Einstein

Ruth Downing Karp
J. Walter Thompson

Ritch Kassof
Benton & Bowles

Gerald Kaufman
Ted Bates Advertising

Allen S. Kay
Korey, Kay & Partners

Jack Keane
Nadler & Larimer

Richard Kiernan
Grey Advertising

Charlie King
Grey Advertising

Fred Kohl
Graber & Cohen

Arthur Korant
Grey Lyon & King

Lois Korey
Korey, Kay & Partners

Diana Kramer
Warwick Advertising

Jerry Lenoff
Rumrill-Hoyt

Robert H. Lenz
Backer & Spielvogel

Paul Levett
Marsteller

Barry Z. Levine
Levy, Sussman & Levine

Ann-Marie Light
Epstein, Raboy Advertising

Joan Lipton
McCann-Erickson

Dick Lopez
Scali, McCabe, Sloves

Dick Lord
Lord, Geller, Federico, Einstein

Judy Lotas
SSC&B

Peter Lubalin
Creamer

Alden R. Ludlow III
Warwick Advertising

Thomas Mabley
Lord, Geller, Federico, Einstein

Malcolm MacDougall
SSC&B

Ira B. Madris
McCann-Erickson

Ken Majka
Calet, Hirsch, Kurnit
& Spector

Edward Mandell
Richards & Edwards

Mike Mangano
Doyle Dane Bernbach

Peggy Bell Masterson
Benton & Bowles

Gerald McGee
Ogilvy & Mather

Lynn McGrath
N W Ayer

Joseph McKenna
Marsteller

William McQuillan
Albert Frank Guenther Law

Richard Mercer
SSC&B

Tom Messner
Ally & Gargano

Bertram Metter
J. Walter Thompson

Rick Meyer
Rosenfield, Sirowitz & Lawson

Livingston Miller
D'Arcy MacManus
& Masius

Robert Minicus
Kenyon & Eckhardt

Marvin Mitchnick
Nadler & Larimer

Mario Morbelli
Young & Rubicam

Jim Morrissey
Grey Advertising

Roger Mosconi
The Marschalk Company

Bill Mullen
Wells, Rich, Greene

Ray Myers
Scali, McCabe, Sloves

Bruce Nelson
McCann-Erickson

John Noble
Doyle Dane Bernbach

Michael Norton
Sudler & Hennessey

Peter Noto
Shaller Rubin Associates

Gerry O'Hara
Epstein, Raboy Advertising

Robert Oksner
Waring & LaRosa

Bernard S. Owett
J. Walter Thompson

Bruce Palmer
Nadler & Larimer

Jim Perretti
Ally & Gargano

Theodore Pettus
Lockhart & Pettus

Charles Piccirillo
Doyle Dane Bernbach

Stuart Pittman
Brainreserve

Faith Popcorn
Brainreserve

John Prizeman
Laurence, Charles & Free

Frazier Purdy
Young & Rubicam

Dick Raboy
Epstein, Raboy Advertising

Michael Randazzo
Mingo-Jones Advertizing

Velve Richey Rankin
Ogilvy & Mather

Sam Reed
Mingo-Jones Advertising

Joey Reiman
D'Arcy MacManus & Masius

Robert Reitzfeld
Altschiller, Reitzfeld, Solin/NCK

Donn Resnick
Grey Advertising

Mike Robertson
Needham, Harper & Steers

Patricia Rockmore
AC&R Advertising

Andrew A. Romano
J. Walter Thompson

Ron Rosenfeld
Rosenfeld, Sirowitz & Lawson

Jim Ross
HBM/Stiefel

Thomas Rost
Ogilvy & Mather

Nat Russo
Levine, Huntley, Schmidt
& Beaver

Ted Sann
BBDO

Jay Schulberg
Ogilvy & Mather

Jerry Shapiro
Grey Lyon & King

Melissa Shapiro
Rosenfeld, Sirowitz & Lawson

Ted Shaw
McCaffrey & McCall

Mervin Shipenberg
Altman, Stoller, Weiss

Bob Singer
Bozell & Jacobs

Don Slater
Slater, Hanft, Martin

Mike Slosberg
Marsteller

Ernie Smith
Sudler & Hennessey

Steve Smith
Ammirati & Puris

Lila Sternglass
Rumrill-Hoyt

Bob Stevenson
D'Arcy MacManus & Masius

Lynn Stiles
Lord, Geller, Federico, Einstein

Kathie Strauss
Marsteller

Carl Stuart
TBWA

Bob Sturtevant
Martin, Sturtevant, Silverman
& Marshall

Len Sugarman
Foote, Cone & Belding

Robert Sullivan
D'Arcy MacManus & Masius

Abie J. Sussman
Levy, Sussman & Levine

Barry L. Tannenholz
Romann & Tannenholz

Eugene H. Tashoff
Campbell-Ewald

Jay Taub
Della Femina, Travisano & Partners

Richard Thomas
Lord, Geller, Federico, Einstein

Tom Thomas
Ammirati & Puris

Ron Travisano
Della Femina, Travisano & Partners

Alex Tsao
Epstein, Raboy Advertising

Eli T. Tulman
McCann-Erickson

Nancy Vaughn
Wells, Rich, Greene

Dan Von Der Embse
Trout & Ries

Kurt Weihs
Lois Pitts Gershon

Gerald Weinstein
Benton & Bowles

Melvin D. Weiss
Altman, Stoller, Weiss

William Wurtzel
Hicks & Greist

Mark Yustein
Della Femina, Travisano & Partners

One Club Members

Donald Aaronson
Michael Abadi
Jeffrey Abbott
Heni Abrams
Lorrie Ader
Judith Alexander
J. Gregory Alderisio
David Altschiller
Arnie Arlow
Deborah Armstrong
George Armstrong
Jeffrey L. Atlas
Susan Attanasio
Roseanne J. Azarian
Ellen Azorin
Carol Ann Baker
Mel Barlin
Anita Baron
Cheryl Baron
Heather Bartling
Brenda Basken
Allan Beaver
Joan Bender
Lois S. Bender
Ron Berger
Sandy Berger
Gail Berk
Noel Berke
Herbert A. Berkowitz
Kiri Bermack
Bennett Bidwell
Paul Biniasz
William Blackman
Paul Blade
Jack Bloom
Richard K. Bloom
Burton Blum
Francesca Blumenthal
Rob Boezewinkel
George R. Bonner, Jr.
Harry M. Braver
Judy Brewton
Marina M. Brock

Ed Brodsky
Scott Bronfman
Audrey Brooks
Ronald A. Brothers
Joe Alec Brown
Lonnie Brown
Casey Burke
Ron Burkhardt
Nelsena Burt
Ed Butler
Larry Cadman
Cathie Campbell
John Caples
Bob Carducci
David Carlin
Jane Carluccio
Barbara Carmack
Earl Carter
Wendy A. Cassel
Earl Cavanah
R. Michael Chapell
Larry Chase
Karen Cherniack
Marcia Christ
Lisa L. Chu
Peter Clarke
Steve Climons
Andrew Cohen
Dale Cohen
Robert I. Cole
Adrienne Collier
Jerry Colman
Kay A. Colmar
Uriah Franklin Corkrum
Robert D. Corwin
Constantin Cotzias
Robert B. Cox
Kathy Crafts
David J. Crain
David Crittenden
Jane L. Cross
Marilyn Cull
Bruce C. Cumsky

Dale Cunningham
James M. Dale
Boris Damast
Wesley Davidson
Diane Davis
Robert A. Degni
Jerry Della Femina
Bob Dion
Diana Dominicci-Stewart
Mary Ann Donovan
Shelley Doppelt
Lynne Doynow
Neil Drossman
Paula Dunn
Laurence Dunst
Tina S. Dyes
Arthur Einstein
Bernadette F. Elias
Barry Epstein
Jerry Esposito
Stephen A. Fales
Suzanne V. Falter
Mary Farrell
Sherie Fas
Stephen M. Fechtor
Oksana Fedorenko
Bob Feig
Steve Feldman
Richard Ferrante
Jerry Fields
Peggy Fields
Sal Finazzo
Carole Anne Fine
Kathleen M. Fitzgerald
Marieve Fitzmaurice-Page
Dudley Fitzpatrick
Carol A. Flynn
John Follis
Mel Freedman
Carl Fremont
Susan Friedman
Harvey Gabor
Judith Gee

John Georges
Sheldon Gewirtz
Gary Geyer
Andrew Giarnella
Frank Ginsberg
Lynne Ginsberg
Pete Glasheen
Sharon Glazer
Irwin Goldberg
Roz Goldfarb
Scott Goldman
David Goldring
Jo Ann Goldsmith
Susan Goodman
Jill Goran
Milt Gossett
Hubert Graf
Paula Green
Jayne Greenstein
Barbara Greer
Daniel Gregory
Dick Grider
Josclynne Grier
Martica Griffin
Robert Haigh
Jim Hallowes
Alan Halpern
Jerome A. Handman
Donna Hanna
Donna Tedesco Hartmann
Nancy Hauptman
Joan Helfman
Joseph M. Heppt
Roy Herbert
Joan Orlian Hillman
Peter Hirsch
Sandra Holtzman
Patrick E. T. Horne
Mike Hughes
Linda Huss
Patricia Hutt
Craig R. Jackson
Richard Jackson

Corrin Jacobsen
Roberta Jaret
JoEllen Johns
Beth Elaine Johnson
James J. Johnson
Caroline Jones
Katherine R. Jordan
Jessica Jossell
John Kaelin
Judy Kaganowich
Barnaby Kalan
David J. Kaminsky
Susan Kantor
Marshall Karp
Daniel S. Karsch
Richard B. Kaufman
Brian M. Kelly
Gail L. Kennedy
Jeffrey Klarik
Murray Klein
Esther Kong
Lois Korey
Haruo Koriyama
Judy Kozuch
Steven Krammer
Henry Kwok
Larry Laiken
Lucille Landini
Andrew Langer
Anthony E. LaPetri
Marybeth Lareau
Doris Latino
Mary Wells Lawrence
David L. Leedy
David J. Leinwohl
Robert N. Lelle
Joyce Lempel
Robert H. Lenz
Robert Levenson
Michael Levine
Georgina Lichtenstein
Marsi S. Liebowitz
Claire O. Lissance

Allison Longo
Jeanne-Marie Lonza
Regina Lorenzo
Kathi Lowe
Marilyn Lowther
Cecile T. Lozano
Margaret Lubalin
Peter Lubalin
Ted Luciani
David Luhn
Karen Lundstrem
Chuck Lustig
Tony Macchia
Georgia Macris
Sandra Marchionda
Celeste Mari
Jack Mariucci
Louise A. Masano
Arthur Cerf Mayer
Ed McCabe
Ruth L. McCarthy
Jennifer L. McCormick
Bill McCullam
Karen McIntosh
Mary Means
Leslie Stokes Mechanic
DeLaine Melillo
Mario G. Messina
Tom Messner
David C. N. Metcalf
Bert Metter
Lyle E. Metzdorf
Beryl Meyer
Lou Miano
Harold Michelson
Tom Millar
S. Michael Minard
Erik Mintz
Michael Miranda
Jack F. Miskell
Susan D. Mitchell
Cathiann Mooney
Rafael Morales

Mark Louis Moretti
Charles Morgan
Linda Morganstern
Katrina Morosoff
Syl M. Morrone
Roger P. Mosconi
Norman Muchnick
Linda J. Mummiani
Ken Musto
Robert Nadler
Thomas Nathan
Simi J. Neger
Celeste Nevler
Keith C. Ninesling
Peter E. Nogueira
Charles Novick
Bill Oberlander
Dick O'Brien
Andrew O'Connor
Robert Oksner
Jane Oriel
Curvin O'Rielly
Rowan O'Riley
Patricia O'Shaughnessy
June Rachelson Ospa
Carol J. Packer
Maxine Paetro
Gail Parker
Carolyn Parrs
Stanley Pearlman
Eleonore Pepin
Ellen Perless
Gail Perry
Patrice A. Peterson
David Piatkowski
Raul Pina
Larry Plapler
Chris Pollock
Shirley Polykoff
Joseph Pompeo
Faith Popcorn
Diane Popinsky
Thomas A. Puckett

Elissa Querze
Brian Quinn
Jane Rabin
Richard Raboy
Jim Raniere
Ted Regan
Brigitte Regout
Jan Rehder
Charles Reich
Michael T. Reid
Anne Reilly
Bob Reitzfeld
Donn H. Resnick
Robert Resnick
Lisa E. Rettig
Ruthann M. Richert
Dorrie Rifkin
L. Kenneth Ritter
Nancy Robbins
Phyllis Robinson
Michael Rosen
Ron Rosenfeld
Robert Rosenthal
Nancy Ross
Susan Rossiello
Mark Rothenberg
Jane Rubini
Bill Ryan
Charlie Ryant
Thomas Sacco
Susan Sacks
Kenneth Sandbank
Jon Sandhaus
Harry Sandler
Bob Sarlin
David Saslaw
Andrew Satter
Louis E. Schiavone III
Julie Schireson
Joyce Schnaufer
Sy Schreckinger
Jay Schulberg
Marjorie E. Schulman

Mike Schwabenland
Claudia Schwartz
Tom Schwartz
Ron Seichrist
Ray Seide
Joan Seidman
Mark Shap
Melisse Shapiro
Vivian Sharton
Daniel Sheehan
Greg Sheldon
Charlotte Sherwood
Brett Shevack
Jamie Shevell
Paul Shields
Jay Shmulewitz
Virgil Cox Shutze
Joe Sicurella
Jonathan Sills
Craig Silverman
Karen L. Simon
Leonard Sirowitz
Howard Smith
Jo Smith
Stephen Smith
Tony Smythe
Martin Solow
Robert Sparks
Mark Spector
Andrea Sperling
Helayne Spivak
Midge Stark
Dean Stefanides
Leon Sterling
Stan Stoj
Debora L. Stone
Charles E. Stramiello
Ira Sturtevant
Thomas B. Stvan
Len Sugarman
Ilene Cohn Tanen
Norman Tanen
Judith Teller

Mike Tesch
Peggy F. Tomarkin
Holly Tooker
Juanita Torrence-Thompson
Ron Travisano
Carol Turturro
Tony Vanderperk
Sharon Vanderslice
Joan Van der Veen
Mary Vanderwoude
Alexa Van de Walle
William F. Vartorella
Stephen Versandi
Larry Vine
Gloria Viseltear
Ned Viseltear
Barbara Vitanza
Dan Von der Embse
Nina Wachsman
Tom Wai-Shek
Sergio Waksman
Judy Wald
Marvin Waldman
Don Walley
Halina V. Warren
Kevin Weidenbacher
Eliot J. Weinstein
Riva B. Weinstein
Ira Weitz
Lynn E. Welsh
Bob Whitworth
Richard Wilde
D. Marc Williams
C. Richard Williams
Kurt Willinger
Cindy Wojdyla
Sandra Wright
Julie Wulff
Carol Wydra
Elizabeth Wynn
Michael Yurick
Mark Yustein
Christine M. Zepf

1983 Gold & Silver Awards

**Consumer Newspaper
Over 600 Lines Single**

1 GOLD
ART DIRECTOR
Anthony Angotti
WRITER
Tom Thomas
DESIGNERS
Anthony Angotti
Barbara Bowman
Dominique Singer
PHOTOGRAPHER
Robert Ammirati
CLIENT
BMW of North America
AGENCY
Ammirati & Puris

2 SILVER
ART DIRECTOR
Seymon Ostilly
WRITER
Kevin O'Neill
DESIGNER
Seymon Ostilly
PHOTOGRAPHER
Manuel Gonzales
CLIENT
IBM
AGENCY
Lord, Geller, Federico,
Einstein

1 GOLD

The life and death of a business deal.

We know that half of all business phone calls never reach the intended party.

The average memo takes a full three days simply to go from one mailroom to another.

IBM office systems can help.

We have a wide range of computers. word processors. electronic typewriters. printers and copiers that help information flow more smoothly.

They can create. file and retrieve documents electronically.

The IBM Audio Distribution System can even do the same for your voice: recording. storing and delivering phone messages. Using ordinary phone buttons. you indicate when you want the message delivered. where. and to whom.

With more than 40 years of experience. no one is more committed to the office than we are—where it is now and where it will be.

Where will you be? IBM

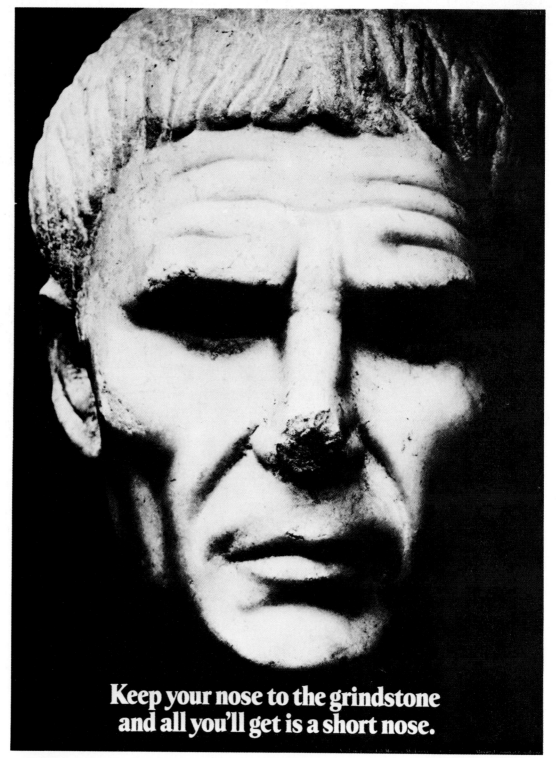

Keep your nose to the grindstone and all you'll get is a short nose.

Sure, success takes hard work. But hard work alone isn't enough.

To make it in business, you also need all the right moves.

You need a clear map of where you're heading, long range and short range.

You need all the smarts, guts, and ambition you can muster.

Ambition? You bet. It's finally out of the closet. At last you can be frank about your drive for success.

That's what the fast track is all about.

If *you're* running on the fast track, your business reading starts with FORTUNE.

For over 50 years, it's been the magazine of business success. It's the authority, the

horse's mouth, the one you rely on when you've *got* to be right.

In marketing, management, technology, the works...FORTUNE's where you get a vital couple of steps on the competition.

It's how to make it—and how to keep it.

So if you want to succeed with the fast-track people, put your advertising in FORTUNE.

FORTUNE
How to succeed.

3 GOLD

We're all created equal.
After that, baby, you're on your own.

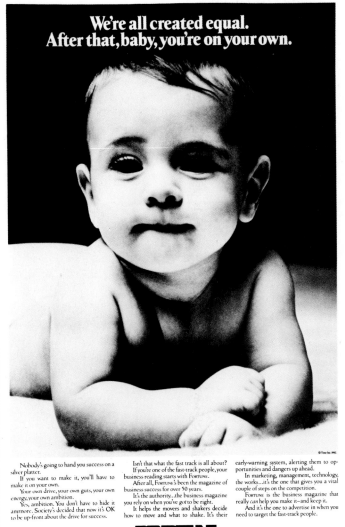

Nobody's going to hand you success on a silver platter.

If you want to make it, you'll have to make it on your own.

Your own drive, your own guts, your own energy, your own ambition.

Yes, ambition. You don't have to hide it anymore. Society's decided that now it's OK to be up-front about the drive for success.

Isn't that what the fast track is all about?

If you're one of the fast-track people, your business reading starts with FORTUNE.

After all, FORTUNE's been the magazine of business success for over 50 years.

It's the authority...the business magazine you rely on when you've *got* to be right.

It helps the movers and shakers decide how to move and what to shake. It's their early-warning system, alerting them to opportunities and dangers up ahead.

In marketing, management, technology, the works...it's the one that gives you a vital couple of steps on the competition.

FORTUNE is the business magazine that really *can* help you make it–and keep it.

And it's the one to advertise in when you need to target the fast-track people.

FORTUNE
How to succeed.

The headhunters will get you
if you really use your brains.

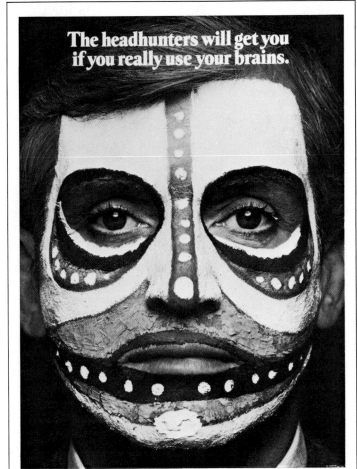

Put all your smarts to work and pretty soon you'll be the one the executive searchers are searching for.

Encourage it. The more headhunters on your trail, the faster you'll get to the top.

The nice thing is, you don't have to hide your ambition under a bushel anymore.

Now you can be up-front about your drive for success.

That's what the fast track is all about.

If *you're* a fast-tracker, your business reading undoubtedly starts with FORTUNE.

It's where you get the help you need to make the most out of your brains.

It's the authority. The last word. The source you rely on when you've just *got* to be right.

FORTUNE's your early-warning system, alerting you to dangers and opportunities up ahead.

In marketing, management, technology, the works–it's where you get a vital couple of steps on the competition.

It's how to make it–and keep it.

And for advertising to the fast-track people, there's nothing else like FORTUNE.

Absolutely nothing!

FORTUNE
How to succeed.

Nead a littel hilp with yur speling?

To err is humin.

To correct that error quickly and accurately, you can count on the IBM Displaywriter, the best-selling stand-alone text processor there is.

It does more than check the spelling of up to 1,000 words a minute. The Displaywriter also has a new spelling aid. Here's how it works: After Spelling Check locates an error, press the AID key and instantly a list of likely choices to replace that misspelled word appears.

The results?

Speed and accuracy on the first try.

Without retyping.

And now the Displaywriter can function as a data processor, too. By running computer programs using the UCSD-p System.*

It also helps speed up editing, revising, merging, formatting, math and footnotes.

In fact, the IBM Displaywriter can save time on almost any office task you can think of.

Except, perhaps, a visit to the water cooler.

Nobody's perfict.

To arrange for a free demonstration of the Displaywriter, call your local IBM representative or IBM's toll-free number listed below.

IBM.

Correct the error of your wayz.

Get an IBM Typewriter. Call 1 800 631-5582.

Every IBM Electronic and Correcting Selectric, III Typewriter gives you Error Correction. For example, let's say you choose one of our electronic typewriters. At the touch of your finger, it can automatically lift a typing error—from a single character up to an entire line—clean off the page. There's no fuss. No mess. No wasted time. For all those evils, the end is near.

IBM

*Ask for Ext. 171 and get details on our discount programs—you could save 5 to 12%. In Hawaii/Alaska, call 1 800 526-2484, Ext. 171.

Buy a computer that leaves you room to grow.

The IBM Datamaster.
If you're about to buy your first computer, you're about to make a big decision.

Before you make that decision, consider the IBM Datamaster, a small business computer that starts at under $10,000.

The IBM Datamaster can meet the data and word processing needs of your growing company.

And as your business grows, you can store more information by adding a disk storage unit that can be shared by up to four work stations. Which means four people can work on the same or different jobs simultaneously.

You can also add one of several printers. Including a new letter-quality printer.

As well as a word processing option that lets you type, edit, format and file text. And offers you a 130,000-word dictionary and synonym assist.

There is a variety of programs available for virtually every industry. Which means

the IBM Datamaster can help you immediately solve problems from simple accounting procedures to complex business analyses.

Of course, the IBM Datamaster is backed by IBM service and support.

So if you're a growing business with big plans for the future, choose your first computer carefully.

After all, a computer shouldn't inhibit your plans.

A computer should help you realize them.

To arrange for a free demonstration of the Datamaster, call your local IBM representative or IBM's toll-free number listed below.

IBM

Call *IBM Direct* 1 800 631-5582 Ext. 171. In Hawaii/Alaska 1 800 526-2484 Ext. 171.

**Consumer Newspaper
600 Lines or Less Single**

5 GOLD
ART DIRECTOR
Ted Shaine

WRITER
Diane Rothschild

DESIGNER
Ted Shaine

PHOTOGRAPHER
Jerry Friedman

CLIENT
Atari

AGENCY
Doyle Dane Bernbach

6 SILVER
ART DIRECTOR
Phil Gips

WRITERS
Robert Fearon
Jan Zlotnick

PHOTOGRAPHER
Jean-Marie Guyaux

CLIENT
Business Week

AGENCY
Fearon O'Leary Kaprielian

WHAT FOOTBALL STRIKE?

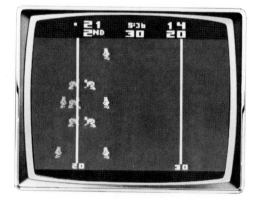

ATARI® REALSPORTS™ FOOTBALL IS ON ITS WAY.

If you own an ATARI Video Computer System,™ you won't have to be without football for long. Because we're about to introduce ATARI RealSports Football. It's one of our new line of highly sophisticated RealSports video games that includes everything from Soccer to Baseball. RealSports Football is so real that the crowd cheers. And the graphics are so sharp the players actually play. They kick. They pass. They block. They tackle. They do virtually everything real players do. Except, of course, strike.

© 1982 Atari, Inc. All rights reserved.

ATARI
A Warner Communications Company

5 GOLD

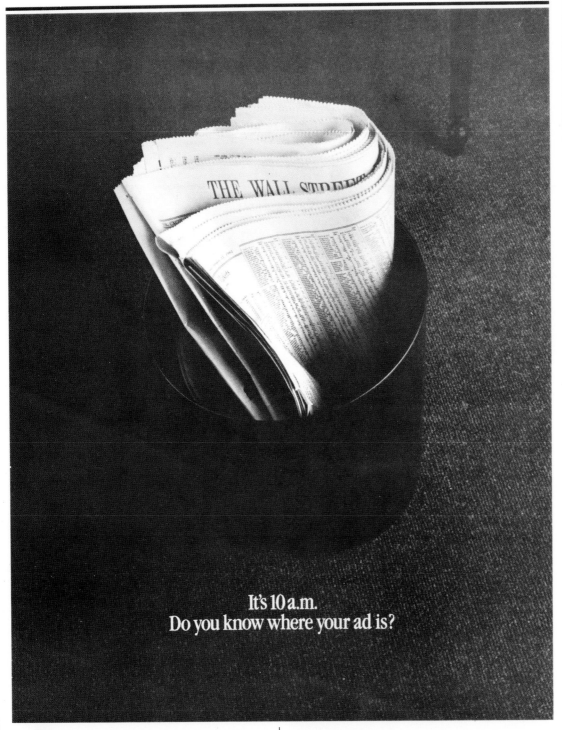

It's 10 a.m.
Do you know where your ad is?

A fast run-through of the capsule business news, a scan of the stock tables, a quick look at some earnings and sales figures, and a glance at an ad or two that catch the eye. Then it's all over for the daily journal. But Business Week and your ad stay with your customers all week long. Most readers get their copies on Friday, read them over the weekend, and keep reading them through the week.

That's because Business Week gives its readers more of what they have to know–concise, yet complete, articles ranging every business concern, from Economics to Corporate Strategies, International Business, Information Processing, Marketing, Investments. And more.

All reported with an interpretive edge that signals business trends to come. An editorial presence that ensures your advertising gets the serious, long-lasting attention you want.

An award-winning thoroughness leaders can't find anywhere else. Not in Forbes. Not in Fortune. And certainly not in the instant media.

Business Week. Where your ad keeps working all week long.

BusinessWeek
The world's leading business magazine.

For information on ordering a subscription to Business Week, please call toll-free 1-800-257-5112. In New Jersey, call 1-800-792-8378.　©1982 McGraw-Hill, Inc

**Consumer Magazine
Black and White
Page or Spread
Including Magazine
Supplements**

7 GOLD

ART DIRECTOR
Dennis D'Amico

WRITER
Ron Berger

PHOTOGRAPHER
Dan Weaks

CLIENT
Timberland

AGENCY
Ally & Gargano

8 SILVER

ART DIRECTOR
Alistair Proctor

WRITER
Billings Fuess

PHOTOGRAPHER
Arnold Newman

CLIENT
International Paper

AGENCY
Ogilvy & Mather

**Consumer Magazine
Color Page or Spread
Including Magazine
Supplements**

9 GOLD

ART DIRECTOR
Lars Anderson

WRITER
Larry Cadman

PHOTOGRAPHERS
Manny Mayes
Mike Verbois
Jerry Friedman

CLIENT
Nikon

AGENCY
Scali, McCabe, Sloves

10 SILVER

ART DIRECTOR
Helmut Krone

WRITER
Peter Bregman

DESIGNER
Helmut Krone

PHOTOGRAPHER
Carl Fischer

CLIENT
Polaroid

AGENCY
Doyle Dane Bernbach

Faster than a speeding bullet.

Introducing the world's fastest 35mm SLR. The Nikon FM2.

Until now, the only way to take a picture of a bullet in flight was with a high-speed electronic strobe.

The picture you see here was taken with a constant light source, a 50mm Nikkor lens, and the remarkable new Nikon FM2.

At 1/4000 sec., the FM2 is twice as fast as any 35mm SLR ever made.

This lightning speed is made possible by an extraordinary Nikon innovation: the first vertically-traveling honeycombed titanium shutter.

Shutter assembly of FM2.

To create a shutter light enough yet strong enough to operate at 1/4000 sec.,

Actual unretouched photo of a 38 caliber bullet, traveling at 400 feet per second, taken at 1/4000 sec. by the FM2.

Nikon engineers used ultra-thin titanium, gave it a patented chemical treatment, then etched it with a honeycomb pattern for extra strength and rigidity.

This major advance in shutter technology not only makes the FM2 the world's fastest 35mm SLR; but one that's more accurate at slower speeds, too.

The fastest flash sync speed of any 35mm SLR: 1/200 sec.

For years, photographers have been haunted by ghosts — fuzzy double images that occur when an electronic flash is used in bright ambient light. The cause of this problem was the slow sync speeds available in 35mm SLRs.

The solution is the Nikon FM2. It has a sync speed of 1/200 sec., more than 50% faster than any other focal plane 35mm SLR.

The ghosts that have plagued most synchro-sunlight photography are gone forever.

There's more to the world's fastest camera than just speed.

One way Nikon improves its products is by listening carefully to the professionals who use them. The FM2 incorporates many features which pros have asked for.

Things like interchangeable focusing screens to facilitate close-up, telephoto and architectural photography.

An on/off switch for the metering system that conserves battery power. A double-exposure control that's easier to operate with one hand. A new viewfinder flash ready light that's compatible with Nikon dedicated strobes.

The FM2 is compatible with all AI Nikkors, Series E and modified AI Nikkors. As well as the optional data back, MD-12 motor drive, and numerous other Nikon accessories.

For photographers interested in complete creative control, the FM2 represents the new state-of-the-art in manual cameras. The features it offers, together with Nikon's legendary ruggedness and reliability, make it like no other camera you've ever seen.

Not only is it faster than a speeding bullet.

It's super in a lot of other ways, too.

Nikon
We take the world's greatest pictures.

We're so confident of the new Polaroid 600 speed instant film and the new Polaroid Sun Cameras that we believe it's possible for you to get 10 good shots for 10 earnest tries every time. 10 for 10! The secret is in having the world's fastest color print film and the unique light mixing cameras that use it. The Polaroid Sun Cameras. In fact, we're so proud, we've even backed it up with Free Smile Insurance: Polaroid

10 hits. No errors.

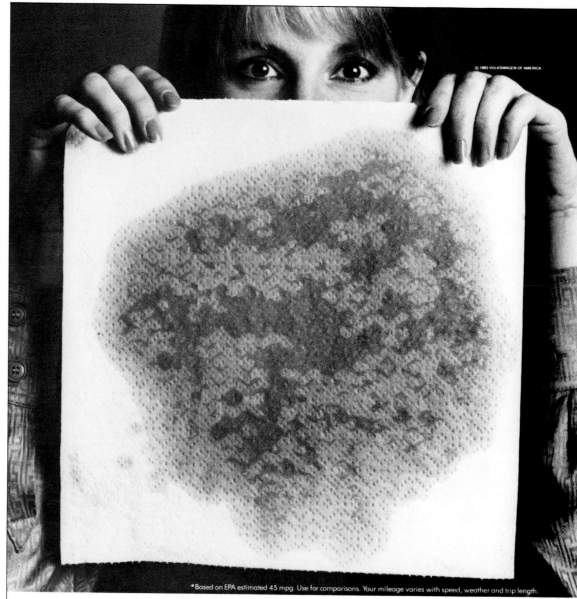

*Based on EPA estimated 45 mpg. Use for comparisons. Your mileage varies with speed, weather and trip length.

This paper towel contains enough fuel to run a Rabbit one half mile.

Astounding, isn't it?

But you probably think we're talking about some wildly advanced engine we put inside a Rabbit.

Perhaps an experiment?

Well, it's quite advanced: it's the Volkswagen Rabbit diesel.

And it makes the Rabbit the best mileage car in America.*

But it's hardly experimental.

Especially when you stop to consider the diesel's legendary reputation for durability.

Now the question is, do you really need the best mileage car in America?

Well, some people will tell you that fuel prices will continue to drop; that gas lines are a thing of the past.

Funny about those folks who made the same predictions in 1974 and again in 1979.

A lot of them now drive Rabbits.

Nothing else is a Volkswagen. ⓥⓦ

Is a cheaper car more expensive?

We readily admit that the Rabbit isn't the cheapest car you can buy.

Or is it?

Before you run out and buy a cheap car, ask yourself a few questions:

Does a cheap car come standard with fuel injection, front-wheel drive, and dual diagonal brakes?

Is a cheap car large enough to carry four large people without forced intimacy, yet agile enough to handle like a sports car?

Is a cheap car cheap to fix?

Or cheap when it's worth next to nothing at trade-in time?

When you take pencil and paper and tally the real cost of owning a Rabbit versus the real cost of owning something cheaper, you'll discover the awful truth about most cheap cars:

They're expensive.

Nothing else is a Volkswagen.

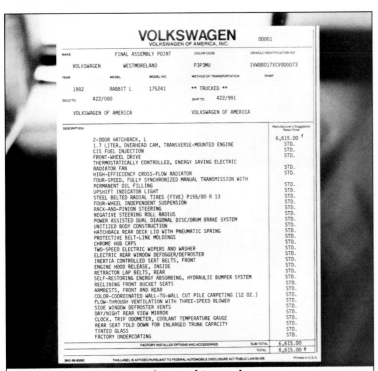

You won't read it and weep.

Much to our consternation, a lot of people think Rabbits cost much more than they really do.

Regrettable, albeit really quite understandable.

Especially when you stop to consider that the Rabbit comes standard with fuel injection, front-wheel drive, and dual diagonal brakes, features usually found on much more expensive cars.

The Rabbit also comes standard with a gas-saving upshift light, not found on any other car regardless of price. Unless, of course, it just happens to be a Volkswagen.

Sure, if you're so inclined, you can indulge yourself with a long list of luxury options that can run up the price of even a Rabbit.

But the way we look at it, the basic Rabbit—reliable, economical* transportation at a reasonable price—may be the greatest luxury of them all.

Nothing else is a Volkswagen.

*EPA estimated 30 mpg, 42 highway estimate. (Use "estimated mpg" for comparison. Mileage varies with speed, trip length, weather. Actual highway mileage will probably be less.)
†Transportation, local taxes and dealer delivery charges additional.

Consumer Magazine
Black and White
Campaign Including
Magazine Supplements

12 SILVER
ART DIRECTOR
Dean Hanson

WRITER
Jarl Olsen

DESIGNERS
Dean Hanson
Jarl Olsen

CLIENT
7 South 8th For Hair

AGENCY
Fallon, McElligott, Rice/Mpls.

A bad haircut can be a real nightmare.

7 South 8th for Hair
804 LaSalle Avenue / Call 333-1376 for appointment

12 SILVER

A bad haircut can make anyone look dumb.

7 South 8th for Hair

804 LaSalle Avenue / Call 333-1376 for appointment

A bad haircut is no laughing matter.

7 South 8th for Hair

804 LaSalle Avenue / Call 333-1376 for appointment

**Consumer Magazine
Color Campaign
Including Magazine
Supplements**

13 GOLD
ART DIRECTORS
Charles Piccirillo
Gary Goldsmith

WRITERS
Ted Bell
Mike Mangano
Diane Sinnott

PHOTOGRAPHERS
Chuck LaMonica
John Paul Endress
Larry Sillen

CLIENT
General Wine & Spirits/
Chivas Regal

AGENCY
Doyle Dane Bernbach

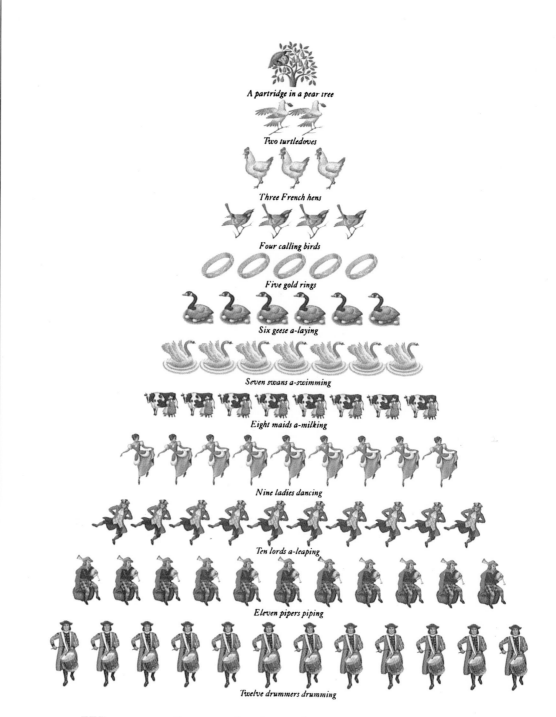

A partridge in a pear tree

Two turtledoves

Three French hens

Four calling birds

Five gold rings

Six geese a-laying

Seven swans a-swimming

Eight maids a-milking

Nine ladies dancing

Ten lords a-leaping

Eleven pipers piping

Twelve drummers drumming

What people gave before there was Chivas Regal.

12 YEARS OLD WORLDWIDE · BLENDED SCOTCH WHISKY · 86 PROOF · © 1982 GENERAL WINE & SPIRITS CO., NEW YORK, N.Y.

13 GOLD

Be careful! That's Chivas Regal!

$45 in Japan.

(Count your blessings.)

Gold & Silver
Awards

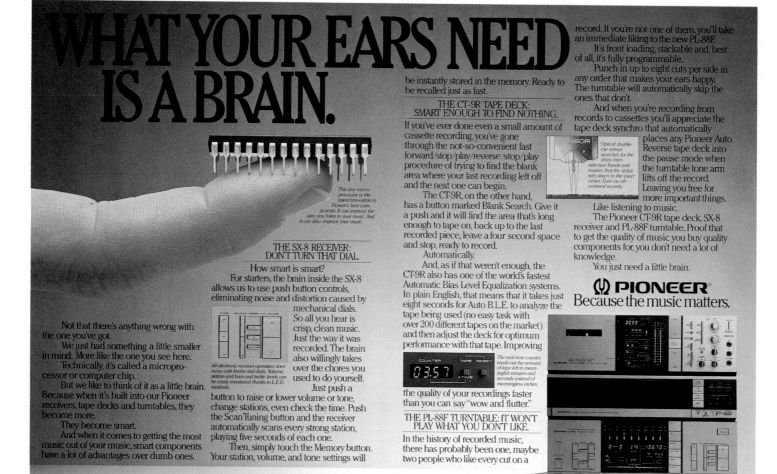

A TAPE DECK SO ADVANCED IT HAS A FEATURE THAT FINDS NOTHING.

We call it Blank Search. You'll no doubt call it the best thing to happen to recording since magnetic tape.

Because, the Pioneer CT-9R tape deck with Blank Search finally puts an end to the old Fast Forward/Stop/Play/Reverse/Stop/Play method of finding where your last recording left off and the next one can begin.

Now, all you have to do is push a button and let the tape deck do the work. It'll find the blank area that's long enough to tape on, back up to the last recorded piece, leave a four second space and stop, ready to record.

And there's more wizardry where that came from. Like Index Scan, Music Search, Blank Skip and a Real Time Counter that reads out the amount of tape left in meaningful minutes and seconds instead of meaningless inches. In other words, features that will revolutionize the way you record and listen to tapes.

But don't thank us.

Thank the little brain that made it all possible. A tiny microprocessor that makes the CT-9R more than a tape deck, it makes it smart.

Smart enough to make your music easier to listen to. Even smart enough to make your music sound better, with Automatic Bias Level Equalization.

What Auto B.L.E. means, to those without a degree in electronics, is that the tape deck automatically analyzes the tape being used (no easy task with over 200 different tapes on the market) and then adjusts itself for optimum recording with that tape. Improving the quality of your recordings faster than you can say "wow and flutter."

Auto B.L.E. aside, all of the CT-9R's features, from Blank Search to Blank Skip, do only one thing.

Let you spend a lot less time looking for your music.

And a lot more time listening to it.

⚛ PIONEER
Because the music matters.

INTRODUCING A TURNTABLE THAT KNOWS A GOOD SONG WHEN IT SEES ONE.

In the history of recorded music, there have probably been one...maybe two people who liked every song on a record.

If you're not one of them, chances are you'll take an immediate liking to the new Pioneer PL-88F turntable. It's programmable.

Which, simply put, means that your index finger can now spare your ears from a less-than-favorite tune. Just push a button or two, and the turntable will play only the cuts you select. And skip right over the ones you don't.

Of course, before you know what order to play them in, you'll want to know what order they're recorded in. And for that, there's Index Scan, which plays the first ten seconds of each cut.

What makes this turntable so smart? A brain.

A tiny microprocessor that works in conjunction with an optical double eye sensor. The sensor actually "reads" the record grooves to carry out the commands you've programmed into the turntable.

That same microprocessor even makes the PL-88F smart enough to improve your recordings. A special deck-synchro system sees to it that the tape deck is placed in the pause mode whenever the turntable tone arm lifts off the record. (Providing that you're smart enough to use a Pioneer Auto Reverse Tape Deck.)

At the touch of a button the PL-88F's platter glides out. Drop a record on, push the button again and the platter retracts and starts to play automatically.

Of course, the most impressive part of the new PL-88F turntable comes when you put on your favorite record, sit down in your favorite spot, relax and do something you've probably been too busy to do with your ordinary turntable.

Listen to music.

Optical double eye sensor searches for the shiny inter-selection bands and insures that the stylus sets down in the exact center. Even on off-centered records.

⚛ PIONEER
Because the music matters.

Gold & Silver Awards

"*Chivas Regal!* . . .
Where do you think you are, heaven?"

Chivas Regal • 12 Years Old Worldwide • Blended Scotch Whisky • 86 Proof. General Wine & Spirits Co., N.Y.

Introducing Tricot Mesh.
It fits like your skin, so it stays on better.

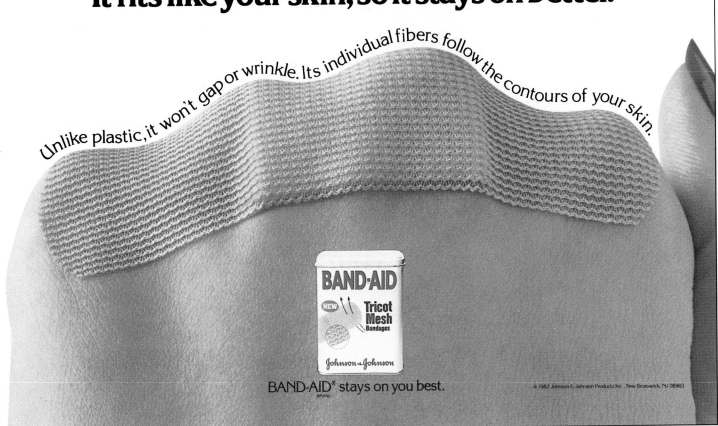

Unlike plastic, it won't gap or wrinkle. Its individual fibers follow the contours of your skin.

BAND-AID® stays on you best.

© 1982 Johnson & Johnson Products Inc., New Brunswick, NJ 08903

The perfect dressing for venison.

This is the Boker 2000 folding lockback, and pure practicality in a field knife was never so beautiful.

Its 440-chrome stainless blade will hold its edge through two or three deer, then come back with a few wipes on a steel. The drop point is a near-perfect extension of your index finger. And the grips are polished rosewood with solid brass bolsters.

For a full-color brochure of the knives they tell the stories about, please send $1 to Boker, Box 30544, Raleigh, N.C. 27612.

Boker, the knives they tell the stories about.

©1981 The Cooper Group

17 SILVER

How to separate the best of the fish from the rest of the fish.

Slice along the spine down to the backbone, and make another bone-deep cut behind the gill flap.

Now, using the flexible stainless blade to "shave" the contours of the rib cage, trim-and-pull the fillet away from the fish.

You now have a perfect fillet. And the polished rosewood handle proves that a functional tool doesn't have to be ugly.

For a full-color brochure of the knives people tell stories about, please send $1 to Boker, Box 30544, Raleigh, N.C. 27612.

Boker, the knives they tell the stories about.

The right knife can save your skin.

The ideal skinning knife has a locking, stainless steel blade with a long "belly" for stripping, and a finely upswept, trailing point for the delicate cape-work.

Its overall design lets you work with confidence, both upward and downward, using any sort of grip.

It has no nooks or notches to collect debris, it cleans up quickly, and it'll last your lifetime with reasonable care.

It's called the Boker 1001. For a full-color brochure of the knives they tell the stories about, please send $1 to Boker, Box 30544, Raleigh, North Carolina 27612.

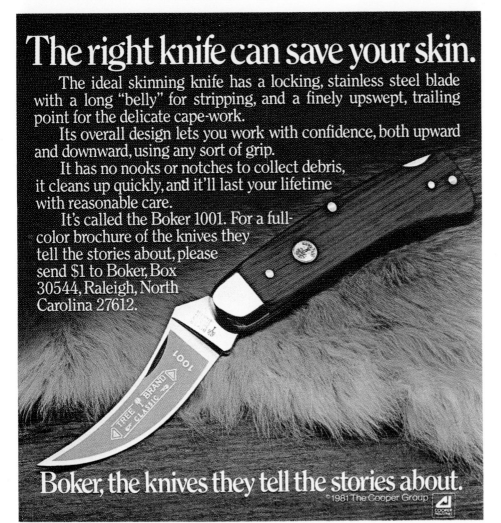

Boker, the knives they tell the stories about.

**Trade
Black and White
Page or Spread**

18 GOLD
ART DIRECTOR
Bob Czernysz

WRITER
Dick Olmsted

PHOTOGRAPHER
Frank Tedesco

CLIENT
Time, Inc./Fortune

AGENCY
Young & Rubicam

19 SILVER
ART DIRECTOR
Stan Schofield

WRITER
Jim Parry

CLIENT
Reader's Digest

AGENCY
Posey, Parry & Quest/
Connecticut

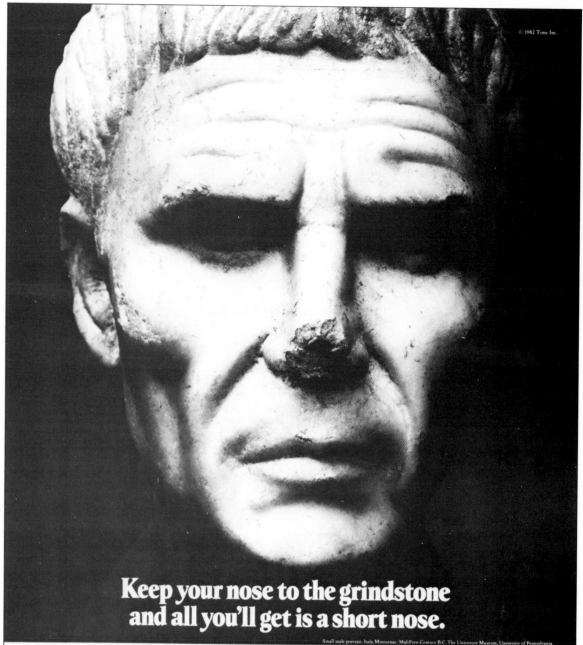

18 GOLD

A man who murdered his parents persuaded psychiatrists to let him live with his aunt and uncle because he loved them "like my own mother and father." Then...

...he murdered them too.

And this is just one true horror story cited by Senator Orrin Hatch in his article, "The Insanity Defense is Insane," written for the October Reader's Digest.

As criminals continue to be acquitted by reason of insanity—and as convicted killers are released from mental hospitals only to kill again—Senator Hatch says we must find a solution to this deadly problem. And he offers one.

It's Digest articles like this that help 40 million readers make sense of an often crazy world.

Reader's Digest

Gold & Silver Awards

Trade
Color Page or Spread

20 SILVER
ART DIRECTOR
Michael Harris

WRITER
Jeff Bockman

PHOTOGRAPHER
Michael Harris

CLIENT
S. Parker Hardware

AGENCY
Big Apple Creative

Trade
Less than One Page
B/W or Color
Single

21 SILVER
ART DIRECTOR
Stan Schofield

WRITER
Jim Parry

CLIENT
Reader's Digest

AGENCY
Posey, Parry & Quest/
Connecticut

WE'RE ABOUT TO SHOOT SOME HOLES IN MASTER LOCK.

Practically any padlock worth its shackle can survive a bullet through the heart.
Including us. S. Parker Hardware. After all, we've been selling quality hardware to the construction trade since 1899. (If anyone knows about a product's quality, it's architects and builders.)
But the real test of how a padlock performs isn't on a firing range. It's in the stores. On the shelves. At the cash register.
This is how Parker is going to blast holes in Master Lock's market: We've created the most exciting and traffic-generating packaging in the industry—it's practically pilfer-proof.
By offering the widest variety of products in the field—50 SKU's—and counting.
By offering terrific delivery. And for ordering purposes, a convenient toll-free number. (1-800-631-1366)
By offering padlocks that are, without question, the best dollar value in the industry.
By offering you quality merchandise which can—and will—increase your gross profit margin by an average of 25%.
The result is quick turnover, fast profits.
That's how you shoot holes in a market. With sound, well-conceived business disciplines. And, of course, giving the consumer their money's worth.
Forget rifles, machine guns or bazookas. Watch yourself, Master Lock.
Parker is ready. We're aiming. And we're about to fire.

S. Parker Hardware Mfg. Corp., Parker Drive, PO. Box 9882, Englewood, New Jersey 07631 Toll-Free 1-800-631-1366.
Visit us at booth 1260 at the Home Center Show.

Car thieves are getting bolder. In Detroit, they started a taxicab company with three stolen police cars.

And in New York, one enterprising thief used his 21 stolen cars to start a rent-a-car company.

These and other stories of America's $1.7-billion-a-year stolen car racket are reported in an original article in the September Reader's Digest, an article that follows a car theft from popped ignition lock to forged vehicle identification number.

It's reporting like this—that shows 40 million readers scenes they'd never see otherwise—that makes the Digest a great vehicle.

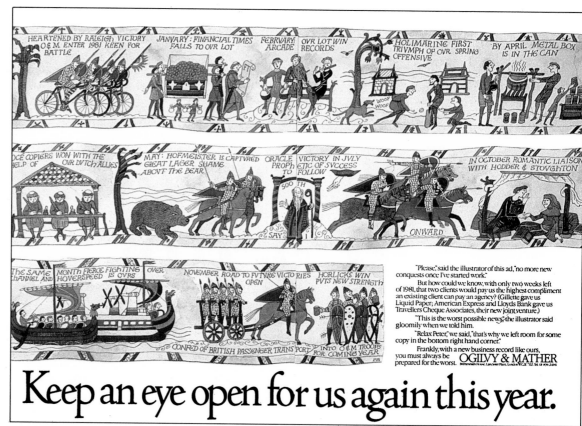

22 GOLD

Gold & Silver Awards

Trade
Any Size
B/W or Color
Campaign

23 SILVER

ART DIRECTOR
Mark Johnson

WRITER
Rav Freidel

DESIGNERS
Mark Johnson
Barbara Bowman
Adrienne Goodman
Dominique Singer

PHOTOGRAPHERS
Steve Steigman
Steve Bronstein

CLIENT
Sony

AGENCY
Ammirati & Puris

IF YOU CAN'T GET BIGGER CAMERAMEN, GET SMALLER CAMERAS.

If your cameramen don't mind packing 30 pounds on their shoulder, you can stop reading right now.

But if they're like most cameramen, mere mortals, they'd much prefer taking on the likes of El Salvador, Beirut or even downtown Topeka shouldering one-third the weight.

Which is precisely why Sony engineered the BVP-110.

Weighing in at just 9½ pounds and measuring only 14" x 3½" x 5", the BVP-110 is the industry's smallest, lightest, most compact full-fledged video camera. (In fact, it's so small,

one network actually strapped it to a sky diver's helmet, while another fastened it to a snow skier traveling at 70 mph, with the results of both being super video.)

The Sony BVP-110 offers distinct advantages beyond compactness. Because it's a one-tube, you're free of the single most difficult and aggravating problem associated with three-tubes: registration error.

You're also free of color drift and black balance errors.

And the Sony one-tube frees you of something else—

toting around loads of extra batteries. This rugged, dependable camera has the lowest power consumption of any broadcast-quality camera in the industry. It'll operate for more than two hours on a single battery pack.

So if you're looking to stay out in front of the news, instead of behind it, and you can't get bigger cameramen, get the next best thing. The Sony BVP-110.

Sony makes a complete line of cameras as well as ½", ¾" and 1" broadcast VTR's, editors, Digital Timebase Correc-

tors, and high-performance monitors.

For more information, call Sony Broadcast Company, in New York/New Jersey at (201) 368-5085; in Chicago at (312) 860-7800; in Los Angeles at (213) 537-4300; in Atlanta at (404) 451-7671; or in Dallas at (214) 659-3600.

SONY Broadcast

Sony is a registered trademark of the Sony Corp. © 1982 Sony Corp. of America, 9 W. 57th St., New York, N.Y. 10019

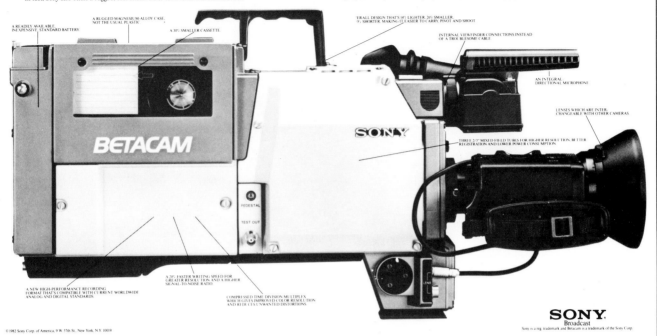

Collateral
Brochures
Other than by mail

24 GOLD

ART DIRECTORS
Paul Regan
William Tomlinson

WRITERS
Peter D. Nichols
Paul Mahoney

DESIGNER
William Tomlinson

PHOTOGRAPHER
Steve Marsel

CLIENT
J&J Corrugated Box

AGENCY
Hill, Holliday, Connors,
Cosmopulos/Boston

25 SILVER

ART DIRECTOR
Kent Eggleston

WRITER
Lew Cady

CLIENT
Art Directors Club of Denver

AGENCY
Broyles, Allebaugh & Davis/
Colorado

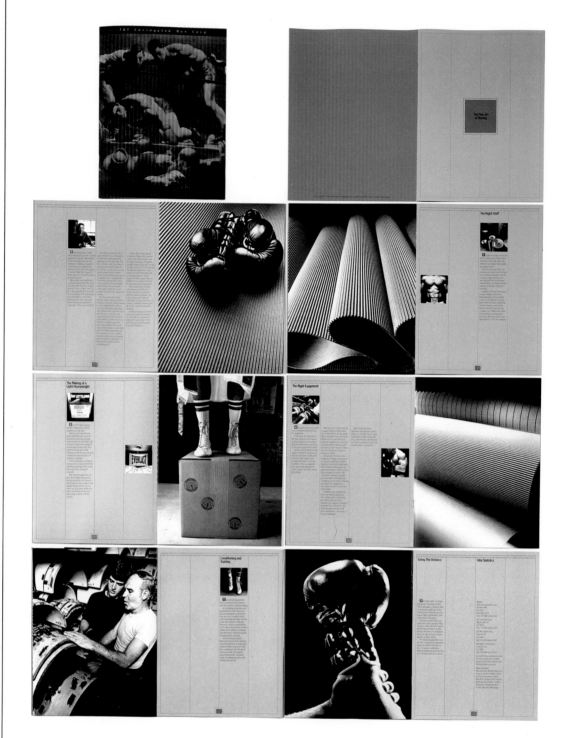

24 GOLD

DRAW ME

and be a
FAMOUS ART GUY*

Talent Test inside!

FAMOUS ART GUYS SCHOOL

Denver, Colorado

YOU CAN BE A FAMOUS ART GUY!

Find out if you have valuable talent. Enter the 1982 Art Directors Club of Denver FAMOUS ART GUYS SHOW.

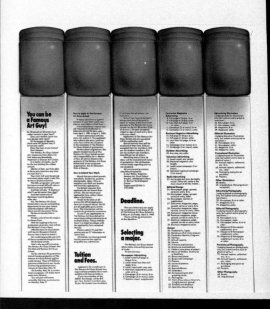

Collateral Sale Kits

26 GOLD

ART DIRECTOR
Lee Einhorn

WRITER
Stuart Nickerson

DESIGNER
Lee Einhorn

PHOTOGRAPHER
Greg Jarem

CLIENT
Saab-Scania

AGENCY
RMI/New Jersey

27 SILVER

ART DIRECTOR
James Sebastian

DESIGNERS
James Sebastian
Michael Lauretano
Rose Biondi

PHOTOGRAPHER
Joe Standart

CLIENT
Martex/West Point Pepperell

AGENCY
Designframe

Collateral Direct Mail

28 SILVER

ART DIRECTOR & WRITER
David Anderson

PHOTOGRAPHER
Dick Kaiser

CLIENT
Western Landscape
Construction

AGENCY
Ogilvy & Mather/Los Angeles

26 GOLD

WESTERN LANDSCAPE CONSTRUCTION
We're helping to build the west.

**Collateral
P.O.P.**

29 GOLD
ART DIRECTOR
Jeffrey Vogt
WRITER
David Tessler
DESIGNERS
Jeffrey Vogt
Denise Monaco
Adrienne Goodman
ARTIST
R&V Studio
PHOTOGRAPHER
Cailor/Resnick Studio
CLIENT
BMW of North America
AGENCY
Ammirati & Puris

30 SILVER
ART DIRECTOR
Jerry Whitley
WRITER
Joe O'Neil
DESIGNERS
Jerry Whitley
Denise Monaco
Adrienne Goodman
PHOTOGRAPHER
Dick James
CLIENT
BMW of North America
AGENCY
Ammirati & Puris

THE FIRST KNOWN EXAMPLE OF A CAR EVALUATING ITS DRIVER.

Until now, timetables for routine automobile maintenance have overlooked one important and generally unpredictable factor: the person behind the wheel.

Obviously, someone who drives mostly on crowded city streets places different stresses on a car than someone who drives mostly on uncluttered highways. Differences in driving techniques (such as how hard one accelerates) are also a significant factor.

Which is why BMW engineers have developed the Service Interval Indicator®— a computer-governed system based on the obvious fact that different people drive differently.

With the aid of electronic sensors, the Service Interval Indicator monitors individual variations in driving habits and environments—as measured by engine speeds, the number of cold starts, and miles driven.

It then processes this information, and calculates when service is actually warranted—not just dictated by an arbitrary schedule.

One of BMW's major preoccupations has always been man's interaction with machine.

And BMW's new Service Interval Indicator represents machine's latest contribution to that end.

THE ULTIMATE DRIVING MACHINE.

29 GOLD

LET THE GOVERNMENT PAY FOR SOME OF YOUR FUN. LEASE A BMW.

There are any number of cars available for leasing that may function beautifully as tax write-offs. BMW's, however, are engineered to function beautifully as cars. To provide exhilaration behind the wheel, not merely behind the calculator.

They were designed, after all, by German engineers who believe that extraordinary performance is the only rational motive for buying, or leasing, an expensive automobile.

And so, they are intended for drivers who are as fond of rounding corners and accelerating up straightaways as they are of eluding taxes.

THE ULTIMATE DRIVING MACHINE.

**Outdoor
Single**

31 GOLD
ART DIRECTOR
Dean Hanson
WRITER
Jarl Olson
PHOTOGRAPHER
Bettmann Archives
CLIENT
7 South 8th For Hair
AGENCY
Fallon, McElligott, Rice/Mpls.

32 SILVER
ART DIRECTOR
Ian Potter
WRITER
Rob Kitchen
CLIENT
Ciba Geigy
AGENCY
FCO Univas/London

A bad haircut can make anyone look dumb.

7 South 8th for Hair
804 LaSalle Avenue / Call 333-1376 for appointment

31 GOLD

32 SILVER

**Outdoor
Campaign**

33 SILVER
ART DIRECTOR
Gordon Bennett
WRITER
Martin Puris
DESIGNERS
Gordon Bennett
Barbara Bowman
PHOTOGRAPHERS
Gilles Bensimon
Oliviero Toscani
CLIENT
Club Med
AGENCY
Ammirati & Puris

CLUB MED. THE ANTIDOTE FOR CIVILIZATION.

33 SILVER

CLUB MED.
THE ANTIDOTE
FOR
CIVILIZATION.

CLUB MED.
THE ANTIDOTE
FOR
CIVILIZATION.

THE DECISION TO HAVE A BABY COULD SOON BE BETWEEN YOU, YOUR HUSBAND AND YOUR SENATOR.

For everyone who thought something like this could never happen. It has.

This week, the United States Senate will vote on two bills which could deprive you of your most fundamental personal rights: the right to have the number of children you want. When you want them. Or to have none at all.

These bills ultimately seek to outlaw all abortion. For all women.

Even if the pregnancy is the result of rape. Or incest.

Sponsoring the bills are Jesse Helms, Orrin Hatch and other right-wing U.S. Senators who will stop at nothing to impose their particular religious and personal beliefs on you. Your family. Your friends. Everyone.

And what's even more frightening, they are acting with the encouragement of President Reagan.

Don't stand by silently. Telephone and telegraph your senators today. Their address is: The United States Senate, Washington, D.C. 20510.

And fill out the Planned Parenthood coupon. Give generously of your time and money.

The fate of safe and legal abortion hangs in the balance.

**JOIN
PLANNED PARENTHOOD**

Planned Parenthood of New York City, Inc.
380 Second Avenue, New York, N.Y. 10010
212/777-2002

☐ I believe abortion is something personal, not political. Please keep me informed and add me to your mailing list.

☐ I want to make a tax-deductible contribution to support Planned Parenthood's work. Here is my check in the amount of $_____

NAME _____

ADDRESS _____

CITY/STATE/ZIP _____

TELEPHONE (DAY) _____ (EVE) _____

A copy of our financial report can be obtained from us or the New York Department of State, Office of Charities Registration, Albany, New York 12231

This advertisement has been paid for with private contributions.

© 1982 Planned Parenthood of New York City, Inc.   NYT 8/15

ABORTION IS SOMETHING PERSONAL. NOT POLITICAL.

WHAT IF YOUR BABY IS GOING TO HAVE A BABY?

40% of all girls who turn 14 this year will become pregnant while they are still teenagers.

Each one is somebody's daughter. With her whole life in front of her.

Yet on March 10th the United States Senate Judiciary Committee took an unprecedented first step which could force a woman to bear a child. Even if she's only a child herself.

They have approved the "Hatch Amendment" to the Constitution which will now go to the Senate floor. And it may very well pass.

If this amendment becomes law, it could ultimately deny you your most fundamental personal rights: The right to have the number of children you want. When you want them. Or to have none at all.

The "Hatch Amendment" will abolish your Constitutional freedom to choose an abortion. And at the same time will allow the states and Congress to outlaw all abortion.

Even if the pregnancy is the result of rape. Or incest.

It is even possible that if you have an abortion you could be prosecuted for murder.

Backing this amendment are right-wing United States Senators who want to impose their religious beliefs on you. Your friends. Your family. Everyone.

Don't stand by silently and let the minority rule. Fill out the Planned Parenthood coupon. Give generously of your time and money. Write to your Senators. Their address is c/o The United States Senate, Washington, D.C., 20510.

Now more than ever, we must fight to keep the government from governing your private life.

The fate of safe and legal abortion lies in the balance.

ABORTION IS SOMETHING PERSONAL. NOT POLITICAL.

Public Service
Newspaper or Magazine
Campaign

36 GOLD
ART DIRECTOR
Nancy Rice
WRITER
Tom McElligott
PHOTOGRAPHERS
Tom Bach
Jim Marvy
CLIENT
The Episcopal Ad Project
AGENCY
Fallon, McElligott, Rice/Mpls.

God didn't give His only begotten Son to be a spokesman for the moral majority.

If you think Jesus loves all people — even those who don't agree with Him —
come and join us in a service where diversity is not only allowed, but welcomed.
The Episcopal Church

Will man destroy in six minutes what it took God six days to create?

If you think it's time Christianity raised its voice in the life and death issues of our age, come and join us in the active worship and fellowship of the Episcopal Church.
The Episcopal Church

You shouldn't have to go through channels to talk to God.

If you believe there ought to be more to God than a flickering image interrupted by commercials, join us as we worship and discover the joy of God together in the Episcopal Church.
The Episcopal Church

**Public Service
Newspaper or Magazine
Campaign**

37 SILVER
ART DIRECTOR
Bill Schwartz
WRITERS
Craig Astler
Dennis Okerbloom
PHOTOGRAPHER
Studio R
CLIENT
United Way
AGENCY
Meldrum & Fewsmith/Ohio

SOME ALCOHOLICS ARE YOUNGER THAN THE BOOZE THEY DRINK.

Lush. Boozehound. Drunk. Alkie. Wino.
These are tragic terms to describe adults.
Apply them to children, and they become heartbreaking.
The reality of the situation is that 75% of all children have tried alcohol or drugs by the age of 17.
Yet we can't wring our hands over the situation. We have to act.
When you give to United Way, you help 175 agencies in our local area. But due to today's economy, those agencies need extra help. Because more people are in need. And fewer can give.
Give generously to United Way. And give to this year's '82 PLUS campaign for today's extraordinary needs.
It might keep a youngster from aging before his time.

United Way.
It works for all of us.

UNFORTUNATELY, SOME PEOPLE HAVE NO PROBLEM LOSING WEIGHT.

Not when you have a can of ravioli for a family of four.
Or half a loaf of bread to last a weekend.
Or low-cost wieners every night for a month.
These are the kind of nutritional problems some poor people face, right in our area.
And it's why United Way is here to help them.
When you give to United Way, you help 175 agencies in our local area. But due to today's economy, those agencies need extra help. Because more people are in need. And fewer can give.
Give generously to United Way. And give to this year's '82 PLUS campaign for today's extraordinary needs.
If people are going to lose weight, let's make it by choice.

United Way.
It works for all of us.

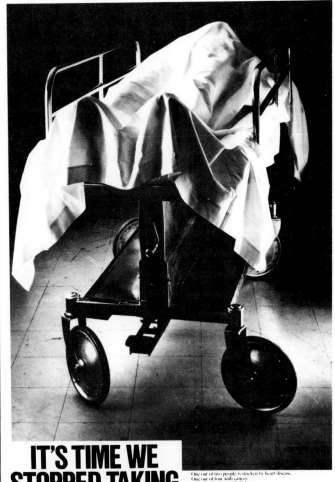

IT'S TIME WE STOPPED TAKING MAJOR ILLNESS LYING DOWN.

One out of two people is stricken by heart disease.
One out of four with cancer.
One out of twenty with diabetes.
Afflictions like these have been around so long, we've almost forgotten it's possible to defeat them.
Now. Today. With current technology. And all that's needed is the proper help.
When you give to United Way, you help 175 agencies in our local area. But due to today's economy, those agencies need extra help. Because more people are in need. And fewer can give.
Give generously to United Way. And give to this year's '82 PLUS campaign for today's extraordinary needs.
With your help, we can beat major illness.
Before it beats us.

United Way.
It works for all of us.

**Public Service
Outdoor Single**

38 SILVER
ART DIRECTOR
Jean-Marie Clarence Poisson
WRITER
Shelley Buber
DESIGNERS & ARTISTS
Jean-Marie Clarence Poisson
Shelley Buber
PHOTOGRAPHER
Michael Pierce
CLIENT
American Heart Association
AGENCY
Poisson & Buber

**Corporate
Newspaper or Magazine
Single**

39 GOLD
ART DIRECTOR
Priscilla Croft
WRITER
Martin Cooke
DESIGNER
Priscilla Croft
PHOTOGRAPHER
Steve Steigman
CLIENT
Xerox
AGENCY
Needham, Harper & Steers

40 SILVER
ART DIRECTOR
Maxeen Smart
WRITER
Frankie Cadwell
DESIGNER
Maxeen Smart
CLIENT
Sotheby Arcade Auctions
AGENCY
Cadwell Davis Partners

38 SILVER

YOU DON'T STAY THE LEADER OF A BUSINESS JUST BY INVENTING THE BUSINESS.

DuMont invented the first commercial television set. Duryea introduced the first automobile. And Hurley, the first washing machine.

Obviously, inventing a business is no guarantee that a company will keep leading that business.

Like these companies, Xerox also invented a business. Unlike them, we're still leading our business.

There's a simple reason: we never stopped inventing. Just as our original 914 was the most advanced copier in 1959, our 9500 is the most advanced today.

The 9500 performs more different tasks than any duplicator ever made. It reduces. It sorts. It collates. It even makes the best looking copies in the business.

And it does all this nearly twice as fast as the next fastest machine on the market. Two copies per second.

We also invented the 8200. It does just about any job you could ever ask of a copier. All at the touch of a few buttons. And it gives you blacker blacks, whiter whites and truer grays than any copier that's gone before.

Then there's the 5600. It's the first and only copier that automatically makes two-sided copies from two-sided originals. It has microcomputer diagnostics like the 8200 and 9500. It has a special document handler to deliver completely collated sets. And it has a very loyal following.

A recent independent survey asked people if they would replace their 5600 with any other brand of copier. Not one would.

You see, you become the DuMont of a business by inventing the business.

You become the Xerox of a business by going on and reinventing it. Year after year after year.

For more information, call 800-828-6210,* operator 100, or your local Xerox sales office.

XEROX

How much would you bid for this?

The world's oldest, most experienced auction house announces Sotheby's Arcade Auctions, specially created to enable you to buy and sell moderately valuable decorative arts. Each Arcade Auction, held for a two-day period every two weeks, will offer approximately 1,500 lots, valued from $50 to $5000.

A fascinating range and diversity of furniture, rugs, silver, porcelain and other decorative works of art make Sotheby's Arcade Auctions an attractive way to buy. 1,500 lots comprising approximately 10,000 items will be auctioned every two weeks in newly designed luxurious space at our York Avenue galleries.

The name of Sotheby's will benefit everything you choose to sell. Your consignments will enjoy exposure to unprecedented numbers of serious and affluent buyers. With Sotheby's Arcade Auctions, turnover will be fast and efficient. It is only about four weeks from consignment to sale and two weeks to payment.

Come July 15th and 16th to York Avenue at 72nd Street, first floor for Sotheby's new Arcade Auction. For dealers, it's an efficient new way to turn inventory. For collectors of every level, it's an exciting way to find what you want and sell what you don't. Visit the exhibitions starting Friday July 10th. Catalogues are available *at the galleries only.* For more information call 212/472-3577 or write: Sotheby's Arcade Auctions, 1334 York Avenue, New York, N.Y. 10021.

SOTHEBY'S

Sotheby's Arcade Auctions.
Every two weeks $50 to $5000.

**Corporate
Newspaper or Magazine
Campaign**

41 GOLD
ART DIRECTOR
Michael Lyons
WRITER
Paul Norris
PHOTOGRAPHERS
Michael Lyons
Sheik Amin
CLIENT
Aramco Services
AGENCY
Ogilvy & Mather/Houston

This plant at Abqaiq, Saudi Arabia,
processes one tenth of all the free
world's oil.

POSTCARD*

True, Long Beach has
better pizza places. But
Saudi Arabia has better
projects for petroleum
engineers like you and
me to work on.
Seriously, you would
envy our assignments.
If an oil company does
it, Aramco probably
does it the most or
the biggest.
Hang loose,
Eddie

Mr. David Newkirk
Hutcheson Oil Company
13500 Harwin Dr

Long Beach, California
90881 U.S.A.

Aramco, the largest oil producer in the world, is currently involved in projects
worth billions. Challenging positions are open for experienced geophysicists,
geologists, and petroleum engineers. Call (713) 750-6965. Aramco Services Company,
Mail Code Z4053-2, P.O. Box 53607, Houston, Texas 77052. **ARAMCO**

Safaniya, off the coast of Saudi Arabia, is the world's largest offshore oilfield.

Dear T.J.
Good thing I'm so modest. That way I won't make you feel bad by bragging about the big projects and big budgets in Saudi Arabia. Seriously though, a geophysicist can really show his stuff here. If an oil company does it, Aramco probably does it the most or the biggest. EAT YOUR HEART OUT!!
Gary

Mr. T.J. Jackson
Stanfeld Engineering
1400 Crane Ave.
Lafayette, Louisiana
70554 U.S.A.   No. 6

Aramco, the largest oil producer in the world, is currently involved in projects worth billions. Challenging positions are open for experienced geophysicists, geologists, and petroleum engineers. Call (713) 750-6965. Aramco Services Company, Mail Code Z4060-2, P.O. Box 53607, Houston, Texas 77052. **ARAMCO**

The Ghawar, in Saudi Arabia, is the largest oilfield in the world.

CAN YOU PUT UP WITH A LITTLE EGO TRIP FROM AN OLD GEOLOGIST BUDDY? THE PART OF OUR GHAWAR FIELD THAT I'M WORKING ON HAS ABOUT THE SAME RESERVES AS OKLAHOMA. NOT BAD FOR AN OLD LUFKIN, TEXAS, BOY, HUH? IF AN OIL COMPANY DOES IT, ARAMCO PROBABLY DOES IT THE MOST OR THE BIGGEST.

TAKE CARE,
GEORGE

M.J. LYONS
NANCO PETROLEUM CO.
8100 MORGAN ROAD
TULSA, OKLAHOMA 74190
U.S.A.   No. 34

Aramco, the largest oil producer in the world, is currently involved in projects worth billions. Challenging positions are open for experienced geophysicists, geologists, and petroleum engineers. Call (713) 750-6965. Aramco Services Company, Mail Code Z4061-2, P.O. Box 53607, Houston, Texas 77052. **ARAMCO**

How much would you bid for this?

The world's oldest, most experienced auction house announces Sotheby's Arcade Auctions, specially created to enable you to buy and sell moderately valuable decorative arts. Each Arcade Auction, held for a two-day period every two weeks, will offer approximately 1,500 lots, valued from $50 to $5000.

A fascinating range and diversity of furniture, rugs, silver, porcelain and other decorative works of art make Sotheby's Arcade Auctions an attractive way to buy. 1,500 lots comprising approximately 10,000 items will be auctioned every two weeks in newly designed luxurious space at our York Avenue galleries.

American Banjo Clock. Est. $100-200

The name of Sotheby's will benefit everything you choose to sell. Your consignments will enjoy exposure to unprecedented numbers of serious and affluent buyers. With Sotheby's Arcade Auctions, turnover will be fast and efficient. It is only about four weeks from consignment to sale and two weeks to payment.

Come July 15th and 16th to York Avenue at 72nd Street, first floor for Sotheby's new Arcade Auction. For dealers, it's an efficient new way to turn inventory. For collectors of every level, it's an exciting way to find what you want and sell what you don't. Visit the exhibitions starting Friday July 10th. Catalogues are available *at the galleries only.* For more information call 212/472-3577 or write: Sotheby's Arcade Auctions, 1334 York Avenue, New York, N.Y. 10021.

SOTHEBY'S

American Duck Decoy (one of three). Est. $200-300

Gothic Revival Style Armchair. Est. $400-600

Art Nouveau Stained Glass Lamp. Est. $1500-2000

Sotheby's Arcade Auctions.
Every two weeks $50 to $5000.

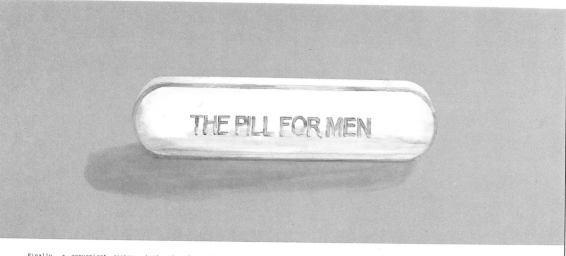

MEN HAVE BABIES TOO.

Finally, a convenient contraceptive for men. The Pill For Men from Johnson & Turturro Laboratories. It's 100% effective, it's risk-free and it's going to revolutionize the course of future relationships.

By introducing freedom. For both you and your partner. From both the fear of pregnancy and the risk of harmful side effects associated with other contraceptives. Freedom to have sex when you want. And to have a family when you want. Because The Pill For Men in no way interferes with a man's ability to father.

We're sure. After 20 years and over 25 million dollars in research, Johnson & Turturro found a way to allow each man to regulate his own fertility. And we backed that up with five years of testing more than two thousand men all across the United States.

So, if you and your partner are tired of the innaccuracies and restrictions associated with other forms of birth control, ask your doctor about Johnson & Turturro's 100% effective contraceptive in a daily tablet, The Pill For Men.

Because the method you're using is now obsolete.

**Introducing The Pill For Men.
A new fact of life.**

43 GOLD

TAKE THIS PILL AND NOTHING WILL HAPPEN.

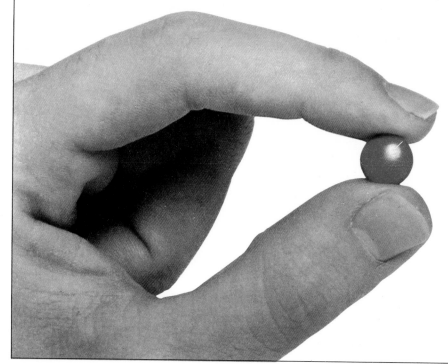

Absolutely nothing.

The pill is Control; the first birth control pill for men. Control provides total protection in a safe and effective way; a promise, that until now, no other male contraceptive could make.

Control is an idea that was conceived over twenty years ago and took twenty-five million dollars and the testing of two thousand men to make it a reality.

With a doctor's prescription, taken daily, Control is all the contraception you will ever need.

So take Control and take contraception into your own hands. Simple. Effective.

CONTROL
The first Birth Control Pill for Men

**The only time it won't work
is when you don't take it.**

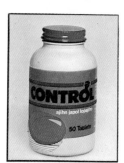

44 SILVER

45 GOLD

Hallo, have you heard about this rather unusual English candy which has a more sophisticated kind of taste than regular candy, not quite as sweet but a very fine classy sort of taste, and it's made by an English firm called Callard and Bowser and it really is jolly good. In fact, the truth is, it's jolly, jolly good, and you'll like it, and as I say it *is* English so please buy it because we need the money in England at the moment, I mean we're all as poor as church mice now, servants are unbelievably expensive and our industry's practically disappeared, about all we make is muffins and cricket bats and really good candy and half the cricket bats come from Hong Kong, so please, do us a favour and just try this Callard and Bowser candy, its rather sophisticated taste and I'm sure you'll approve of it and after all, I mean we did fight on your side in the War and we always let you beat us at golf and incidentally, let's not forget you pinched our language, if we hadn't forgotten to copyright that you'd be paying us the most amazing royalties every week so instead please buy Callard and Bowser's rather sophisticated English candy and help England back on its feet, frankly I think it's the least you can do.

46 SILVER

Hallo there. Look, apparently last time I was on the radio, talking about this frightfully good rather sophisticated English candy, when I said the name of the people who make this candy, which is Callard and Bowser, I didn't say Callard and Bowser terribly clearly and so all you good American persons have been going into Supermarkets and Drugstores asking for Bollard and Trouser, and Callous and Grocer, Gizzard and Powder, so let's get the name straight, shall we, it's Callard and Bowser. Cal-lard... Cal as in *Cal*vin Coolidge and lard as Jess Wil*lard* and Bowser, that's Bow as in the *Bau*haus, or better still Mutiny on the *Bou*nty and - ser, as in Pan*zer* Division. So if you want to try the best most sophisticated and upper class candy we make in England, it's quite simple, all you have to do is think of *Cal*vin Coolidge and Jess Wil*lard, and* as in Hans Christian *And*ersen and then the *Bau*haus or Mutiny on the *Bou*nty and a Pan*zer* Division, Callard and Bowser. It may take a little time to get hold of but I think you'll find it's worth it.

Gold & Silver Awards

Consumer Radio Campaign

47 GOLD
WRITERS
John Cleese
Lynn Stiles
CLIENT
Callard & Bowser/USA
AGENCY PRODUCER
Robert L. Dein
AGENCY
Lord, Geller, Federico,
Einstein

48 SILVER
WRITERS:
Steve Sandoz
Palmer Pettersen
CLIENT
Pizza Haven
AGENCY PRODUCERS
Palmer Pettersen
Steve Sandoz
AGENCY
John Brown & Partners/
Washington

47 GOLD

Hallo there. Look, apparently last time I was on the radio, talking about this frightfully good rather sophisticated English candy, when I said the name of the people who make this candy, which is Callard and Bowser, I didn't say Callard and Bowser terribly clearly and so all you good American persons have been going into Supermarkets and Drugstores asking for Bollard and Trouser, and Callous and Grocer, Gizzard and Powder, so let's get the name straight, shall we, it's Callard and Bowser. Cal-lard... Cal as in *Cal*vin Coolidge and lard as Jess Wil*lard* and Bowser, that's Bow as in the *Bau*haus, or better still Mutiny on the *Boun*ty and - ser, as in Pan*zer* Division. So if you want to try the best most sophisticated and upper class candy we make in England, it's quite simple, all you have to do is think of *Cal*vin Coolidge and Jess Wil*lard, and* as in Hans Christian *And*ersen and then the *Bau*haus or Mutiny on the *Boun*ty and a pan*zer* Division, Callard and Bowser. It may take a little time to get hold of but I think you'll find it's worth it.

47 GOLD

Hallo, have you heard about this rather unusual English candy which has a more sophisticated kind of taste than regular candy, not quite as sweet but a very fine classy sort of taste, and it's made by an English firm called Callard and Bowser and it really is jolly good. In fact, the truth is, it's jolly, jolly good, and you'll like it, and as I say it *is* English so please buy it because we need the money in England at the moment, I mean we're all as poor as church mice now, servants are unbelievably expensive and our industry's practically disappeared, about all we make is muffins and cricket bats and really good candy and half the cricket bats come from Hong Kong, so please, do us a favour and just try this Callard and Bowser candy, its rather sophisticated taste and I'm sure you'll approve of it and after all, I mean we did fight on your side in the War and we always let you beat us at golf and incidentally, let's not forget you pinched our language, if we hadn't forgotten to copyright that you'd be paying us the most amazing royalties every week so instead please buy Callard and Bowser's rather sophisticated English candy and help England back on its feet, frankly I think it's the least you can do.

47 GOLD

Hallo... Um... look there's some frightfully good rather sophisticated English candy now being sold in the US of A, it's terribly popular among the upper classes here in England so please do try some. It's called Callard and Bowser candy and it's butterscotch and toffee and toffee comes in seven exciting new flavours, Raspberry, Aubergine, Smoky Passionfruit, Mackerel, Pork and Prune, Lamb and Banana, and the flavour of the month Leather, Tangerine and Raccoon, a new taste sensation... I'm sorry those aren't the flavours at all, I made them up, it was a cheap trick to catch your attention, and I'm very ashamed of myself because the real flavours are perfectly sensible and quite delicious, and rather sophisticated because Callard and Bowser candy isn't quite as sweet as ordinary candy, so it appeals to rather sophisticated, urbane, educated people who wouldn't like silly publicity stunts about Leather Tangerine and Raccoon flavoured toffee *at all*. So please forgive me; completely ignore this commercial. Forget all about it and simply try some of Callard and Bowser's candy and I promise not to be naughty again.

ANNCR: And now it's time for Pizza Haven's afternoon sing-along, led today by that popular youth group "Up With Pizza."

LEADER: Here's a song most of you should know, so sing along. Hit it, Cubby.

(MUSIC: MUSIC BEGINS WITH SINGLE GUITAR AND A CHORUS OF VOICES SINGING TO THE TUNE OF "MICHAEL ROW THE BOAT ASHORE".)

SINGERS: *Michael bring a pizza home,*
From Pizza Haven
It's the place where the pizza comes from,
That tastes like heaven.

LEADER: O.K., now boys only...

BOYS: *Haven hero sixteen inches wide,*
It's a great deal.

LEADER: Now just the girls...

GIRLS: *Fifteen toppings from side to side,*
What a tasty meal.

LEADER: Now, all you on the freeway...

(SFX: HORNS HONKING, PEOPLE CLAPPING.)

THRONG: *Stop by Pizza Haven tonight,*
On your way home.
Michael, make your family feel all right,
Bring a pizza.

(SFX: APPLAUSE AND HORNS HONKING UP AND UNDER.)

ANNCR: Pizza Haven *is* pizza heaven.

(MUSIC: PIANO INTRO TO HALLELUJAH CHORUS UP AND UNDER.)

ANNCR: And now, the 18 fresh toppings of Pizza Haven as sung by the Jalapeno Chorus.

(MUSIC: SUNG TO TUNE OF HALLELUJAH CHORUS)

LARGE CHORUS: *Jalapeno, jalapeno,*
Pepperoni, pepperoni,
Green peppers and mushrooms.

CHORUS: *Fresh tomato, delicious sausage,*
With anchovies or pineapple,
We top it just for you.

MEN: *For the best pizza you have eaten.*

CHORUS: *Salami, fresh onions,*
Black olives with bacon.

SOPRANOS: *Have your choice,*

MEN: *Extra cheese or shrimp and ham.*

SOPRANOS: *Choose your size,*

MEN: *Sauerkraut or lean ground beef.*

CHORUS: *And we shall eat for ever and ever.*
Pizza Haven, pizza heaven, Pizza Haven, pizza heaven, Piz-za Hav-en.

ANNCR: Pizza Haven *is* pizza heaven.

(SFX: TELEPHONE RINGS)

ANGEL OVER PHONE: Halo. Pizza Haven. Can I help you?

MAN AT HOME: (SUNG TO THE TUNE OF "KUMBYAH")
Want a pizza here, come by truck.

ANGEL: Okay, what kind would you like?

MAN'S WIFE: *Pepperoni, come by truck.*

ANGEL: Anything else on it?

THEIR SON: *Olives and mushrooms, come by truck.*

ANGEL: And, what to drink?

ALL: *3 big cokes, come by truck.*

ANGEL: Very good. How big a pizza, now?

MAN: *Sixteen inches, come by truck.*

ANGEL: Sixteen inches, then.

MAN & WIFE: *Bring it hot, please, come by truck.*

ANGEL: Absolutely! Any salads there?

MAN: *Not this evening, thanks, come by truck.*

ANGEL: Okay, we'll send a truck right out.

ALL: *Thank you very much, come by truck.*

ANGEL: We always do.

ALL: *We'll hang up now, come by truck.*

ANGEL: Great. Enjoy your pizza.

ALL: *Hanging up now, come by truck.*

ANGEL: On it's way.

ALL: *We'll hang up now, come by truck.*

ANGEL: I will too, then.

ALL: *Hanging up now, come by truck.*

ANGEL: You bet.

ANNCR: Pizza Haven *is* Pizza Heaven.
Call, and ye shall receive.

Gold & Silver
Awards

**Consumer Television
60 Seconds Single**

49 GOLD
ART DIRECTOR
Dave Davis
WRITER
Bob Meury
CLIENT
Sony Corporation–
Betamax Components
DIRECTOR
Gary Princz
PRODUCTION CO.
EUE Productions
AGENCY PRODUCERS
Lois Rice
Bruce Giuriceo
AGENCY
Backer & Spielvogel

50 SILVER
ART DIRECTORS
Mark Nussbaum
Bob Lenz
WRITER
Barry Lisee
CLIENT
Miller Brewing/
High Life
DIRECTOR
Joe Hanwright
PRODUCTION CO.
Larkin Productions
AGENCY PRODUCER
Barry Lisee
AGENCY
Backer & Spielvogel

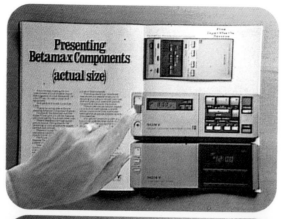

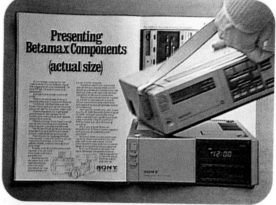

49 GOLD

ANNCR: Have you seen the latest ad for Sony
Betamax Components? There they are. Actual
size.

I can't believe it. They look so real. Oh. They are
real! This is terrific.

And look. A wireless remote control that does
just about everything. Let's see. Umm. Reverse,
whoh...whoh. And forward. In almost any
speed you want. Boy, that was fast. Umm, I'd
better put it back.

And Betamax Components are so compact and
lightweight, you can take the recorder anywhere
to shoot your own movies. This could be my big
chance!

Let's see. What else is there to play with. Oh, a
coupon. Oh, there's the Sony Trinicon Color
Camera. It gives you instant replay right
through the eyepiece...There's even an offer for
free tapes. Mmm...I think I'll keep the
coupon.

The Sony Betamax Component System.

You know what?

I think I'll keep the whole thing.

50 SILVER

(MUSIC UNDER)

(VO): 'Round here, well I guess we take work about as serious as anybody else. But I'll tell you somethin' boys, come sundown ain't nobody more serious about havin' a good time.

(MUSIC IN): *Welcome to Miller Time. It's all yours, and it's all mine. Bring your thirsty self right here, you've got the time we've got the beer for what you had in mind. Welcome to Miller Time.*

(VO): The best beer for the best time of the day. Miller High Life.

(MUSIC): *Bring your thirsty self right here, you've got the time, we've got the beer for what you have in mind. Oh-oh; Welcome, you know you're welcome, welcome, everybody's welcome. Welcome to Miller Time. Yours and mine.*

Gold & Silver Awards

**Consumer Television
60 Seconds Campaign**

51 GOLD

ART DIRECTORS
Mark Nussbaum
Bob Lenz
Gerald Pfiffner
Jim Anderson

WRITERS
Barry Lisee
Gerald Pfiffner

CLIENT
Miller Brewing/
High Life

DIRECTORS
Joe Hanwright
Steve Horn
Joe Pytka

PRODUCTION COS.
Larkin Productions
Steve Horn Productions
Levine Pytka

AGENCY PRODUCERS
Barry Lisee
Andy Cornelius
Tom Dakin

AGENCY
Backer & Spielvogel

51 GOLD

(MUSIC UNDER)

(VO): 'Round here, well I guess we take work about as serious as anybody else. But I'll tell you somethin' boys, come sundown ain't nobody more serious about havin' a good time.

(MUSIC IN): *Welcome to Miller Time. It's all yours, and it's all mine. Bring your thirsty self right here, you've got the time we've got the beer for what you had in mind. Welcome to Miller Time.*

(VO): The best beer for the best time of the day. Miller High Life.

(MUSIC): *Bring your thirsty self right here, you've got the time, we've got the beer for what you have in mind. Oh-oh; Welcome, you know you're welcome, welcome, everybody's welcome. Welcome to Miller Time. Yours and mine.*

(MUSIC UNDER)

ANNCR (VO): When you live and work around the water you put in some pretty long days. But y'know... I guess that's what makes us really enjoy our nights.

SINGERS: *Welcome to Miller Time. It's all yours and it's all mine. Bring your thirsty self right here... You've got the time, we've got the beer for what you have in mind. Welcome to Miller Time.*

ANNCR (VO): The best beer for the best time of the day. Miller High Life.

SINGERS: *Bring your thirsty self right here... you've got the time, we've got the beer for what you have in mind. Welcome to Miller Time. Yours and mine.*

(SFX: MUSIC IN BACKGROUND.)

ANNCR (VO): This place is real special. We wouldn't trade one of our days up here for anything. Except maybe for one of our nights.

SONG: *Welcome to Miller Time. It's all yours, and it's all mine. Bring your thirsty self right here, you've got the time, we've got the beer, for what you have in mind. Welcome to Miller Time.*

ANNCR (VO): The best beer for the best time of the day. Miller High Life.

SONG: *Bring your thirsty self right here, you've got the time, we've got the beer, for what you have in mind. Oh, welcome, you know you're welcome, welcome, everybody's welcome.*
Welcome to Miller Time.
Yours and mine.

**Consumer Television
60 Seconds Campaign**

52 SILVER

ART DIRECTORS
Lee Gleason
Ralph Love

WRITERS
David Lamb
Larry Simon
David Klehr

CLIENT
Anheuser-Busch/
Budweiser Light

DIRECTOR
Joe Pytka

PRODUCTION CO.
Levine Pytka

AGENCY PRODUCERS
David Lamb
Gary Conway

AGENCY
Needham, Harper & Steers/
Chicago

52 SILVER

(MUSIC)

GOALIE (VO): You can protect everything but your ego. "Cause they know how it hurts."

SINGERS: *Bring out your best.*

GOALIE: And they'll go for it again.

ANNCR (VO): The best never comes easy. That's why there's nothing else like it. Budweiser Light.

SINGERS: *Bring out your best
You've got to reach deep inside.
Bring out your best
Budweiser Light
Bring out your best
Budweiser Light.*

ANNCR (VO): The best. You've found it in yourself and now you've found it in the beer you drink

SINGERS: *Budweiser
Budweiser Light*

SCOUT #1: When did they move him down?

SCOUT #2: Couple of years ago when he hurt his arm.

PITCHER (VO): Early in the year these guys were down here scouting the kids. Now they're looking for help.

SINGERS: *Bring out your best.*

ANNCR (VO): The best never comes easy. That's why there's nothing else like it.
Budweiser Light.

SINGERS: *Bring out your best
Budweiser Light
Bring out your best
Budweiser Light
Bring out your best*

ANNCR (VO): The best, you've found it in yourself. And now you've found it in the beer you drink.

SCOUT: Hey Bob, you gotta minute?

SINGERS: *Budweiser Light*

(MUSIC)

COACH: No second shots, Wallace.
No second shots.

PLAYER: I'm used to him yelling.

COACH: Wallace, you've got to keep him out of there.

PLAYER: But not at me.

COACH: Box him out. Box him out.

ANNCR: The best never comes easy.
That's why there's nothing else like it.
Budweiser Light

SINGERS: *Bring out your best*
Bring out your best
Budweiser Light
Bring out your best
Budweiser Light

ANNCR: The best.

COACH: Nice game

ANNCR: You've found it in yourself. And now you've
found it in the beer you drink.

SINGERS: *Budweiser*
Budweiser Light

Gold & Silver Awards

CLUB MED®
The antidote for civilization.™

53 GOLD

ANNCR: At Club Med you can water ski…play tennis…snorkel…or sail…wind surf…or play volley ball…

At Club Med you can exercise everything. Including your right not to exercise anything.

SONG: *The Club Med vacation. The antidote for civilization.*

54 SILVER (TIE)

CLARA: Ed, it's time to take the rabbits to the pet store. I better rent a trailer.

ANNCR (VO): A lot of folks call Jartran when their business expands faster than expected.

CLARA: Ed, I think we need a truck.

ANNCR (VO): You see, most Jartran trucks have automatic transmission. And they all have a low price.

CLARA: Ed, I think we need a bigger truck. (PAUSE) Ed…

ANNCR (VO): So when you need a truck for your business or your family, just call your Jartran dealer. And he'll hop right to it.

55 SILVER (TIE)

(MUSIC UNDER)

MAN: Have you been talking to our son on long distance again?

WOMAN: (NODS AND WHIMPERS)

MAN: Did he tell you how much he loves you?

WOMAN: (NODS AND WHIMPERS)

MAN: Did he tell you how well he's doing in school?

WOMAN: (NODS AND WHIMPERS AND CRIES)

MAN: All those things are wonderful. What on earth are you crying for?

WOMAN: Did you see our long distance bill?

(MUSIC)

ANNCR (VO): If your long distance bills are too much, call MCI. Sure, reach out and touch someone. Just do it for a whole lot less.

Consumer Television
30 Seconds
Campaign

56 GOLD

ART DIRECTOR
Michael Tesch

WRITER
Patrick Kelly

CLIENT
Federal Express

DIRECTORS
Patrick Kelly
Joe Sedelmaier

PRODUCTION COS.
Kelly Pictures
Hampton Road Films
Sedelmaier Films

AGENCY PRODUCER
Maureen Kearns

AGENCY
Ally & Gargano

56 GOLD

GUY: I need that package of slides for a major presentation tomorrow at 10:30 a.m.

COMPETITOR: You got it!

GUY: Not noon, not 3:00, 10:30 a.m.

COMPETITOR: You got it!

GUY: Listen to me. No slides, no presentation.

COMPETITOR: You got it!

GUY: Well, where is it?

COMPETITOR: You'll get it!

(SFX: BARKING)

ANNCR (VO): Next time send it Federal Express.
Now Federal schedules delivery by 10:30 a.m.
So when we say you got it, you'll get it.

POSTAL CLERK: And on top of that, I only have 6,542 days till retirement.

(SFX: BELL)

CUSTOMER: Uh, I'd like to send some Express Mail letters to...

CLERK: We don't go there.
And with the insurance plan and other little tidbits, that adds up to a nice little piece of change, don't you see.

CUSTOMER: Uh, what about...

POSTAL CLERK: We don't go there.
Evelyn and I, you know Evelyn...

ANNCR (VO): At Federal Express we go to thousands more cities and communities with our Overnight Letter than the Post Office goes with Express Mail. So now when you have to send an important letter... you don't have to deal with the Post Office.

CUSTOMER: Uh...

POSTAL CLERK: We don't go there either.

(SFX: PULLS DOWN SHADE)

FEEMER: Schtoolum, do you know how to get this big package to Seattle overnight?

SCHTOOLUM:: Gee I don't know, Feemer, let's go up and bounce it off Boomer.

(SFX: ELEVATOR)

BOOMER: Gosh, I don't know fellas, let's go up and run it by Rizzo.

RIZZO: Let's parade it by Pooperman.

POOPERMAN: Let's waltz it by Wimpus.

WIMPUS: Let's dance it by Dolt.

ANNCR (VO): If more people knew that Federal Express handles great big packages even up to 70 pounds, it sure would save everybody a whole lot of trouble.

**Consumer Television
30 Seconds
Campaign**

57 SILVER
ART DIRECTOR
George Euringer

WRITERS
Helayne Spivak
Tom Messner

CLIENT
MCI

DIRECTOR
Bob Giraldi

PRODUCTION CO.
Giraldi Productions

AGENCY PRODUCER
Jerry Haynes

AGENCY
Ally & Gargano

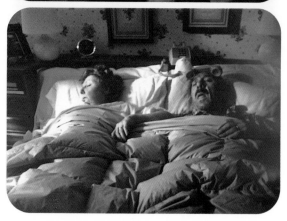

57 SILVER

(MUSIC UNDER)

MAN: Have you been talking to our son on long
distance again?

WOMAN: (NODS AND WHIMPERS)

MAN: Did he tell you how much he loves you?

WOMAN: (NODS AND WHIMPERS)

MAN: Did he tell you how well he's doing in school?

WOMAN: (NODS AND WHIMPERS AND CRIES)

MAN: All those things are wonderful. What on earth
are you crying for?

WOMAN: Did you see our long distance bill?

(MUSIC)

ANNCR (VO): If your long distance bills are too much,
call MCI. Sure, reach out and touch someone.
Just do it for a whole lot less.

(PHONE RINGS. A VERY SLEEPY WOMAN PICKS UP THE
PHONE)

MOM: Hullo?

DAVE: Mom? Surprise! It's Dave.

MOM: Dave?

DAVE: Your son. I'm sorry I woke you but the long
distance rates are cheapest after 11 p.m.

MOM: (SNORES)

DAVE: Mom? Put Dad on, Mom.
Dad? Dad? Mom?...

ANNCR (VO): To save 15 to 50% on long distance before
as well as after 11 p.m., call MCI.
And never reach out and wake someone again.

(SOUND OF PHONE RINGING. IT'S PICKED UP AND A VERY
SLEEPY VOICE SPEAKS):

LYN: Hullo?

HAROLD: Lyn? It's Harold. I'm calling long distance.

LYN: What time is it?

HAROLD: 2 a.m. your time, sleepy head!

LYN: 2 a.m.?

HAROLD: Oh, you wouldn't believe the money I save
by calling after 11 p.m.

LYN: Oh, really?

HAROLD: For sure.

LYN: I can save you even more money, Harold.

HAROLD: How, baby?

LYN: (CLICK AT RECEIVER IS HEARD)

ANNCR (VO): To save 15 to 50% on long distance before
as well as after 11 p.m., call MCI.

And stop talking in someone else's sleep.

Consumer Television 10 Seconds Single

58 GOLD

ART DIRECTOR
Mike Tesch

WRITER
Patrick Kelly

CLIENT
Federal Express

DIRECTOR
Patrick Kelly

PRODUCTION COS.
Hampton Road Films
Kelly Pictures

AGENCY PRODUCER
Maureen Kearns

AGENCY
Ally & Gargano

59 SILVER

ART DIRECTOR
Dean Stefanides

WRITER
Earl Carter

CLIENT
Nikon

DIRECTOR
Dennis Chalkin

PRODUCTION CO.
Dennis Chalkin Productions

AGENCY PRODUCER
Gary Grossman

AGENCY
Scali, McCabe, Sloves

Television Technique Best Slice of Life 60 or 30 Seconds Single

60 GOLD

ART DIRECTOR
George Euringer

WRITER
Tom Messner

CLIENT
MCI

DIRECTOR
Bob Giraldi

PRODUCTION CO.
Giraldi Productions

AGENCY PRODUCER
Jerry Haynes

AGENCY
Ally & Gargano

61 SILVER

ART DIRECTOR
George Euringer

WRITER
Helayne Spivak

CLIENT
MCI

DIRECTOR
Bob Giraldi

PRODUCTION CO.
Giraldi Productions

AGENCY PRODUCER
Jerry Haynes

AGENCY
Ally & Gargano

58 GOLD

(SFX: PAPER RUSTLING, SHAKING)

ANNCR (VO): You've got a lot riding on this letter. And you going to hand it over to the Post Office. Federal Express has an alternative.

59 SILVER

VO: When the space shuttle took off, one of the few things on board that didn't have a backup system... was a Nikon camera.

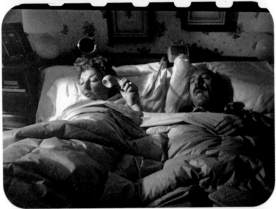

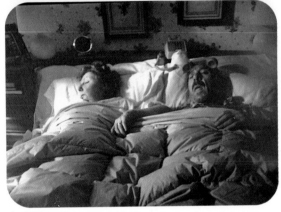

60 GOLD

(MUSIC UNDER)

MAN: Have you been talking to our son on long distance again?

WOMAN: (NODS AND WHIMPERS)

MAN: Did he tell you how much he loves you?

WOMAN: (NODS AND WHIMPERS)

MAN: Did he tell you how well he's doing in school?

WOMAN: (NODS AND WHIMPERS AND CRIES)

MAN: All those things are wonderful. What on earth are you crying for?

WOMAN: Did you see our long distance bill?

(MUSIC)

ANNCR (VO): If your long distance bills are too much, call MCI. Sure, reach out and touch someone. Just do it for a whole lot less.

61 SILVER

(PHONE RINGS. A VERY SLEEPY WOMAN PICKS UP THE PHONE)

MOM: Hullo?

DAVE: Mom? Surprise! It's Dave.

MOM: Dave?

DAVE: Your son. I'm sorry I woke you but the long distance rates are cheapest after 11 p.m.

MOM: (SNORES)

DAVE: Mom? Put Dad on, Mom.

Dad? Dad? Mom?...

ANNCR (VO): To save 15 to 50% on long distance before as well as after 11 p.m., call MCI.

And never reach out and wake someone again.

Gold & Silver Awards

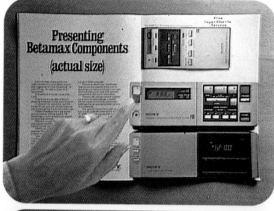

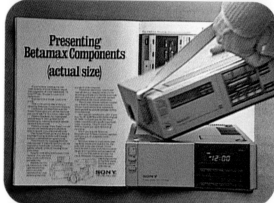

62 GOLD

ANNCR: Have you seen the latest ad for Sony Betamax Components? There they are. Actual size.

I can't believe it. They look so real. Oh. They are real! This is terrific.

And look. A wireless remote control that does just about everything. Let's see. Umm. Reverse, whoh...whoh. And forward. In almost any speed you want. Boy, that was fast. Umm, I'd better put it back.

And Betamax Components are so compact and lightweight, you can take the recorder anywhere to shoot your own movies. This could be my big chance!

Let's see. What else is there to play with. Oh, a coupon. Oh, there's the Sony Trinicon Color Camera. It gives you instant replay right through the eyepiece...There's even an offer for free tapes. Mmm...I think I'll keep the coupon.

The Sony Betamax Component System.

You know what?

I think I'll keep the whole thing.

63 SILVER

(DRAMATIC MUSIC)

VO: Since 1975 we changed a few things on the Rabbit.

We made it faster.

We made it more economical.

We made it more reliable.

Seven years and 15,000 changes later, we improved the way the Rabbit runs,

not the way it looks.

64 GOLD

(MUSIC UNDER)

MAN: Have you been talking to our son on long distance again?

WOMAN: (NODS AND WHIMPERS)

MAN: Did he tell you how much he loves you?

WOMAN: (NODS AND WHIMPERS)

MAN: Did he tell you how well he's doing in school?

WOMAN: (NODS AND WHIMPERS AND CRIES)

MAN: All those things are wonderful. What on earth are you crying for?

WOMAN: Did you see our long distance bill?

(MUSIC)

ANNCR (VO): If your long distance bills are too much, call MCI. Sure, reach out and touch someone. Just do it for a whole lot less.

65 SILVER

(MUSIC UNDER)

(VO): 'Round here, well I guess we take work about as serious as anybody else. But I'll tell you somethin' boys, come sundown ain't nobody more serious about havin' a good time.

(MUSIC IN): *Welcome to Miller Time. It's all yours, and it's all mine. Bring your thirsty self right here, you've got the time we've got the beer for what you had in mind. Welcome to Miller Time.*

(VO): The best beer for the best time of the day. Miller High Life.

(MUSIC): *Bring your thirsty self right here, you've got the time, we've got the beer for what you have in mind. Oh-oh; Welcome, you know you're welcome, welcome, everybody's welcome. Welcome to Miller Time. Yours and mine.*

Gold & Silver Awards

**Public Service Television
Any Length
Single**

66 GOLD

ART DIRECTORS & WRITERS
Steve Diamant
Rick Boyko

CLIENT
Handgun Control

DIRECTOR
Cosimo

PRODUCTION CO.
Cosimo Productions

AGENCY PRODUCERS
Steve Diamant
Rick Boyko

67 SILVER

ART DIRECTOR
Gary Alfredson

WRITERS
Mabon Childs
John Dymun

CLIENT
PA Committee for
Effective Justice

DIRECTOR
John Pytka

PRODUCTION CO.
Joseph Pytka Productions

AGENCY
Ketchum Advertising/
Pittsburgh

66 GOLD

ANNCR (VO): In Japan last year, 48 people lost their
lives to handguns...

ANNCR (VO): In Great Britain...8.

ANNCR (VO): In Canada 52.

ANNCR (VO): And in the United States...10,728.

ANNCR (VO): God bless America

P42980
SERVING LIFE

P68147
SERVING LIFE

COMMIT A CRIME WITH A GUN
AND THIS IS WHAT YOU'RE IN FOR.
FOR FIVE YEARS.

67 SILVER

INMATE #1: Have you ever heard a tough guy cry?
Yeah, I hear 'em crying here every night.

VO: Pennsylvania has a new law.

INMATE #2: Steel, concrete, cold, hatred, bitterness.
This is every single day.

VO: From now on, a crime with a gun means you're
in for five years.

INMATE #3: Imagine being in a cell, 5 ft. by 8 ft.,
with a guy you don't even like.

VO: No deals. No parole, no exceptions.

INMATE #4: There are times in here when you
become so desperate you want to call out to
someone, you want to talk to someone, but there
is nobody who cares.

VO: Five years is a ton of time.

INMATE #5: Sometimes you wake up in the night-time
and you will scream. That's how bad it is in here.
This is a hard situation. You don't want to come
in here.

VO: Commit a crime with a gun and this is what
you're in for.

(SFX: CELL DOOR SLAMS.)

VO: For five years.

Gold & Silver Awards

**Public Service Television
Any Length
Campaign**

68 GOLD
ART DIRECTOR
Gary Alfredson

WRITERS
Mabon Childs
John Dymun

CLIENT
PA Committee for
Effective Justice

DIRECTOR
John Pytka

PRODUCTION CO.
Joseph Pytka Productions

AGENCY
Ketchum Advertising/
Pittsburgh

COMMIT A CRIME WITH A GUN AND YOU'VE SHOT 5 YEARS OF YOUR LIFE.

COMMIT A CRIME WITH A GUN AND YOU'VE SHOT 5 YEARS OF YOUR LIFE.

68 GOLD

INMATE: Hey! You think you're tough? You don't want to come to prison. Because they'll show just how tough that you're not.

(SFX: CELL DOOR SLAMS.)

INMATE: In prison you're afraid all the time. But you can't never show it.

(SFX: CELL DOOR SLAMS.)

INMATE #1: What is prison like? It . . . It hurts . . . prison hurts.

(SFX: CELL DOOR SLAMS.)

**Public Service Television
Any Length
Campaign**

69 SILVER
ART DIRECTOR
Gary Alfredson
WRITERS
Mabon Childs
John Dymun
CLIENT
PA Committee for
Effective Justice
DIRECTOR
John Pytka
PRODUCTION CO.
Joseph Pytka Productions
AGENCY
Ketchum Advertising/
Pittsburgh

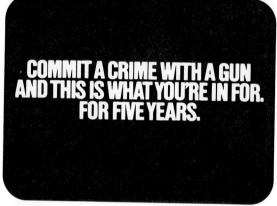

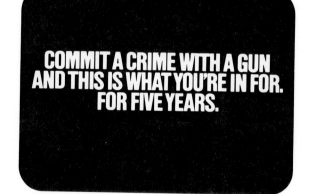

69 SILVER

INMATE #1: Have you ever heard a tough guy cry? Yeah, I hear 'em crying here every night.

vo: Pennsylvania has a new law.

INMATE #2: Steel, concrete, cold, hatred, bitterness. This is every single day.

vo: From now on, a crime with a gun means you're in for five years.

INMATE #3: Imagine being in a cell, 5 ft. by 8 ft., with a guy you don't even like.

vo: No deals. No parole, no exceptions.

INMATE #4: There are times in here when you become so desperate you want to call out to someone, you want to talk to someone, but there is nobody who cares.

vo: Five years is a ton of time.

INMATE #5: Sometimes you wake up in the night-time and you will scream. That's how bad it is in here. This is a hard situation. You don't want to come in here.

vo: Commit a crime with a gun and this is what you're in for.

(SFX: CELL DOOR SLAMS.)

vo: For five years.

vo: Commit a crime with a gun in Pennsylvania and this is what you're in for.

For five years.

And five years in prison is a ton of time.

But it takes just one day to learn that these bars do more than keep you in.

They keep the other inmates out.

Before you pull a gun...think about it.

No matter how bad you think it is where you are now, it's worse in here.

(SFX: CELL DOOR SLAMS.)

COMMIT A CRIME WITH A GUN AND THIS IS WHAT YOU'RE IN FOR. FOR FIVE YEARS.

vo: Imagine five years in prison. You're just a number. You're what everyone else wants you to be. You're not even sure you're a man anymore. Imagine being cut off from the world. Cut off from your family. For five years.

(SFX: CELL DOOR SLAMS.)

Commit a crime with a gun in Pennsylvania and this is what you're in for.

And five years in prison is worse than anything you can imagine.

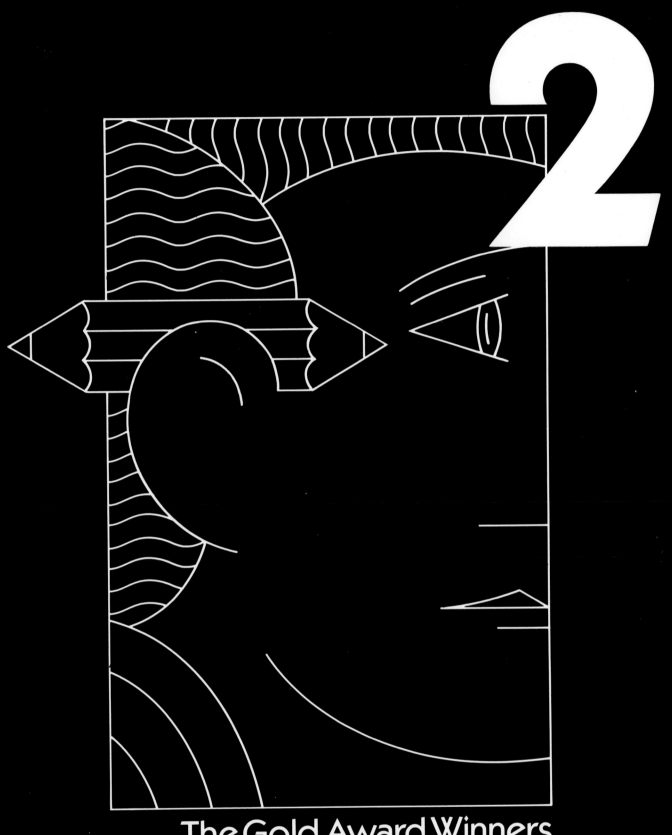

2

The Gold Award Winners
On The Gold Award Winners

The Gold Award Winners on The Gold Award Winners

**Consumer Newspaper
Over 600 Lines Single**

AGENCY: Ammirati & Puris
CLIENT: BMW of North America

It was late in the fall of 1981, a time when, if you believed certain economists, the End of the World Was Near.

Interest rates were astronomical, the stock market was plummeting, and we had to do an ad for early '82 which was to interest people in an investment called a BMW 320i.

We'd solved the problem several months earlier with an ad that said BMW's performed better, in terms of resale value, than 318 stocks on the New York Stock Exchange. The strategy here was simple. A BMW is almost indecent fun to drive. Positioning it as a great investment allows you to tell yourself, your spouse, or whoever controls you through guilt, that you're being prudent rather than self-indulgent when you buy one.

As the closing drew near, it became clear that our story had gotten even better: BMW's were holding more of their resale value while stocks were holding less of theirs. But we didn't want to simply set new figures and rerun the old ad, because the news might have been lost on people who'd already seen it. On the other hand, we didn't want to abandon the ad altogether since it had been very successful.

So instead we set a new headline, defaced the mechanical with a grease pencil, and sent it off to the engraver's. The result is shown below—maybe the first time in history someone committed an act of public graffiti in full view of millions and walked away with an award instead of a misdemeanor.

Tom Thomas: Senior Vice President; Copy Supervisor
Anthony Angotti: Senior Vice President; Art Supervisor

1 GOLD

**Consumer Newspaper
Over 600 Lines Campaign**

**Trade
Black and White
Page or Spread**

AGENCY: Young & Rubicam
CLIENT: Time Inc./Fortune

In a way, the "how to succeed" campaign grew out of the fact that Fortune magazine had *too* much prestige. Research had shown us that people still thought it was read mostly by heads of companies... by the rich man in the big house on top of the hill... by the old, the staid, and the stodgy. It was, they thought, a coffee table magazine: plenty of cachet, but not something people actually read and put into action. The truth, of course, was something else. As the magazine had evolved (toward more and shorter articles, more accessible information), the readership had grown a lot younger and more "fast-track."

It seemed to us that a key to this changing audience was its attitude toward ambition and succeeding. *Success was out of the closet.* Suddenly people didn't have to hide their urge to get to the top. It was OK to want to make it—and keep it.

The "how to succeed" ads have come at this central idea from a variety of angles. But always, we've tried to make the ads young, contemporary, a little humorous, realistic. And yes, even a bit wiseass—as in the ground-off nose ad that proposes the philosophy that "keeping your nose to the grindstone" can be carried too far. To be sure, there's an element of "get yours" in all this, but with humor... with any edge of meanness taken off.

Has the campaign worked? You never know for sure with advertising promotion campaigns. But the fact that Fortune's just had the most successful first-half in its history (as of June, 1983) at least tells us it's not *not* working.

*Bob Czernysz
Dick Olmsted*

**Consumer Newspaper
600 Lines or Less Single**

AGENCY: Doyle Dane Bernbach
CLIENT: Atari

'What football strike?' actually began life as 'What baseball strike?'

Unfortunately, the baseball strike ended before the ad was ready.

Luckily the NFL players went on strike six months later, and through clever rewriting of the headline we were able to salvage the original concept.

*Ted Shaine, Art Director
Diane Rothschild, Copywriter*

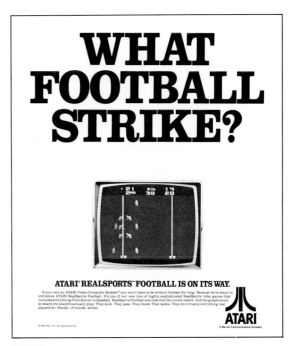

5 GOLD

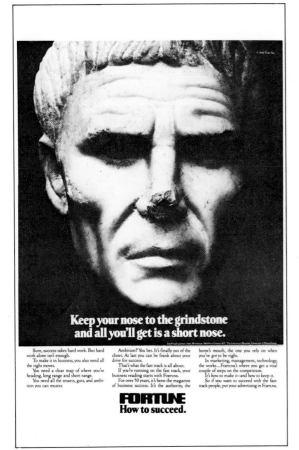

3 GOLD AND 18 GOLD

Consumer Magazine Black and White Page or Spread Including Magazine Supplements

AGENCY: Ally & Gargano, Inc.
CLIENT: Timberland

The story behind the Timberland Gold Award goes back to a day last year when Dennis D'Amico and I were sitting around talking about what to do for Timberland's line of handsewn shoes. We agreed on a direction and called our client.

"Hi, Stan, we want to talk to you about an idea for handsewns, when can we get together?"

"How about Thursday night at the Palm?"

(THURSDAY NIGHT AT THE PALM)

"Hi, Stan, how you been?"

"Hey, guys, what do you want to drink?"

"A couple of Heineken's, thanks."

"You guys have something for handsewns?"

"We're thinking about positioning them as classics that get better over time, you know, like old jeans, and clothes like that."

"Sounds interesting. You happen to see the Knick-Celtic game last night? That Bird is something."

"Stan, don't you want to talk about handsewns anymore?"

"Not really. Why ruin a nice business dinner by talking about business?"

(ONE WEEK LATER AT ALLY & GARGANO)

"Well, Stan, here's the handsewn ad."

"When did I agree on that direction?"

"Last week at the Palm, don't you remember?"

"Oh, yeah."

"So do you like it?"

"Who doesn't? They've got the best cottage fries and steaks around. And the *Clams Oreganate* are killers."

"No, the ad."

"That's pretty good, too. Where's the copy?"

"It'll be ready next week, when can we get together?"

"How about Tuesday night at Smith & Wollensky?"

Ron Berger

Consumer Magazine Color Page or Spread Including Magazine Supplements

AGENCY: Scali, McCabe, Sloves
CLIENT: Nikon

This is how I came up with the award-winning "Faster Than A Speeding Bullet" ad.

I was sitting in the office of my art director Lars Anderson one day. On the desk in front of us was a brand new Nikon camera called FM2. Its shutter speed of 1/4000th second made it the fastest 35mm camera in the world. But how could we communicate that?

Lars said, "Why don't we see if we can take a picture of a bullet in flight?"

I said, "Good idea, Lars."

We searched around for a headline with no result.

The next day I was sitting in my office thinking of something else when Lars stuck his head in. "Faster than a speeding bullet," he said.

I looked up. "What?" I asked.

"That should be the headline."

"Good idea, Lars."

Lars Anderson then went to California to the Brooks Institute of Photography and after several determined days came back with a picture of a speeding bullet taken by the Nikon FM2.

That's how I came up with the idea for this award-winning ad.

Moral: When your art director has a good idea, ride on his coattails. And collect the awards without guilt. Because someday he may have to ride on yours.

Larry Cadman
Associate Creative Director
Senior Vice President

9 GOLD

7 GOLD

**Consumer Magazine
Black and White
Campaign Including
Magazine Supplements**

AGENCY: Doyle Dane Bernbach
CLIENT: Volkswagen of America

These ads simply represent a continuation of a campaign begun 23 years ago by Doyle Dane Bernbach.

Volkswagen ads are legendary. Careers have been built on them. Books in every language have been written about them. They have been emulated, duplicated, and debated for over 20 years.

These particular ads, however, represent a return to this format after a seven year hiatus.

And what happened?

Of course we won a Gold Medal.

But as gratifying was the consumer response: our client received letters saying that seeing provocative, informative, black and white Volkswagen ads in the magazines once again was not unlike unexpectedly encountering an old and treasured friend.

*Irwin Warren
Roy Grace*

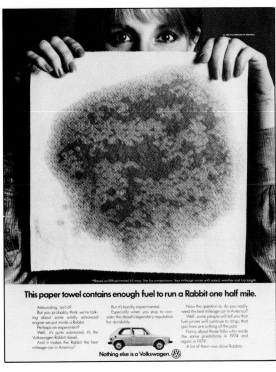

11 GOLD

**Consumer Magazine
Color Campaign
Including Magazine
Supplements**

AGENCY: Doyle Dane Bernbach
CLIENT: Chivas Regal

The tone and style of Chivas Regal advertising was created some 20 years ago at Doyle Dane Bernbach. It has always been assumptive and provocative, but what is interesting about this year's campaign is that each ad has a slightly different graphic approach. Proving that a good campaign doesn't have to consist of look-alike ads.

*Charles Piccirillo
Gary Goldsmith
Ted Bell
Mike Mangano
Diane Sinnott*

13 GOLD

Consumer Magazine
Less Than One Page
B/W or Color
Single

AGENCY: Doyle Dane Bernbach
CLIENT: General Wine & Spirits/Chivas Regal

"Chivas Regal? Where do you think you are, heaven?"
It happens to us all occasionally. We're in hell and we ask for a drink of Chivas Regal—not just because of its grand taste, but also to impress the hell out of everybody. And we're shattered to learn that life has dealt us more than a deadly blow: we're in the wrong place. MORAL: Find the right place—the right agency and the right client. Show up occasionally and appear alert and conscientious. And you'll be rewarded—if not here, then in heaven—with Chivas Regal and other riches galore. You'll even get to meet us.

Charles Abrams
George Rike

"Chivas Regal!...
Where do you think you are, heaven?"

Chivas Regal • 12 Years Old Worldwide • Blended Scotch Whisky • 86 Proof. General Wine & Spirits Co., N.Y.

15 GOLD

Trade
Any Size
B/W or Color
Campaign

AGENCY: Ogilvy & Mather/London
CLIENT: Ogilvy & Mather

Garry Horner and I work closely with our bearlike type-director Geoff Pearson, who asks anxiously after each presentation: "How'd it go, lads?"
To which we invariably reply: "They love the ads, Geoff, but they hate the typography". He always believes us and sulks.
When our Chairman refused to allow us to run the ad that said: "The C.I.A. isn't the only agency selling information to the Russians," Geoff sulked for a week.
(Anyone who wants the background to that story can ring us on London 836 2466.)
Geoff was bitter when the Chairman insisted we remove the hammer and sickle from between the words "Ogilvy" and "Mather" on the version that ultimately ran.
"Who does he think he is?" he shouted.
Garry and I hold Geoff entirely to blame for the part he played in helping these ads win your gold pencil.
Okay, Geoff, you can stop sulking now.

Indra Sinha
Garry Horner

22 GOLD

**Collateral
Brochures
Other than by mail**

AGENCY: Hill, Holliday, Connors, Cosmopulos/Boston
CLIENT: J & J Corrugated Box

"Who'd like to go down to Fall River, Massachusetts, to talk to a box company about a collateral project...?"

Sometimes the rainbow ends in the strangest places.

In this case, it turned out to be a corrugated box full of gold located 50 miles southeast of Boston.

We found J & J Box cared about quality.

They worked hard.

They were proud.

They did good work.

And that's what they asked of us.

All we did is add a few new wrinkles.

...Sometimes it pays to go out of your way.

Paul Regan
William Tomlinson
Peter D. Nichols
Paul Mahoney

24 GOLD

**Collateral
Sales Kits**

AGENCY: RMI, Inc.
CLIENT: Saab-Scania of America

The range of work RMI has been doing for Saab-Scania of America over the years runs from creating brochures for showroom use to producing sales training materials.

So when Dick Rochford, Saab's National Merchandising Manager, called Rick Henry, Account Supervisor on Saab, and me to meet with him to discuss Saab's new model introduction, we were ready to tackle almost anything.

What they needed was a communications piece designed to orientate the Saab dealer network about new product changes and to show them samples of support material they would be receiving throughout the model year.

How do you package a variety of information in one neat package that looks attractive and is guaranteed to be opened and gone through by every department of a dealership?

First, you design or photograph a dramatic visual to use as a box wrap.

Second, come up with a slogan that works well with the graphic as well as an incentive theme for dealers.

Third, design and construct a box that will hold 20 pounds worth of advertising, collateral, training, service and parts materials that will be sent to each dealer.

Finally, hope that what you have just created will be enthusiastically received by Saab dealers across the country and be used as an incentive for them to sell more cars than the year before.

An unusual project? You bet. But do you know something? It worked!

Lee Einhorn, Creative Director
Rick Henry, Account Supervisor

26 GOLD

**Collateral
P.O.P.**

AGENCY: Ammirati & Puris
CLIENT: BMW of North America

The reactions of most people to the subject of technology range anywhere from boredom to intimidation.

For those of us working on BMW, this creates an interesting challenge—to communicate BMW's technological superiority without making people's eyes glaze over.

So when we set out to do an ad for this particular BMW innovation—an electronic system that monitors driving habits and calculates when a BMW needs to be serviced—we tried to emphasize the humanity of the product instead of trying to dazzle people with its technological sophistication.

In so doing, we ended up with a headline that employs one of the most basic precepts of journalism—namely, that "Dog bites man" isn't news, but "Man bites dog" is.

*David Tessler
Jeff Vogt*

29 GOLD

**Outdoor
Single**

AGENCY: Fallon McElligott Rice
CLIENT: 7 South 8th for Hair

There is an advantage to working on a limited budget: it forces you to be simple.

Dean and I have been simple for years.

Although no one has ever given us a medal for it until now.

*Jarl Olsen
Dean Hanson*

31 GOLD

AGENCY: Levine, Huntley, Schmidt & Beaver
CLIENT: Planned Parenthood of New York City

For some reason, we always assumed that making a baby was something that went on between a man and a woman.

However, last year, a few United States Senators felt it was their job to interfere in this process by attempting to outlaw all abortion. For all women. Under all circumstances.

The strength of this ad, we believe, lies in the use of humor to demonstrate our outrage.

And apparently, Americans were outraged too. Coupons, contributions and letters poured into Planned Parenthood. And we'd like to think that our ad played a part in helping to defeat the anti-abortion legislation.

Tana Klugherz, Art Director
Deborah Kasher, Copywriter

34 GOLD

AGENCY: Fallon McElligott Rice
CLIENT: The Episcopal Ad Project

These ads are the latest examples of a campaign which we began in 1977 for the Episcopal Church. The campaign grew out of a local effort by a single Minneapolis church to attract new members. Since that time, these and other ads in the series have appeared in all fifty of the United States, Canada, the British Isles and parts of the Caribbean.

From the beginning, the strategy of the campaign has been simply to position the Episcopal Church as a moderate, thoughtful and reasonable worship alternative to fundamentalist and television Christianity.

While the campaign sadly lacks a national media plan, it has been successful in attracting trial and growth on a church-by-church, state-by-state basis.

Since production money has been extremely modest from the beginning, the campaign has been heavily dependent upon gratis contributions of time, craftsmanship and materials. In this case, not only did the agency offer its time free, but a number of photographers, retouchers, typesetters, engravers and printers often gave their services at cost or less.

It's a good example of a grass-roots, shoestring budget advertising campaign that succeeded and grew ·beyond all expectation, largely because the clear positioning and strong concepts were never bitten to death by the usual array of committee guppies.

It's been fun.

Tom McElligott
Nancy Rice

36 GOLD

Corporate
Newspaper or Magazine
Single

AGENCY: Needham, Harper & Steers
CLIENT: Xerox "DuMont"

We were very pleased at the One Show's response to our ad.

The initial response hadn't been so good.

A man who had revived the old DuMont name to sell new television sets practically threatened to sue us. (We talked our way out of that one by promising to send him 500 reprints of the ad.)

Another guy who was making DuMont oscilloscopes politely told us he hated it.

And the word "hate" doesn't begin to describe how the late Allen B. DuMont's daughter felt about it.

After that, most of the responses were just peaceful requests for more information about Xerox copiers.

And right up until awards night, we kept telling ourselves that that was the kind of response we had gone into this business for.

Now, at least we can afford to be more honest with ourselves.

Marty Cooke
Priscilla Croft

39 GOLD

Corporate
Newspaper or Magazine
Campaign

AGENCY: Ogilvy & Mather/Houston
CLIENT: Aramco Services

Companies who talk about themselves are usually bores, just like people who talk about themselves. It's so hard to do good corporate advertising because you have to communicate something about the company, but you can't just talk about the company.

Aramco wanted this campaign to communicate the colossal size of their projects in Arabia. It would help them recruit some very hard-to-get people.

In a way this campaign is a demonstration. The benefit is a job worth bragging about. The demonstration is an employee bragging about his job.

We like this campaign best when we think of all the professional, acceptable, safe ways in which we didn't do it.

Mike Lyons
Paul Norris

41 GOLD

Student Competition

SCHOOL: School of Visual Arts

We set out to win The One Show Student Competition because we felt that would boost our careers like nothing else could. We were wrong. Yes, winning was thrilling and rewarding, but working for an extended period of time on one assignment taught us more than we imagined it could.

Because, as students, our work so far had been on one product for a period of one week. Here, we had to sustain our energy about ten times as long, finding new perspectives into what we thought we had already explored inside and out.

We had The One Club's factual work order for the first male birth control pill, but being two nice, Catholic, Italian girls, we needed more. So, we put together a survey. And we talked to a lot of men. We found one common denominator:

All men, no matter how conservative or egalitarian they may be, believe that birth control is basically a woman's responsibility, because she's the one who goes through the physical act of birthing a baby. But, men have babies too. Hmmm. No. That's too easy and too feminist. We have to push further.

So we did. Every lunch hour. Every day after work. For two months.

But when it came down to making a choice, "MEN HAVE BABIES TOO," said it all.

As we sit here, writing this during our lunch hour, still secretaries at Needham, Harper & Steers, it seems as though some things never change. But as we look back on all this, it's obvious that they do.

Hopefully we'll go through some more change in the very near future. If not, you know where to reach us.

Beth Johnson
Carol Turturro

MEN HAVE BABIES TOO.

THE PILL FOR MEN

43 GOLD

Consumer Radio
Single
Consumer Radio
Campaign

AGENCY: Lord, Geller, Federico, Einstein, Inc.
CLIENT: Callard & Bowser/USA

Arthur Einstein had the idea.
John Molyneux, president of Callard & Bowser USA, had the courage.
John Cleese had the genius.
And I'm the one who had to say, "It's funny, John, but they won't let us say it on the radio."
Here are some of those banned bits:
"shoot-outs at the check-out counters,
lumpen proletariat,
slaughtering pheasants on the croquet lawn,
handful of salt and some twigs or a turnip,
God bless your esteemed highness,
Colonel Jim Bowie of cutlery fame,
packed off to Siberia,
construction workers, tramps and politicians,
a taffy is a Welshman and not good to eat at all,
yeoman storekeeper,
no matter what sort of riff-raff you are,
that's the price you pay for not being Communist."
There, luv, we've said it all.

Lynn Stiles

SEE GOLD AWARD WINNERS 45 AND 47.

**Consumer Television
60 Seconds Single**

**Television Technique
Best Demonstration
60 or 30 Seconds
Single**

AGENCY: Backer & Spielvogel
CLIENT: Sony-Betamax Components

This commercial and its companion magazine ad were simply intended to demonstrate a product that had a lot to demonstrate.

All we did was get out of the way.

*Dave Davis
Bob Lenz
Bob Meury*

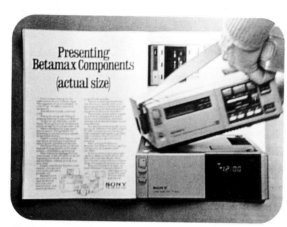

49 GOLD AND 62 GOLD

**Consumer Television
60 Seconds Campaign**

AGENCY: Backer & Spielvogel
CLIENT: Miller Brewing/High Life

This campaign was fourteen years in the making. Its ancestry goes back to the first "Miller Time" spot.

*If you've got the time
We've got the beer
Miller Beer
Tastes too good to hurry thru
But when it's time to relax
One beer stands clear*

So, first off, much credit must go to those who came up with the "Miller Time" concept. Also, to those who recognized a good thing when they saw it and, more importantly, resisted the "gimme somethin' new" urge all those years.

"Welcome to Miller Time" evolved with the need to speak to a younger audience and the way they drink beer.

Again, a great piece of music led the way. "When it's time to relax" became a rousing "Welcome, everybody's welcome."

*Welcome to Miller Time
It's all yours
And it's all mine
Bring your thirsty self right here
You've got the time
We've got the beer
For what you have in mind*

And the visual beat picked up accordingly—from maybe four scenes in sixty seconds to more like forty.

The number of scenes per sixty seconds is probably exceeded only by the number of very caring people who helped make them happen. They have made these things fun to do. It shows on the film.

*Gerald Pfiffner
Barry Lisee
Mark Nussbaum
Bob Lenz
Jim Anderson*

51 GOLD

**Consumer Television
30 Second Single**

AGENCY: Ammirati & Puris
CLIENT: Club Med

Club Med is an all-inclusive vacation with every activity imaginable. People know that.

In fact, they know it so well that many think of it as the adult equivalent of a summer camp—with all the regimentation that implies.

So we decided to do a commercial that promised them nothing—or everything, or any combination thereof they chose.

*Tony Angotti
Joe O'Neill*

53 GOLD

**Consumer Television
30 Seconds Campaign**

**ConsumerTelevision
10 Seconds
Single**

AGENCY: Ally & Gargano
CLIENT: Federal Express

What more can we say?
*Mike Tesch
Patrick Kelly*

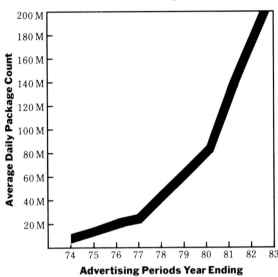

56 GOLD

58 GOLD

**Television Technique
Best Slice of Life
60 or 30 Seconds
Single**

**Television Technique
Best Brand Image
60 or 30 Seconds
Single**

AGENCY: Ally & Gargano
CLIENT: MCI

All of us at MCI and Ally & Gargano would like to take this opportunity to thank the folks at Bell Telephone and N.W. Ayer for producing as pointed and poignant a commercial as "Joey Called."

We'd also like to encourage them in their future efforts. It's very, very difficult to satirize the mediocre. And impossible to satirize that which has not forced its way into the national consciousness.

Q: Why do art directors and copywriters enter award shows?
A: To break out of anonymity.
Q: Any other reason?
A: To take the ephemera they produce and immortalize it, in a sense, in annuals such as this.
Q: Why do agencies enter award shows?
A: Giant agencies, to prove that bigness doesn't mean an atrophied creative department. Small agencies, to prove that they can mix it up with anybody.
Q: Does it work?
A: Ogilvy has demonstrated that you can get better as you get bigger. McElligott has demonstrated that Minneapolis is the new standard by which all advertising should be measured.
Q: What about London?
A: It's nice to see an emerging third world nation such as Great Britain making such strides in the world of commerce.
Q: Is that meant to be taken seriously?
A: Of course not. Saatchi, Collett, DDB London were all doing great stuff long before the alleged New Wave. As were Samuel Johnson, Marlowe, and Chesterton.
Q: Chesterton? What did he sell?
A: He sold himself.
Q: Is that why you entered the same commercial in both the "Slice of Life" and the "Brand Image" categories? To sell yourself?
A: Unless you can write a best-seller (*Confessions* or *From those Wonderful People*), there's no other medium for advertising people to advertise themselves.

*George Euringer
Tom Messner*

60 GOLD AND 64 GOLD

**Public Service
Television Single**

CLIENT: Handgun Control

One of the best things about winning a Gold Medal in The One Show is that you get to thank all the people who transformed your piece of paper into an award-winning commercial.

With this commercial, it's even more meaningful because everyone worked for free.

Cosimo, our film director, worked his artistry so well you could never imagine the amount of painstaking effort he devoted to it.

John Fogelson, our film editor, hand-carved it into a thing of beauty and hand-carried it the rest of the way.

Film mixer Ed Golya got us louder gunfire than we ever hoped to get and still hear Alan Keyes' splendid voiceover.

Visual Effects and Perfect Timing got the picture perfect.

And Frank Sobocienski's insights and wisdom made it better than it ever could have been without him.

Thanks again, everybody. We owe you.

About the concept:

When we found out how many people die by the handgun each year in America, we were stunned. When we found out how many people die by the handgun in countries so similar to ours in other ways, we were even more stunned. So we searched for the kind of visual that would hold people still long enough for us to ram these incredible statistics home.

After all that, "God Bless America" seemed the only thing left to say.

*Steve Diamant
Rick Boyko*

66 GOLD

**Public Service
Television Campaign**

AGENCY: Ketchum Advertising
CLIENT: PA. Committee for Effective Justice

On March 24th, we went to prison. Western State
Penitentiary.

"Here. Wanna see what it's like inside a cell?" Slam.

One hundred years of stone and steel, Western Pen
looms over the Ohio River like a million bad dreams.

"It's fight or be somebody's boy."

We talk to guards, deputy wardens, psychologists
and prisoners. Lots of prisoners.

"Try to grab an extra 15 seconds of sleep and you're
liable to find a sock stuffed in your mouth."

We walk across an empty prison yard. A bell goes off.
Convicts everywhere. As they file past, one thing hits
us straight in the eyes. It's their eyes. They're filled
with a combination of fear and hate you just don't see
anywhere else.

"If you're little, better pretend to be crazy. Real
crazy. And bad."

Whistles and bells. Catcalls and shouts. Cell doors
slamming. Eerie echoes. And those eyes.

"I been in here so long...I can't even dream about
the outside anymore."

A hulking steel door slams. And we're outside again.
But we've all been back. In nightmares.

John Dymun
Mabon Childs

68 GOLD

3

1983 Print Finalists

1983 Print Finalists

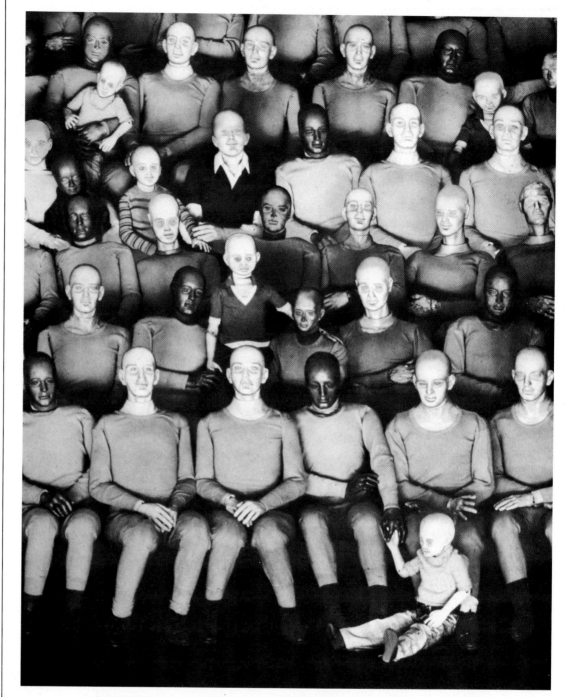

Volkswagen is at the mercy of a bunch of dummies.

Our dummies simulate the human body.

Their bones are ceramic. Their insides are computers which record their every jiggle, bounce and temperature change.

And they never lie.

Day after day we subject our dummies to the kind of torture that would make even a sadist wince.

They crash into brick walls going 50 miles an hour.

That's how we learned how to make seat belts that the United States government thinks are just as good as air bags.

It also helped us design a car body that's no ordinary car body: it's an impact absorbing safety cell. In an accident, it just might save your life.

Our dummies freeze for hours in arctic cold and swelter in tropical heat. And then they tell us about it.

That's why our cars come with heaters that really heat, defrosters that really defrost, and a ventilation system that provides plenty of fresh air without providing a draft.

We monitor our dummies while they ride, uninterrupted, for days at a time on miserable roads through blinding snow, driving sleet, and torrential rain.

Maybe that's why an excellent time to test drive a Volkswagen is during a blizzard, preferably on an icy road.

People who own Volkswagens marvel at how well they handle and how safe and comfortable they are.

All of which leads to the inevitable question:

Does Volkswagen employ the most intelligent engineers in Germany?

Or the smartest dummies?

Or both?

Nothing else is a Volkswagen.

THIS MAN DIED AND LIVED TO TALK ABOUT IT.

"DEATH AND BEYOND"

What happens to us after we die? This is possibly the most provocative question of all time.

Some people think there's an afterlife. Others think it's just a void. Yet some people, such as 33 year old John Migliaccio, believe they've experienced the answer.

This week, in a Special Report on The 5 o'clock Eyewitness News, Rose Ann Scamardella talks to people who've died. Then returned to life. And finds out what happened in between.

Watch "Death and Beyond". And hear what death is like, from people who've been there.

THE 5 O'CLOCK EYEWITNESS NEWS ⑦

71

AIRLINE OFFERS BUS FARES.

TEXAS INTERNATIONAL	BUS
HARTFORD $39	HARTFORD $45.75
HOUSTON $79	HOUSTON $98.70
NEW ORLEANS $78	NEW ORLEANS $98.75
SAN ANTONIO $98	SAN ANTONIO $98.90
ALBUQUERQUE $98	ALBUQUERQUE $98.90
LOS ANGELES $98	LOS ANGELES $98.90

FARES QUOTED BY GREYHOUND AND TRAILWAYS RESERVATIONS CENTERS. FEB. 3, 1982

Buses have always been slower and less convenient than planes. But they've also been cheaper. A lot cheaper.

Now thanks to Texas International Airlines, taking a plane is cheaper than the bus.

Just follow these rules:

1. You must reserve and buy your seat from now through March 8, and do your flying between February 23 and April 7. You should buy your seat as far ahead as possible, but you must buy it at least two weeks before you fly.

2. Seats are limited, so call early.
3. You must pay for your tickets when you make your reservation. Give us your credit card number or see your travel agent.
4. Tickets are valid on Texas International only, and are non-refundable.

For more information and reservations, call 347-4777, or your professional travel agent. But do it quickly. Because at these rates, if you wait, you may have to take a bus.

Texas International

72

It makes impossibel impossible.

The IBM Displaywriter System.

When an error in spelling mars an otherwise perfect piece of work, a strange thing happens:

People remember the spelling error more than they remember the otherwise perfect piece of work.

The IBM Displaywriter helps stop spelling errors like these from happening.

Because it's more than just a text processor. It's a text processor that lets you check the spelling of up to 50,000

words electronically. At up to 1,000 words a minute. In 11 different languages.

The Displaywriter also lets you edit, revise, change your format, do math, merge, and file with electronic speed.

All of which goes toward giving you a flawless finished document.

Which is exactly what you want to stick in people's minds.

As opposed to the alternative.

I am interested in learning more about the IBM Displaywriter System. Please have your representative get in touch with me.

NAME_____ TITLE_____
COMPANY_____
ADDRESS_____
CITY_____ STATE_____ ZIP_____
BUSINESS PHONE_____

IBM
400 Parsons Pond Drive—Dept. 804
Franklin Lakes, N.J. 07417

Call IBM Direct 800-631-5582 Ext. 141. In New Jersey 800-352-4960 Ext. 141
In Hawaii/Alaska 800-526-2484 Ext. 141

73

PUT ASIDE YOUR 35MM SLR FOR JUST ONE INSTANT.

With the development of the Polaroid SLR 680, instant photography has reached a new level of sophistication.

And yet, not even we would suggest that it is the only camera for you.

Because as we all know, your 35mm SLR is suitable for a wide range of photographic situations.

We do feel that the SLR 680 should be one of your cameras. For more than one reason, the first of which is instantly apparent.

IT GIVES YOU THE PICTURE RIGHT AWAY. (DON'T YOU WISH YOUR 35MM DID?)

Think about that for a moment. You must admit, it's a wonderful thing for a camera to be able to do: to take a picture, then give it up for inspection a few seconds later. To be admired, peered at, passed around.

To be shared.

It's so simple. The Polaroid SLR 680 hands you a developing picture. Which you, in turn, can hand to someone else.

This act, examined, reveals itself to be a very satisfying form of human communication.

Unexamined, it's just lots of fun.

Although, when we consider the design of the SLR 680, we doubt that fun has ever been taken more seriously.

IT USES THE FASTEST COLOR PRINT FILM IN THE WORLD. INSTANT OR OTHERWISE.

Perhaps the most basic element of the new camera is the film around which it is designed: Polaroid 600 High Speed. At 600 ASA, it is a remarkable achievement in itself: the world's fastest color print film.

It permits smaller apertures, thereby increasing depth-of-field.

POLAROID PRESENTS THE $265* SLR 680.
A SERIOUS INSTANT CAMERA FOR THE FUN OF IT.

And it helps you freeze the action, rather than blur it.

The camera's optics are also noteworthy. It is the world's only folding single-lens-reflex camera. It gives you through-the-lens viewing of the scene you wish to photograph.

The camera has a four-element, coated-glass lens. Designed by computer, it has been called one

of the most innovative camera lenses ever made.

IT'S COMPLETELY AUTOMATIC. IT'S ALSO MANUAL.

The SLR 680 has sonar Autofocus, and an automatic strobe.

This strobe is unique in several ways. It is designed

to be used indoors and out. To supply conventional flash illumination when necessary, or to provide supplemental fill, in order to minimize shadows that bright sun can cast under subjects' eyes, noses and chins.

It also aims itself. It tilts sharply downward, when the subject is close, points straight ahead if the subject is distant, or assumes any appropriate angle in between. Automatically.

You can use the strobe on every shot, thanks, in part, to its fast recharging time: in less than 3 seconds, you're ready to shoot another picture. Or you can shut off the strobe, mount the camera on your tripod, and take time exposures of up to 14 seconds.

The sonar Autofocus can be disengaged, too, if you want to focus manually.

IT'S A LOT LIKE YOUR 35MM CAMERA. THEN AGAIN, IT ISN'T.

The SLR 680 can be completely automatic, or fully manual; it's very flexible that way. In this regard, we think you'll find it reminiscent of your 35mm camera.

But that is where the similarity ends.

The SLR 680, after all, lets you see your pictures. Immediately. And even better, the people you're with get to see, too.

Visit your Polaroid dealer soon. He will demonstrate state-of-the-art optics, electronics and film technology.

In an instant.

POLAROID

For more information, call 800-225-1384 in the continental U.S. (or 617-864-4568 collect, in Mass. and Alaska) Mon.-Fri. 8AM-5PM, EST.

74

THE NIGHT WE GOT ALL THE HOLLYWOOD DIRT.

Whenever stars get together, somebody gets trampled. In this case it was a carpet.

And even though it was seen with over 200 of Hollywood's heaviest stars during the filming of "Night of 100 Stars," nobody spotted it. You see, it was a carpet of soil resistant Anso* IV nylon.*

If you missed this walk-on, you can catch twenty others just like it at Einstein Moomjy.

Where you'll see a collection of Anso IV carpets that goes on forever. Like "War and Peace."

The latest velours, silkies, saxonies and suedes. All as repelled by dirt as you are.

Pin dots, plaids, true grids and industrial carpets that don't like to dirty themselves either.

In color by Moomjycolor. Lilacs, peaches and roses.

Pastels so fresh they're not on T.V. yet.

And while it may not be nice to fool mother nature, we have some natural shades that will sure keep her guessing.

We'd like to take this opportunity to thank all our other broadloom, our area rugs and Orientals. Without which we wouldn't be here.

What's more, for a 2 week limited engagement, these Anso IV's go from as little as $19.99 a sq. yd.—installation and padding included.

Hurry, they'll be playing to a full house.

So if you'd like to see any of them in person (or in carpet), stop at Einstein Moomjy.

Don't be surprised if you see some stars. In person (and on carpet).

Einstein Moomjy. The Carpet Department Store®

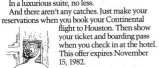

THE BMW 733i. IT DOESN'T SCREAM WEALTH. IT JUST QUIETLY REWARDS INSIGHT.

It's no secret that there are some expensive sedans that are purchased for their sheer expensiveness.

Sedans that serve as a sort of public declaration of status and prosperity.

Such cars are the antithesis of the BMW 733i—the luxury sedan engineered in the belief that performance, not self-congratulation, is the ultimate measure of a car's worth.

A PANACEA FOR PURISTS.

The 733i is a car whose subtleties of engineering and technology place it beyond the needs of all but a handful of purists. (Which is perhaps just as well, given its limited supply.)

For those serious drivers, however, it is as close to a necessity as a $35,000* sedan can come.

Its fuel-injected engine delivers the sort of heady response that suggests an oversized power-plant beneath the hood. Not so. The 733i's 6-cylinder engine arrives at high performance through refinement, not brute force.

A system of microprocessors gathers data on fuel mixtures, engine speed and other factors. It then orders ignition to occur at the optimum moment—accomplishing through elegance of design what might otherwise require additional cylinders and extra girth.

Its suspension handles the landscape with precision instead of bluntness—removing almost surgically the wallowing, skittishness and related uncertainties from bumps and curves. (One reason: a new suspension that uses one of the most important breakthroughs in independent rear suspension design in a generation.)

The 733i is also engineered for those who prefer the subtleties of road topography to the anesthetizing ride of limousine-like sedans. Its highly tactile steering places you in touch with that alternately pleasant and harsh reality called the road—filtering out just enough of its harshness without removing the reality.

The result is a machine that is as much system as car, one so perfectly balanced and rigorously self-policing that it even calculates when routine service is needed.

ENGINEERED FOR DRIVING, NOT JUST SITTING.

Inside, the 733i is engineered for activities of considerably more subtlety than sitting.

Its interior literally helps you drive, rather than merely accompanying you on the trip.

Its supple leather seats are designed to follow the curvature of the spine, placing the driver in postures that are anatomically correct and help reduce driver fatigue.

An Active Check/Control provides readings on 7 different measures of the car's operational readiness.

An on-board computer provides all manner of trip information, such as the distance remaining to your destination.

In fact, no detail in a BMW 733i ever suffers from inattention because it's judged 'minor.' And its warranty reflects this obsessiveness.

The 733i is backed by BMW's 3-year/36,000-mile limited warranty and a 6-year limited warranty against rust perforation.

The result is a car that can stand up both over time and under scrutiny. Leading Car and Driver magazine to conclude that the 733i's "parts and pieces…work so well together that they must have been melded in another world."

It may be seen, however, in much more convenient locations.

Your BMW dealer will be happy to arrange a thorough test drive.

THE ULTIMATE DRIVING MACHINE.

*Manufacturer's suggested retail price $34,300. Actual price depends on dealer. Price excludes state and local taxes, dealer prep, destination and handling charges. *Warranty applies to automobiles purchased from authorized U.S. BMW dealers only. See your BMW dealer for details. © 1982 BMW of North America, Inc. The BMW trademark and logo are registered. European Tourist Delivery can be arranged through your authorized U.S. BMW dealer

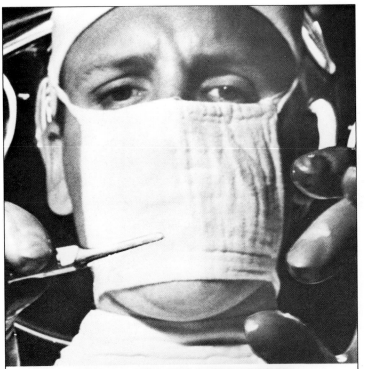

NOW IS NOT THE TIME TO FIND OUT YOU PICKED THE WRONG DOCTOR.

When it comes to picking a doctor, most people follow someone else's prescription.
But the doctor that's right for someone else might not be exactly right for you.
Tonight, find out how to find a doctor properly.

A 2-part Special Report by Earl Ubell.

"FINDING DR. RIGHT" BEGINNING TONIGHT AT 5 AND 11. CHANNEL ⓞ 2 NEWSBREAKERS

If it concerns you, it concerns us.

© 1982 WCBS-TV

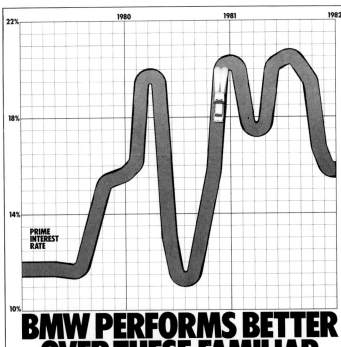

BMW PERFORMS BETTER OVER THESE FAMILIAR PEAKS, VALLEYS AND HAIRPIN TURNS.

Over the past three years, the Dow Jones Industrial Average fluctuated between 759 and 1024.
Gold careened from $217 an ounce to $850 and back down to $391.
And the prime interest rate soared from 11.75% to over 20% before sinking to 15.75%.
One of the most serene vantage points from which to observe all this volatility was behind the wheel of a BMW 320i.
Over the same three years, a new 320i fluctuated hardly at all. In fact, according to the December 1981 NADA Used-Car Guide, a 1979 320i closed out the period with a retained value of 97.3% of its purchase price.*
Meanwhile, the 320i's performance over more tangible peaks, valleys, etc., was equally surefooted.
"Not only does the fully independent suspension flatten mountainous bumps," Car and Driver wrote, but it will also "gobble serpentine asphalt all day without breathing hard."

Even its warranty outperforms most other cars: a 3-year/36,000-mile limited warranty plus a 6-year limited warranty against rust perforation.†
So before you invest a five-figure sum in a lesser car, we suggest you visit your nearest BMW dealer—and test drive the alternative:
A car that handles the economy with the same ease with which it handles the topography.
THE ULTIMATE DRIVING MACHINE.

The first problem it solves is what to give for Christmas.

More people in more places solve more problems with Apples than with any other personal computer in the world.
And now Apple solves one more.
The authorized Apple dealers listed below are offering very special prices on Apple Christmas packages—complete Apple Personal Computer systems with everything you need to get started, including software.
So there's never been a better season to buy the world's most popular personal computer, the Apple II.

Or our most powerful, the Apple III.
And you can choose from packages tailored for small business, big business, education or home use.
Of course, this is a limited time offer. So visit your authorized Apple dealer or call for an appointment today. Before his evergreen turns brown.
And save yourself a merry little bundle.

The most personal computer. 🍎 **apple**

© 1982 Apple Computer Inc.

Ra bbit

The cheapest way to go from a to b

Diesel
45 EPA est. mpg.*
58 EPA est. highway mpg.*

The best mileage car in America

*Use "estimated mpg" for comparison; mileage will vary with speed, trip length, weather. Actual highway mpg will probably be less.

THE NEW VOLVO 760 GLE. ITS SHAPE HAS MET WITH SOME RESISTANCE IN THE PRESS BUT VERY LITTLE ON THE ROAD.

In a world where it's often difficult to tell one car from another, no-one can mistake the new Volvo 760 GLE.

Its elegant profile is instantly recognisable.

Basically a wedge shape, it has a low bonnet, clearly sculptured edges and a steeply raked rear windscreen.

It is extremely aerodynamic giving a resistant co-efficient of just under 0.40.

(Equally important, it also gives three rear seat passengers the chance to sit up in comfort.)

A few journalists were surprised by the car's unusual profile but no-one has questioned its efficiency.

Although a roomy 5-seater, 6-cylinder saloon, the new Volvo is surprisingly economical.

The automatic model gives you 25 mpg (at 75 mph) 32.1 mpg (at 56 mph) and 17.9 mpg (Urban).

Of course, this economy is not solely due to the car's styling.

The 760 GLE is some 88 lbs lighter than Volvo's previous 6-cylinder saloon.

While the car's new automatic transmission is equipped with an overdrive that reduces the engine's fuel consumption at speed, quite dramatically.

A DRIVER'S CAR.
Economy, however, is rarely the main reason for buying a car of this class.

The Volvo 760 GLE has to meet the needs of the driver as well as the needs of society.

It does it triumphantly.

"Ultimate handling is a delight with total predictability and neutral balance in fast curves, gentle understeer in the slower ones." AUTOCAR

"The car showed excellent stability at all speeds." MOTOR TREND.

The Volvo 760 GLE is very much a driver's car.

Top speed is 118 mph and 60 mph can be reached in just under 10 seconds, but it's the sheer driveability of the car that marks it out as special.

The long wheelbase and wide track give the car wonderful stability - even when buffeted by side winds, but the biggest contribution to the outstanding handling is made by the new rear suspension.

Volvo have introduced an entirely new constant track rear axle with a patented sub-frame.

This not only improves road holding but gives less vibration and lower noise levels.

Motor Trend summed it up this way:

"The new 760 saloons are capable of getting from Point A to Point B in a better than average hurry. With reassuring stability. Traditional Volvo comfort. And a level of luxury that is new for this company."

Inside, the car is indeed extremely comfortable.

The new front seats have been developed in co-operation with orthopaedic experts at the Sahlgrenska Hospital in Gothenburg.

Both are electrically heated. The seats automatically warm up at temperatures below 14°C.

You can choose leather or plush velour and the upholstery colour is repeated on the door panels and dashboard.

The dashboard itself is angled towards the driver so all the controls are within easy reach.

"Ergonomically the 760 GLE is excellent." AUTOCAR.

It is also extremely well-equipped.

Full air conditioning, electric windows and door mirrors, central locking, metallic paint, tinted glass, power steering and alloy wheels are all standard.

You'll also find a host of extra little touches that make the 760 GLE a very satisfying car to live with.

For example, when you close the driver's door after getting in the car the courtesy light stays on for 15 seconds giving you time to put the key in the ignition.

There are no less than 10 different storage areas inside the car and there are reading lamps for both front and rear seats.

The boot, too, is especially accommodating.

And if the 760 GLE does well by your suitcases it does even better by your rear seat passengers.

The rear seat is unusually wide due to the absence of any wheel arches and the high roof line gives plenty of headroom.

THE TRADITIONAL VIRTUES.
Underlying all this enjoyment, of course, is Volvo's traditional concern with safety and reliability.

The new Volvo more than meets every international safety regulation.

For example, the USA authorities demand that a car must meet stringent frontal collision standards.

The Volvo 760 GLE easily exceeds these standards, being able to absorb an impact some 36% greater than the regulations require.

When a car maker goes to that kind of trouble when it doesn't have to, you know you're in safe hands.

But if longevity of the occupants is a Volvo pre-occupation so is the longevity of the car.

Nobody makes longer lasting cars than Volvo.

The latest statistics to come from the Swedish Motor Inspection Company show that the Volvo has an average life expectancy of 19.3 years.

Longer than any other car in the survey.

The 760 GLE more than matches the quality of past Volvos, it improves on it.

To help prevent rust approximately one-third of the Volvo's bodywork is Zincrometal or zinc-coated sheet metal. About 18 square metres in all.

HOW MUCH? WHERE CAN I SEE IT?
The Volvo 760 GLE is at your nearest Volvo showroom now.

Prices start at £12,041, a figure that compares very favourably with other luxury cars on the market.

However, as with the car's looks, we're happy for you to judge the car's value for yourself.

If you'd like a colour brochure, ask your secretary to call us at the number below or send us your business card and we'll do the rest.

Better still, call in and see the car in the showroom.

You'll find, even standing still, it overcomes any resistance. **VOLVO**

PRICES FOR THE NEW VOLVO 760 SERIES START AT £12,041 FOR MANUAL MODEL. CAR TAX & VAT INCLUDED: DELIVERY & NUMBER PLATES EXTRA: BROCHURES & SALES INFORMATION TEL. HIGH WYCOMBE (0494) 13444 OR WRITE TO DEPT FT5, VOLVO CUSTOMER SERVICES, HIGH WYCOMBE, BUCKS HP12 8PN EXPORT SALES TEL. 01 494 1111/2

**Consumer Newspaper
Over 600 Lines Single**

86
ART DIRECTOR
Tod Seisser
WRITER
Jay Taub
PHOTOGRAPHER
David Langley
CLIENT
WABC-TV
AGENCY
Della Femina, Travisano
& Partners

87
ART DIRECTOR
Jim Cox
WRITER
Marc Deschenes
PHOTOGRAPHER
James Wood
CLIENT
Fotomat
AGENCY
Chiat/Day-Los Angeles

88 GOLD
ART DIRECTOR
Anthony Angotti
WRITER
Tom Thomas
DESIGNERS
Anthony Angotti
Barbara Bowman
Dominique Singer
PHOTOGRAPHER
Robert Ammirati
CLIENT
BMW of North America
AGENCY
Ammirati & Puris

SOME PEOPLE ARE SO OPPOSED TO MURDER THEY'LL KILL ANYONE WHO COMMITS IT.

"DO YOU WANT THEM DEAD?"

There are now thirty-seven states that stand united behind the death sentence. And a total of five methods by which it's carried out. The electric chair, cyanide gas, hanging, lethal injection and firing squad.

But no matter which method is used, the result is the same. The taking of a human life.

This week, in an Eyewitness News Special Report, Roger Grimsby takes a good hard look at capital punishment.

You'll meet murderers on death row who are waiting to die. And families of their victims. Who can't wait to see them dead.

Watch "Do You Want Them Dead?" Then decide for yourself if the death penalty should become a way of life.

EYEWITNESS NEWS 6PM ⑦

"I developed 37% bigger muscles at Fotomat."

"My rippling biceps at a puny 3½ x 5."

"My biceps at a massive 4 x 6."

So can you.

Just bring your film to Fotomat and ask for their new Custom Series Prints.

Bingo!

Your 35mm prints will be 37% bigger than usual.

Your 126 prints will be 31% bigger. And your 110, 33% bigger.

But not just bigger. Better, too.

Your film will be processed with extra time and care in Fotomat's own labs by their most experienced photofinishers.

So not only will your muscles look bigger, they'll be real sharp. And your skin tone will be just right. Like mine.

New Custom Series Prints come in glossy or studio finish.

And, if you clip the coupon, they also come with a buck off.

$1.00 off 110,126,35mm

Custom Series Print developing at your participating Fotomat store. One roll per coupon. Offer expires 00/00/00.

Custom Series Prints

FOTOMAT

87

LAST YEAR, A CAR OUT-PERFORMED 318 STOCKS ON THE NEW YORK STOCK EXCHANGE.

If you'd bought a new BMW 320i in the beginning of 1980, and sold it at the end, your investment would have retained 92.5% of its original value. If you'd done the same with any of 318 NYSE stocks, you'd have done less well. And you'd have forfeited an important daily dividend: The unfluctuating joy of driving one of the world's great performance sedans.

BMW
THE ULTIMATE DRIVING MACHINE.

BMW UPDATES ITS ANNUAL REPORT TO PERFORMANCE-MINDED INVESTORS.

88 GOLD

89
ART DIRECTOR
Phil Gips

WRITERS
Robert Fearon
Jan Zlotnick

PHOTOGRAPHERS
Jean-Marie Guyaux
Peter Kane

CLIENT
Business Week

AGENCY
Fearon O'Leary Kaprielian

90
ART DIRECTOR
Alex Tsao

WRITERS
Dick Raboy
Mitch Epstein
Debbie Polenberg

DESIGNER
Alex Tsao

ARTISTS
Tim Belair
Alex Tsao

PHOTOGRAPHER
Gordon Munro

CLIENT
Barney's New York

AGENCY
Epstein, Raboy Advertising

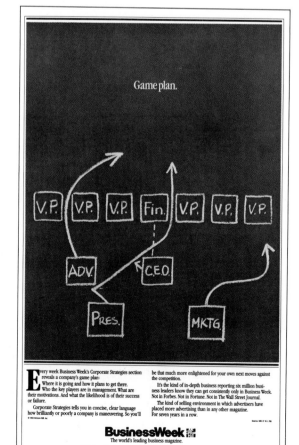

The British tradition of service is much in evidence in the English Room at Barney's. Here, and nowhere else outside London, a gentleman may see the complete offerings of the great British makers Kilgour, French & Stanbury, Daks, Burberrys, Rodex and Aquascutum. And he may, should he prefer, review them as he would on Savile Row, which is to say by appointment.

THE ENGLISH ROOM AT BARNEY'S

In an age when there is perhaps too much new under the sun, the tailoring at Barney's is a vestige of another era.

Our tailors today pursue their craft as it was practiced 59 years ago: with needle, thimble, thread. And pride. Equally rare, the 250 tailors at Barney's outnumber the sales staff—by almost two to one. This, to provide a level of service that has all but vanished over the past half-century.

After all, no matter how well a suit may be made, ultimately, we feel it's an obligation to see that it's tailored to fit, as well.

When a store offers the service that recalls another age, it does, indeed, seem like old times.

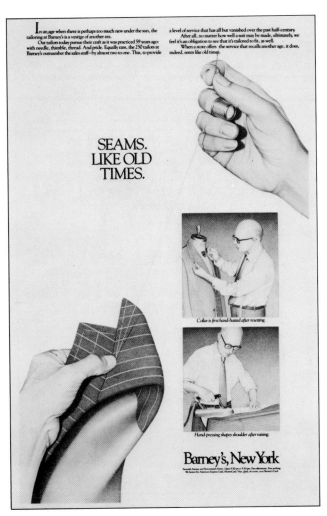

SEAMS. LIKE OLD TIMES.

Collar is first hand-basted after resetting.

Hand-pressing shapes shoulder after raising.

Barney's, New York

Nothing is quite as flattering to a man as a tuxedo.

The R.S.V.P. Room at Barneys provides the opportunity to be flattered fourteen different ways.

Oxxford

Hickey Freeman

Lanvin

Kilgour, French & Stanbury

Giorgio Armani

Bruno Piattelli

Ermenegildo Zegna

Cerruti 1881

Basile

Gianfranco Ferrè

Pierre Cardin

Bill Blass

Lord West

After Six

THE R.S.V.P. ROOM AT BARNEYS NEW YORK

**Consumer Newspaper
Over 600 Lines Campaign**

91
ART DIRECTOR
Tod Seisser

WRITER
Jay Taub

PHOTOGRAPHERS
Steve Steigman
David Langley

CLIENT
WABC-TV

AGENCY
Della Femina, Travisano
& Partners

92
ART DIRECTOR
Stan Kovics

WRITER
Michael Lipton

PHOTOGRAPHER
Dan Rubin

CLIENT
Chelsea Gym

AGENCY
Great Scott Advertising

IF THIS NUCLEAR PLANT MELTS DOWN TOMORROW, 250,000 PEOPLE WILL HAVE TO SHARE 30 HOSPITAL BEDS.

"NUCLEAR ACCIDENTS: ARE WE PREPARED?"

This is the Indian Point nuclear generating station in Westchester County. It provides electricity for millions of New York State residents. But for the 250,000 people who live in the area, it also provides cause for alarm.

If it experienced a major radiological leak, could the hospitals within the surrounding high-risk area handle all the victims?

The State of New York says yes. But the people in charge of the hospitals say there's not enough bed space. And not enough training.

This week, watch a 5 o'clock Eyewitness News Special Report with Storm Field – "Nuclear Accidents: Are We Prepared?"

Because after all you've heard about nuclear contamination, it's time you were exposed to something different. The facts.

THE 5 O'CLOCK EYEWITNESS NEWS

THIS MAN DIED AND LIVED TO TALK ABOUT IT.

"DEATH AND BEYOND"

What happens to us after we die? This is possibly the most provocative question of all time.

Some people think there's an afterlife. Others think it's just a void. Yet some people, such as 33 year old John Migliaccio, believe they've experienced the answer.

This week, in a Special Report on The 5 o'clock Eyewitness News, Rose Ann Scamardella talks to people who've died. Then returned to life. And finds out what happened in between.

Watch "Death and Beyond". And hear what death is like, from people who've been there.

THE 5 O'CLOCK EYEWITNESS NEWS

SOME PEOPLE ARE SO OPPOSED TO MURDER THEY'LL KILL ANYONE WHO COMMITS IT.

"DO YOU WANT THEM DEAD?"

There are now thirty-seven states that stand united behind the death sentence. And a total of five methods by which it's carried out. The electric chair, cyanide gas, hanging, lethal injection and firing squad.

But no matter which method is used, the result is the same. The taking of a human life.

This week, in an Eyewitness News Special Report, Roger Grimsby takes a good hard look at capital punishment. You'll meet murderers on death row who are waiting to die. And families of their victims. Who can't wait to see them dead.

Watch "Do You Want Them Dead?" Then decide for yourself if the death penalty should become a way of life.

EYEWITNESS NEWS 6PM

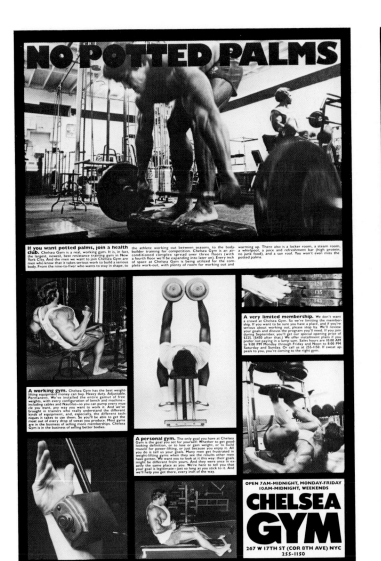
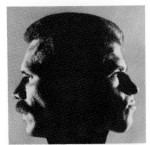

Consumer Newspaper
Over 600 Lines Campaign

95
ART DIRECTOR
Dennis D'Amico
WRITER
Bob Martell
DESIGNER
Dennis D'Amico
CLIENT
MCI
AGENCY
Ally & Gargano

96
ART DIRECTORS
Jean Marcellino
Seymon Ostilly
WRITER
Kevin O'Neill
DESIGNER
Seymon Ostilly
ARTIST
Fred Marcellino
PHOTOGRAPHER
Manuel Gonzales
CLIENT
IBM
AGENCY
Lord, Geller, Federico,
Einstein

Old Habits vs. Common Sense

LONG DISTANCE CALLS	MINS.	BELL	MCI	SAVINGS
New York City to Trenton	15	$4.40	$2.90	34.1%
Washington, D.C. to Atlanta	2	1.05	.75	28.6
San Francisco to Denver	7	3.28	2.69	18.0
Philadelphia to Wilmington	20	5.80	3.87	33.3
Chicago to Milwaukee	5	2.05	1.64	20.0
Boston to Providence	2	.76	.39	48.7
Hartford to Springfield, MA	17	4.96	3.29	33.6
New Haven to New York City	1	.57	.25	56.1
Los Angeles to Chicago	16	7.24	6.14	15.2
Richmond to Baltimore	1	.58	.34	41.4
Cincinnati to Louisville	4	1.68	1.31	22.0
Cheyenne to Fort Collins	30	8.60	5.81	32.4
Houston to Phoenix	5	2.40	1.92	20.0
New Orleans to Cincinnati	17	7.50	6.36	15.2
San Diego to Indianapolis	10	4.60	3.84	16.5
Chicago to Cleveland	18	7.73	6.54	15.4
Los Angeles to St. Louis	9	4.16	3.46	16.8
New York City to Miami	8	3.72	3.07	17.5
Denver to Washington, D.C.	16	7.24	6.14	15.2
Baltimore to Houston	4	1.96	1.54	21.4

Old habits don't die easily.

Sometimes, even when they come face-to-face with overwhelming common sense.

Look at our chart.

Common sense would dictate that when you can place the same call to the same place and save 15 to 50%, it would be foolish not to.

That's why half the Fortune 500 and nearly 200,000 other companies, large and small, have joined MCI.

But some companies are still thinking about it.

And while they think about it, their competitors are enjoying the savings you see on the chart.

How can MCI charge less than Bell for the same service?

Very simply, MCI is more efficient than Bell. We've built our own coast-to-coast network exclusively for long distance calling. Our equipment is newer and more advanced.

We work to hold our costs down, so we can pass

the long distance savings along to you.

We can also give you flexibility. Every business has different needs. So we have different plans for you to choose from.

They all have one thing in common. You save on every long distance call you make. From 15 to 50%.

The total savings in a year can be enormous. A computer company saved a million dollars. An airline saved $800,000. A bank, $750,000.

No capital investment. No installation. No nothing.

These savings are pure profit because there's no capital investment whatsoever. No installation. From the very first moment you start using MCI, it's cost-effective.

You place the same calls to the same places you're calling now. But you start paying less. A lot less. With every phone call.

Naturally, you may have some questions about MCI. We'd be happy to send you a free brochure.

Simply fill out the coupon and mail it to us. Or call your local MCI sales office.

Let common sense prevail.

MCI
The nation's long distance phone company.

MCI Telecommunications Corp.
P.O. Box 611
Vienna, VA 22180

Please send me more information on how to cut long distance costs 15 to 50%.
☐ For Business   ☐ For Home
Name
Title
Company _____ Telephone
Address _____ City
State _____ Zip

You have a choice. You can contribute to Bell's profits. Or yours.

LONG DISTANCE CALLS	MINS.	BELL	MCI	SAVINGS
New York City to Trenton	15	$4.40	$2.90	34.1%
Washington, D.C. to Atlanta	2	1.05	.75	28.6
Erie to Cleveland	3	1.31	.98	25.2
Philadelphia to Wilmington	20	5.80	3.87	33.3
Chicago to Milwaukee	5	2.05	1.64	20.0
Boston to Providence	2	.76	.39	48.7
Hartford to Springfield, MA	17	4.96	3.29	33.6
New Haven to New York City	1	.57	.25	56.1
Scranton to Newark	2	2.79	2.30	17.6
Richmond to Baltimore	1	.58	.34	41.4
Cincinnati to Louisville	4	1.68	1.31	22.0
Cheyenne to Fort Collins	30	8.60	5.81	32.4
Houston to Phoenix	5	2.40	1.92	20.0
New Orleans to Cincinnati	17	7.50	6.36	15.2
San Diego to Indianapolis	10	4.60	3.84	16.8
Chicago to Cleveland	18	7.73	6.54	15.4
Pittsburgh to St. Louis	3	1.48	1.12	24.3
Atlanta to Birmingham	9	3.70	3.08	16.8
Denver to Washington, D.C.	16	7.24	6.14	15.2
Baltimore to Houston	4	1.96	1.54	21.4
Wash., D.C. to Baltimore	25	7.20	4.84	32.8
Miami to San Francisco	10	5.15	4.32	16.1
Los Angeles to Phoenix	23	9.83	8.35	15.1
Detroit to Minneapolis	6	2.77	2.25	18.8
Newark to Albany	7	2.92	2.40	17.8
Syracuse to Harrisburg	4	1.75	1.37	21.7
Detroit to Toledo	18	5.24	3.48	33.6

Usually, there are a lot of pros and cons to any decision.

With this decision, you'll find there are all pros and no cons.

You can keep paying the full rate to Bell. Or you can join MCI and cut your long distance costs 15 to 50%. Without giving up anything.

You'll be in good company. Today, half the Fortune 500 and 170,000 other companies are enjoying the savings you see on the chart.

How can MCI charge less than Bell?

The secret is efficiency. MCI operates a long distance system more efficiently than Bell. We're a newer company and we're not saddled with outdated equipment. We work to keep our costs low, so we can pass the savings along to you.

We're also able to offer you flexibility. Every business has different needs. So we have a number of different plans for you to choose from.

They all have one thing in common. You save on every phone call you make. From 15 to 50%.

The total savings over a year can be enormous. A computer company saved over a million dollars. An airline, $800,000. A bank, $750,000.

No capital investment. No installation. No nothing.

You get these savings with absolutely no capital investment. No new equipment of any kind. So, from the first moment you start using MCI, the savings are pure profit.

All you need are the same pushbutton phones you're using now. You punch a few extra buttons. That's it. Everything else is exactly the same. Except you start paying a lot less.

MCI now provides service to over 80% of the nation's area codes. To and from over 4000 cities. And every day, another little piece of America's geography is being added.

Naturally, you may have some questions about MCI. We'd be happy to send you a free brochure. Simply fill out the coupon and mail it to us.

Or call your local MCI sales office.

And start putting your money into your profits. Instead of Bell's.

MCI
The nation's long distance phone company.

MCI Telecommunications Corp.
1133 19th Street, N.W.
Washington, D.C. 20036

Please send me more information on how to cut long distance costs 15 to 50%.
Name
Company
Address _____ City
State _____ Zip

Put your money into your profits. Instead of your phone.

LONG DISTANCE CALLS	MINS.	BELL	MCI	SAVINGS
San Diego to Houston	4	$1.96	$1.54	21.4%
Albany to Lancaster	3	1.36	1.03	24.3
Syracuse to Akron	8	3.53	2.91	17.6
Minneapolis to Kalamazoo	5	2.27	1.82	19.8
Kansas City to Tulsa	9	3.70	3.08	16.8
Louisville to St. Louis	7	2.92	2.40	17.8
New Haven to New York City	1	.57	.25	56.1
New York City to Miami	5	2.40	1.92	20.0
Atlanta to Boston	2	1.08	.77	28.7
Phoenix to San Francisco	15	6.64	5.62	15.4
Austin to Nashville	3	1.48	1.12	24.3
Fresno to Denver	8	3.63	3.00	17.4
Newark to Erie	2	1.01	.73	27.8
Gary to Flint	6	2.53	2.05	19.0
Baltimore to Cleveland	4	1.85	1.45	21.6
Chicago to Ann Arbor	11	4.48	3.77	15.8
Dallas to Memphis	3	1.43	1.09	23.8
Jacksonville to Atlanta	7	2.92	2.40	17.8
Okla. City to Wichita Falls	1	.57	.33	42.1
Cincinnati to Detroit	10	4.09	3.42	16.4
Baton Rouge to Birmingham	5	2.27	1.82	19.8
Pittsburgh to Columbus	1	.58	.34	41.4
Wash., D.C. to Philadelphia	10	3.90	3.28	15.9
Morristown to Bridgeport	2	.94	.66	29.8
Fredericksburg to Annapolis	3	1.31	.98	25.2
Trenton to Detroit	1	.62	.37	40.3
Charlotte to Richmond	12	4.87	4.11	15.6
New York City to Wash., D.C.	13	5.26	4.45	15.4

Take a look at our chart. Then decide where you want to put your money.

Into Bell's profits. Or yours.

Long distance costs are a necessary part of doing business. But a large part of what you're paying Bell is not a necessary expense.

Not when you can make the same call to the same place with MCI. And save 15 to 50%.

That's why half the Fortune 500 and nearly 200,000 other companies across the country have joined MCI.

How can MCI charge less than Bell for the same service?

MCI has built its own coast-to-coast network exclusively for long distance calling.

Our system is newer and more efficient. We're a newer company, so we're not saddled with outdated equipment. We also work to hold our costs down, so we can pass the long distance savings along to you.

We also know that every company has different long distance needs. An insurance company has different needs than a travel agency. So we have a number of different plans for you to choose from.

No matter which plan you choose, you save on every long distance call you make with MCI. From 15 to 50%.

The savings over a year can be enormous. A computer company saved over a million dollars. An airline, $800,000. A bank, $750,000.

No capital investment. No installation. No nothing.

You get these savings with absolutely no capital investment. No new equipment of any kind. You use the same push-button phones you're using now. So from the first moment you start using MCI, the savings are pure profit.

MCI now reaches most of the phones in the country. In fact, in a growing number of cities, you can use MCI to call any other phone in any other state in the continental United States.

Naturally, you may have some questions about MCI. We'd be happy to send you a free brochure. Simply fill out the coupon and mail it to us.

Or call your local MCI sales office.

Let Bell profit at someone else's expense.

MCI
The nation's long distance phone company.

MCI Telecommunications Corp.
P.O. Box 611
Vienna, VA 22180

Please send me more information on how to cut long distance costs 15 to 50%.
☐ For Business   ☐ For Home
Name
Title
Company
Address _____ City
State _____ Zip

There was a time when all computers were big. They were also costly and complex.

Nevertheless, they were very well-suited to the jobs they had to do. But the average person rarely saw one of these computers and certainly didn't consider using one. At IBM, something has been happening to computers. They have been getting smaller. Their prices have been shrinking. And the special knowledge required to use one has been reduced dramatically. Our IBM Personal Computer, for example, is small enough to fit on a desk blotter but its power is equal to older computers many times its size. Today, small IBM computers can help businesses of all sizes manage their growth. Or families handle their bank accounts. Even very small people (kids for example) will find them just the right size. Of course there is something else that's small about our small computers. The price: they start at under $1,600. You see, it always pays to read the small print.

IBM

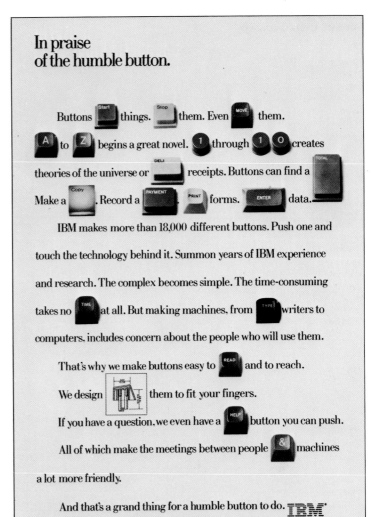

In praise of the humble button.

Buttons [Start] things. [Stop] them. Even [MOVE] them. [A] to [Z] begins a great novel. [1] through [1] [O] creates theories of the universe or [DEL] receipts. Buttons can find a [TOTAL] Make a [Copy]. Record a [PAYMENT]. [PRINT] forms. [ENTER] data.

IBM makes more than 18,000 different buttons. Push one and touch the technology behind it. Summon years of IBM experience and research. The complex becomes simple. The time-consuming takes no [TIME] at all. But making machines, from [TYPE]writers to computers, includes concern about the people who will use them.

That's why we make buttons easy to [READ] and to reach.

We design [⊔] them to fit your fingers.

If you have a question, we even have a [HELP] button you can push.

All of which make the meetings between people [&] machines a lot more friendly.

And that's a grand thing for a humble button to do. **IBM**

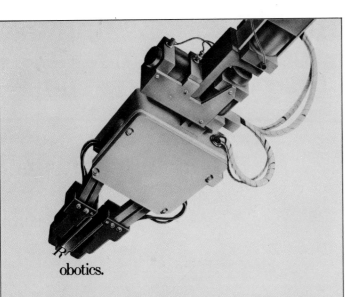

obotics.

This story begins with the period at the end of this sentence. The robotic arm above can locate a hole half that size and accurately insert a pin, once or thousands of times.

Today, IBM robotic systems controlled by computers are doing precision work on complex, tedious or even hazardous tasks. Using special sensors in the "gripper," they are assembling complicated mechanisms, rejecting defective parts, testing completed units and keeping inventories.

Communication between the system and its computer is made possible by the most advanced robotic programming language yet reported. The language and the robotic systems it controls are part of our continuing commitment to research and development — a commitment funded with more than $8 billion over the past seven years.

IBM robotic systems can improve productivity, worker safety and product quality.

And that's precisely why we're in business. **IBM**

97

98

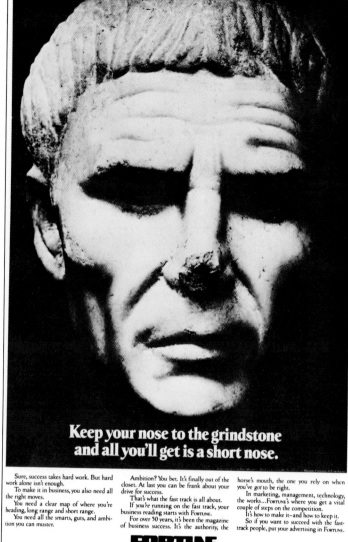

99 GOLD

We're all created equal.
After that, baby, you're on your own.

Nobody's going to hand you success on a silver platter.

If you want to make it, you'll have to make it on your own.

Your own drive, your own guts, your own energy, your own ambition.

Yes, ambition. You don't have to hide it anymore. Society's decided that now it's OK to be up-front about the drive for success.

Isn't that what the fast track is all about?

If you're one of the fast-track people, your business reading starts with FORTUNE.

After all, FORTUNE's been the magazine of business success for over 50 years.

It's the authority...the business magazine you rely on when you've *got* to be right.

It helps the movers and shakers decide how to move and what to shake. It's their

early-warning system, alerting them to opportunities and dangers up ahead.

In marketing, management, technology, the works...it's the one that gives you a vital couple of steps on the competition.

FORTUNE is the business magazine that really *can* help you make it—and keep it.

And it's the one to advertise in when you need to target the fast-track people.

FORTUNE
How to succeed.

The headhunters will get you
if you really use your brains.

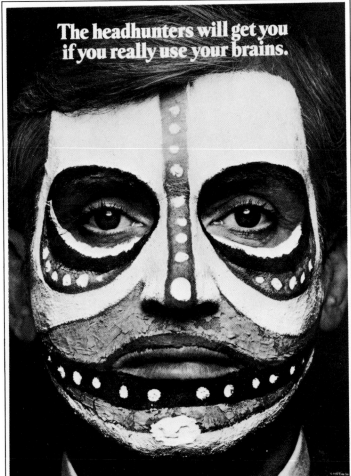

Put all your smarts to work and pretty soon you'll be the one the executive searchers are searching for.

Encourage it. The more headhunters on your trail, the faster you'll get to the top.

The nice thing is, you don't have to hide your ambition under a bushel anymore.

Now you can be up-front about your drive for success.

That's what the fast track is all about.

If *you're* a fast-tracker, your business reading undoubtedly starts with FORTUNE.

It's where you get the help you need to make the most out of your brains.

It's the authority. The last word. The source you rely on when you've just *got* to be right.

FORTUNE's your early-warning system,

alerting you to dangers and opportunities up ahead.

In marketing, management, technology, the works—it's where you get a vital couple of steps on the competition.

It's how to make it—and keep it.

And for advertising to the fast-track people, there's nothing else like FORTUNE.

Absolutely nothing!

FORTUNE
How to succeed.

HOW TO MAKE THE BEST OF YOUR WURST.

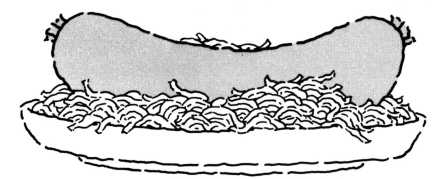

Start with the best. Steinfeld's Sauerkraut. Always moist and crisp. With just the right amount of zest to spice up your favorite recipe.

100

VERMONT.
A LOT GOES ON WHEN THE SKIS COME OFF.

You could float across a steaming pool.

Feast on a filet of sole poached in white Bordeaux.

Bargain for an antique oak icebox. A gramophone. Or a big brass carriage lamp.

Skate across a frozen pond. Fish a frozen lake.

Fire a racquetball.

Dance all night in a 150-year-old country inn to the best band

you'll swear you've ever heard.

Browse through an afternoon of surprises in a genuine general store.

Or snowshoe through a silent forest a million miles from nowhere.

Of course, Vermont means excellent skiing, too. On some of the most breathtaking Alpine and cross country trails in America.

To find out more, just mail the coupon. And for daily ski conditions, call 802-229-0531.

Please send me:

☐ Vermont Alpine Ski Guide

☐ Vermont Cross Country Ski Guide

Name _____
(Please print)

Address _____

City _____

State _____ Zip _____

Mail to: State of Vermont, Room 13,
Montpelier, VT 05602

VERMONT
A SPECIAL WORLD.

SHE HAS HER MOTHER'S EYES, HER FATHER'S CHIN AND HER DOCTOR'S NOSE.

More and more men and women are accentuating the positive and eliminating the negative through cosmetic surgery. But before you decide to modify your features, join us for a look at some new techniques, the befores and afters, the successes and disasters.

A 2-part Special Report by Betsy Ashton.

"OPERATION BEAUTY"
BEGINNING TONIGHT AT 6 AND 11.
CHANNEL ⊙2 NEWSBREAKERS

If it concerns you, it concerns us.

It's 10 a.m.
Do you know where your ad is?

A fast run-through of the capsule business news, a scan of the stock tables, a quick look at some earnings and sales figures, and a glance at an ad or two that catch the eye. Then it's all over for the daily journal.
But Business Week and your ad stay with your customers all week long. Most readers get their copies on Friday, read them over the weekend, and keep reading them through the week.
That's because Business Week gives its readers more of what they have to know–concise, yet complete, articles ranging

every business concern, from Economics to Corporate Strategies, International Business, Information Processing, Marketing, Investments. And more.
All reported with an interpretive edge that signals business trends to come. An editorial presence that ensures your advertising gets the serious, long-lasting attention you want.
An award-winning thoroughness leaders can't find anywhere else. Not in Forbes. Not in Fortune. And certainly not in the instant media.
Business Week. Where your ad keeps working all week long.

BusinessWeek
The world's leading business magazine.

103 SILVER

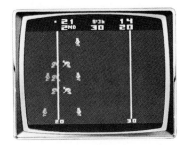

WHAT FOOTBALL STRIKE?

ATARI® REALSPORTS™ FOOTBALL IS ON ITS WAY.

If you own an ATARI Video Computer System,™ you won't have to be without football for long. Because we're about to introduce ATARI RealSports Football. It's one of our new line of highly sophisticated RealSports video games that includes everything from Soccer to Baseball. RealSports Football is so real that the crowd cheers. And the graphics are so sharp the players actually play. They kick. They pass. They block. They tackle. They do virtually everything real players do. Except, of course, strike.

© 1982 Atari, Inc. All rights reserved

ATARI
A Warner Communications Company

COME HELL OR HIGH WATER, IT TALKS UP A STORM.

The Sailor RT 144 AC VHF radio has proved itself in the most punishing field test imaginable: the real world.

It's been beaten, banged and battered in high winds and hurricanes. In gales, squalls and storms. In North Sea fishing boats, Navy lifeboats and desert outposts.

And time and again, when lesser radios would have been long shaken or shattered into oblivion, the Sailor keeps on working.

That's why in Europe, where for centuries fishermen have demanded the most of their boats, the radio most in demand is Sailor.

The fact is, fishing boats in Europe use Sailor more than all other radios combined.

Is it because Sailor is cased in heavy gauge steel—not thin plastic or sheet metal—to withstand as much as a 4,000 pound load?

Is it that all electrical connections are hard wired—not slid into a mechanical connector—to hold up under vibration and resist corrosion on the contacts?

Is it the speaker magnet, some three times the size of competitors' to give more hi-fi clarity and avoid blowout?

Or is it the warranty, a full four years on every part?

Get the Sailor at your nearest Racal-Decca dealer. The best reason to do it is, quite simply, this:

Come hell or high water, you can depend on the Sailor to talk up a storm.

Send me more information and the name of my nearest Racal-Decca dealer.

Name

Address

City   State   Zip

Racal-Decca Marine Inc
4200 23rd Ave. W. Seattle WA 98199
Phone (206) 285-3992

106

108 GOLD

How to enjoy poetry

by James Dickey

International Paper asked James Dickey poet-in-residence at the University of South Carolina, winner of the National Book Award for his collection of poems, "Buck-dancer's Choice," and author of the novel "Deliverance," to tell you how to approach poetry so it can bring special pleasure and understanding to your life.

What is poetry? And why has it been around so long? Many have suspected that it was invented as a school subject, because you have to take exams on it. But that is not what poetry is or why it is still around. That's not what it feels like, either. When you really feel it, a new part of you happens, or an old part is renewed, with surprise and delight at being what it is.

Where poetry is coming from

From the beginning, men have known that words and things, words and actions, words and feelings, go together, and that they can go together in thousands of different ways, according to who is using them. Some ways go shallow, and some go deep.

Your connection with other imaginations

The first thing to understand about poetry is that it comes to you from outside you, in books or in words, but that for it to live, something from within you must come to it and meet it and complete it. Your response with your own mind and body and memory and emotions gives the poem its ability to work its magic; if you give to it, it will give to you, and give plenty.

When you read, don't let the poet write down to you; read up to him. Reach for him from your gut out, and the heart and muscles will come into it, too.

Which sun! Whose stars?

The sun is new every day, the ancient philosopher Heraclitus said. The sun of poetry is new every day, too, because it is seen in different

"The things around us—like water, trees, clouds, the sun—belong to us all. How you see them can enhance my way of seeing them. And just the other way around."

ways by different people who have lived under it, lived with it, responded to it. Their lives are different from yours, but by means of the special spell that poetry brings to the *fact* of the sun—everybody's sun; yours, too—you can come into possession of many suns: as many as men and women have ever been able to imagine. Poetry makes possible the deepest kind of personal possession of the world.

The most beautiful constellation in the winter sky is Orion, which ancient poets thought looked like a hunter, up there, moving across heaven with his dog Sirius. What is this hunter made out of stars hunting for? What does he mean? Who owns him, if anybody? The poet Aldous Huxley felt that he did, and so, in Aldous Huxley's universe of personal emotion, he did.

*Up from among the emblems of the
wind into its heart of power,
The Huntsman climbs, and all his
living stars
Are bright, and all are mine.*

Where to start

The beginning of your true encounter with poetry should be simple. It should bypass all classrooms, all textbooks, courses, examinations, and libraries and go straight to the things that make your own existence exist: to your body and nerves and blood and muscles. Find your own way—a secret way that just maybe you don't know yet—to open yourself as wide as you can and as deep as you can to the moment, the *now* of your own existence and the endless mystery of it, and perhaps at the same time to one other thing that is not you, but is out there: a handful of gravel is a good place to start. So is an ice cube—what more mysterious and beautiful *interior* of something has there ever been?

As for me, I like the sun, the source of all living things, and on certain days very good-feeling, too. "Start with the sun," D.H. Lawrence said, "and everything will slowly, slowly happen." Good advice. And a lot *will* happen.

What is more fascinating than a rock, if you really feel it and *look* at it, or more interesting than a leaf?

*Horses, I mean; butterflies, whales;
Mosses, and stars; and gravelly
Rivers, and fruit.*

*Oceans, I mean; black valleys; corn;
Brambles, and cliffs; rock, dirt, dust, ice...*

Go back and read this list—it is quite a list, Mark Van Doren's list!—item by item. Slowly. Let each of these things call up an image out of your own life.

Think and feel. What moss do you see? Which horse? What field

of corn? What brambles are *your* brambles? Which river is most yours?

The poem's way of going

Part of the spell of poetry is in the rhythm of language, used by poets who understand how powerful a factor rhythm can be, how compelling and unforgettable. Almost anything put into rhythm and rhyme is more memorable than the same thing said in prose. Why this is, no one knows completely, though the answer is surely rooted far down in the biology by means of which we exist; in the circulation of the blood that goes forth from the heart and comes back, and in the repetition of breathing. Croesus was a rich Greek king, back in the sixth century before Christ, but this tombstone was not his:

*No Croesus lies in the grave you see;
I was a poor laborer, and this suits me.*

That is plain-spoken and definitive. You believe it, and the rhyme helps you believe it and keep it.

Some things you'll find out

Writing poetry is a lot like a contest with yourself, and if you like sports and games and competitions of all kinds, you might like to try writing some. Why not?

The possibilities of rhyme are great. Some of the best fun is in making up your own limericks. There's no reason you can't invent limericks about anything that comes to your mind. No reason. Try it.

The problem is to find three words that rhyme and fit into a meaning. "There was a young man from..." *Where* was he from? What

situation was he in? How can these things fit into the limerick form—a form everybody knows—so that the rhymes "pay off," and give that sense of completion and inevitability that is so deliciously memorable that nothing else is like it?

How it goes with you

The more your encounter with poetry deepens, the more your experience of your own life will deepen, and you will begin to see things by means of words, and words by means of things.

You will come to understand the world as it interacts with words, as it can be re-created by words, by rhythms and by images.

You'll understand that this condition is one charged with vital possibilities. You will pick up meaning more quickly—and you will *create* meaning, too, for yourself and for others.

Connections between things will exist for you in ways that they never did before. They will shine with unexpectedness, wide-openness, and you will go toward them, on your own path. "Then..." as Dante says, "...Then will your feet be filled with good desire." You will know this is happening the first time you say, of something you never would have noticed before, "Well, would you look at *that!* Who'd 'a thunk it?" (Pause, full of new light)

"I thunk it!"

James Dickey

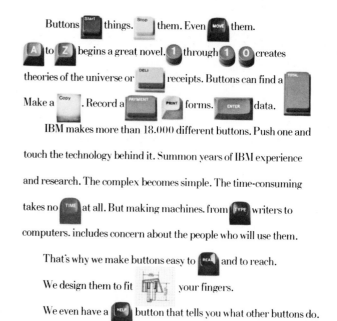

110

111

Just when you thought you understood Brie, Sainsbury's create delicious confusion.

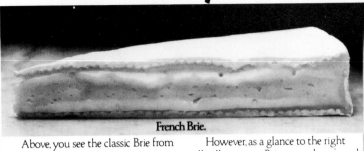

French Brie.

Bavarian Brie with Mushrooms.

Bavarian Brie with Peppers.

Bavarian Blue Brie.

Above, you see the classic Brie from France.

In 1815, at the Congress of Vienna it was voted the "King of Cheeses".

It's a cheese that can cause ecstasy amongst its admirers and its taste has been described as "part mushrooms, part cream, part cognac, part earth".

Surprisingly, it's often served hot in France.

Recipes for Brie tart go back to the 15th century and if you haven't tried Brie dipped in a mustard sauce, rolled in breadcrumbs and then deep fried, you're missing a treat.

Naturally, you'll find such classic French Brie at Sainsbury's.

And it goes without saying you'll find it in perfect condition.

However, as a glance to the right will tell you, our Brie story doesn't end there.

We also sell Bavarian Brie.

It's a slightly higher fat cheese than the French Brie and though it goes soft it doesn't run.

We sell it as a natural or blue cheese and also with mushrooms, herbs or peppers.

It's a subtle, interesting cheese and we're happy to say, increasingly popular.

If you hadn't heard of it before, perhaps it's time you took a closer look at Sainsbury's cheese.

With around 100 different cheeses we can promise you even more confusion.

Of the nicest possible kind.

Good food costs less at Sainsbury's.

Go Bass or go barefoot.

We're so confident of the new Polaroid 600 speed instant film and the new Polaroid Sun Cameras that we believe it's possible for you to get 10 good shots for 10 earnest tries every time. 10 for 10! The secret is in having the world's fastest color print film and the unique light mixing cameras that use it. The Polaroid Sun Cameras. In fact, we're so proud, we've even backed it up with Free Smile Insurance: Polaroid

10 beauties in a row.

114

THE PRICES ARE SO LOW, OUR FOUNDERS WOULD HAVE BEEN EMBARRASSED TO SHOW THEIR FACES. BUT AT LEAST IT'S ALMOST OVER.

"Just $329 for a genuine leather reclining chair? What will our friends say?"

"Just $239 for a solid mahogany Queen Anne silver chest? It's so humiliating."

"Just $799 for a 91" trapunto pillow-back sofa... in velvet? I can't wait until September 11."

"Just $129.95 for a mattress from Paine's own Louisburg mattress line? Where is our sense of tradition?"

"A large selection of Stiffel table and floor lamps for up to $75 off? I could just die."

"I have nothing to do with Paine. You've obviously mistaken me for someone else."

The storewide price reductions at this year's Summer Sale are among the most dramatic in our 147-year history.
So hurry to Paine before this sale ends on Saturday, September 11.
Happily, you won't have to face our founders.

THE PAINE SUMMER SALE.
THE SAVINGS ARE NON-TRADITIONAL.

BOSTON, 81 Arlington St., 426-1500. NATICK, 323 Speen St., 655-2200. HOURS: Boston: 9:30-5:30 Mon.-Sat. Natick: Mon.-Tues., Sat. 9:30-5:30, Weds., Thurs., Fri. 9:30-8:30.
Doorman parking available at our Boston store. Paine charge, MasterCard, Visa and American Express accepted. Interior design service available at no extra cost.

115

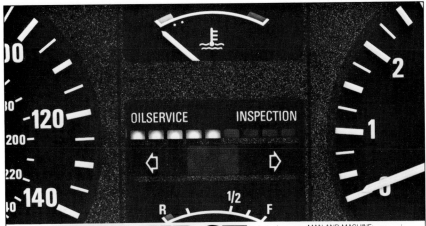

THE FIRST KNOWN EXAMPLE OF A CAR EVALUATING ITS DRIVER.

MAN AND MACHINE: IMPROVING COMMUNICATIONS.

With the aid of electronic sensors, the Service Interval Indicator monitors individual variations in driving habits and environments—as measured by engine speeds, the number of cold starts, and miles driven.

It then processes this information, and calculates when service is warranted—according to how the car is actually driven, not the dictates of an arbitrary schedule.

But BMW's aren't only engineered to evaluate their drivers.

They're also engineered to evaluate themselves.

TAPPING AN ALTERNATIVE SOURCE OF ENERGY: INFORMATION.

Another BMW innovation called Digital Motor Electronics constantly monitors the engine. It uses microprocessors to read all types of engine data— such as idling speed, air/fuel mixture, and throttle openings—and assures that fuel ignition occurs at the optimum moment.

And yet another BMW innovation monitors developments in other places. The On-Board Computer provides everything from outside temperature readings to anti-theft protection.*

The reason for this abundance of technology?

Simply that at BMW, one of our major preoccupations has always been heightening man's interaction with machine.

And all these improvements in communications are machine's latest contributions to that end.

Until now, timetables for routine automobile maintenance have overlooked one important and unpredictable factor: the person behind the wheel.

Obviously, someone who drives mostly on crowded city streets places different stresses on a car than someone who drives mostly on uncluttered highways. Differences in driving techniques (such as how hard one accelerates) are also a factor.

Which is why BMW engineers have developed the Service Interval Indicator— a computer-governed system based on the obvious fact that different people drive differently.

THE ULTIMATE DRIVING MACHINE.
BMW, MUNICH, GERMANY.

*Optional on the 528e. Otherwise, all features discussed are standard on all 6-cylinder BMW's. ©1982 BMW of North America, Inc. The BMW trademark and logo are registered trademarks of Bayerische Motoren Werke, A.G.

$9.35

60¢ EXTRA FOR PROOF OF DELIVERY

$5.60 EXTRA FOR PICK-UP WITH SERVICE AGREEMENT ONLY

NO COMMITMENT TO DELIVER BY NOON

TRACING TAKES DAYS OR WEEKS

SERVICE AVAILABILITY VARIES BY LOCATION

**$11.00
NO STRINGS ATTACHED**

For $11.00, Federal Express will come to your office, pick up your Overnight Letter,℠ deliver it to any of 13,000 communities, trace it any time of the day or night in seconds, get your letter where it's going by noon the next business day,* and send you free proof of delivery.

The choice is yours. But Federal Express has enough confidence in your good judgment to have included the coupon to your right.

For a free kit of Overnight Letter Materials, send to: Overnight Letter Kit, Federal Express Corp., P.O. Box 727, Memphis, TN 38194-2481.
Name_____ Title_____
Company_____
Address_____
City_____ State_____ Zip_____
Phone#_____ Account # (if any)_____

FEDERAL EXPRESS

118

119

THE CAR THAT CAUGHT THE AUTOMOTIVE ESTABLISHMENT WITH ITS TECHNOLOGY DOWN.

We are living in an era whose most celebrated automotive innovation may very well be exotically named upholstery fabrics.

An era of "preventive" technology, characterized by emission controls, anti-pollution devices, and the like.

An era that has witnessed the resurrection of diesel engines whose performance may charitably be described as uninspired.

At BMW, we have no easy remedy for the times. Just a new luxury car engineered to defy them.

THE BMW 528e: HIGH PERFORMANCE THROUGH HIGH TECHNOLOGY.

The 528e is a $24,000[^+] sedan that runs not just on gasoline (in modest amounts) but on information (in massive amounts).

The information is managed by microprocessors deep within the engine. They read all manner of engine data—speed, air/fuel mixture, throttle openings—and then tell the engine what to do in the next thousandth of a second.

This system, called Digital Motor Electronics (DME), acts as both ego and conscience to the engine.

Conscience, because it helps purify emissions and metes out fuel at an EPA-estimated 22 mpg, 32 mpg highway.*

Ego, because it assures that the engine will always deliver what it was bred to deliver: high performance. (Ignition is continuously "ordered" to occur at the optimum time for optimum performance.)

DME is aided in these efforts by a supremely willing accomplice: the new BMW "Eta" engine.

It has the uncanny ability to match energy consumption to driving conditions, running on 6 cylinders when necessary, or, under some conditions, none at all. (During deceleration, fuel is shut off until 960 rpm.)

And it is matched with a suspension equally-sophisticated. One based on a design Car and Driver magazine judged the "most significant breakthrough in front suspension design in this decade."

WHY BMW OWNERS ARE BETTER INFORMED THAN OTHER PEOPLE.

The 528e assumes that the driver, no less than the car, runs on information.

An electronic control system constantly monitors and reports on some 8 different operating functions, including such vital but usually unreported details as brake lining wear.

The sum is a car characterized not just by spacious and thoroughly civilized interiors, but by "superb engineering" (Motor Trend), one able to carry a warranty that makes others read like votes of no confidence: A 3-year/36,000-mile limited warranty and a 6-year limited warranty against rust perforation.**

If you'd prefer that your next luxury car not be another expensive surrender to the times, we suggest you state your preference where it will do some good.

At your nearest BMW dealer. Where the new 528e awaits your test drive.

THE ULTIMATE DRIVING MACHINE.
BMW MUNICH, GERMANY

Manufacturer's suggested retail price: $23,325. Actual price will depend upon dealer. Price does not include state and local taxes, dealer prep, destination and handling charges. *Fuel efficiency figures are for comparison only. Your actual mileage may vary, depending on speed, weather and trip length; actual highway mileage will most likely be lower. **See your BMW dealer for complete details. © 1982 BMW of North America, Inc. The BMW trademark and logo are registered trademarks of Bayerische Motoren Werke, A.G.

We're so confident of the new Polaroid 600 speed instant film and the new Polaroid Sun Cameras that we believe it's possible for you to get 10 good shots for 10 earnest tries every time. 10 for 10! The secret is in having the world's fastest color print film and the unique light mixing cameras that use it. The Polaroid Sun Cameras. In fact, we're so proud, we've even backed it up with Free Smile Insurance: Polaroid

10 hits. No errors.

122

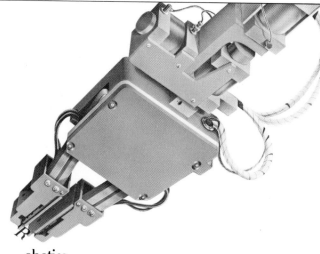

obotics.

This story begins with the period at the end of this sentence.
The robotic arm above can locate a hole that size and accurately insert a pin, once or thousands of times.

Today, IBM robotic systems controlled by computers are doing precision work on complex, tedious or even hazardous tasks. Using special sensors in the "gripper," they are assembling complicated mechanisms, rejecting defective parts, testing completed units and keeping inventories.

Communication between the system and its computer is made possible by the most advanced robotic programming language yet reported. The language and the robotic systems it controls are part of our continuing commitment to research and development — a commitment funded with more than $8 billion over the past seven years.

IBM robotic systems can improve productivity, worker safety and product quality.

And that's precisely why we're in business. **IBM**

126

WE SUPPORT THE WOMEN'S MOVEMENT.

It is not mere coincidence that some of the swiftest women in the world wear Brooks shoes.

The fact is, no other running shoes have as much cushioning as our Lady Vantage and Lady Hugger GT. And no other shoe company has the Varus™ Wedge to control pronation and help prevent running injuries.

So, whether you're a woman who's setting records or just setting out on your first mile, we want you to know one thing. We support your efforts completely.

BROOKS
Feel the difference.

127

128

129 GOLD

**Consumer Magazine
Color Page or Spread
Including Magazine
Supplements**

130
ART DIRECTOR
Bernie Vangrin
WRITER
Don Hadley
DESIGNER
Bernie Vangrin
ARTIST
Carl Filkorn
CLIENT
State of Alaska Div. of Tourism
AGENCY
Foote, Cone & Belding/
Honig–San Francisco

131
ART DIRECTOR
John D'Asto
WRITER
Ron Hawkins
PHOTOGRAPHER
David Deahl
CLIENT
Parker Pen
AGENCY
Ogilvy & Mather/Chicago

132
ART DIRECTOR
Earl Cavanah
WRITER
Larry Cadman
PHOTOGRAPHER
Art Staff, Inc.
CLIENT
Volvo
AGENCY
Scali, McCabe, Sloves

Arctic Grayling

Northern Pike

Silver Salmon

Rainbow Trout

King Salmon

Steelhead

COME TO ALASKA FOR A GOOD FIGHT.

If you like your fish wild, come to Alaska.

Alaska offers you your choice of twelve native species, all of them pugnacious.

Alaska has salt-water fishing: two oceans, two seas and hundreds of bays.

Alaska has fresh-water fishing: Three million lakes and thousands of streams and rivers.

In fact, the only problem with fishing Alaska is knowing where to begin.

Write us or call us, and we'll help you get started.

For *free* Alaska Travel Brochure, write: Alaska Division of Tourism, Pouch E-38, Juneau, Alaska 99811. OR CALL TOLL FREE 800-228-3777, *anytime.*

A L A S K A

130

Give them something they don't have.

One good pen.

Consider a Parker Arrow ball pen. It won't smudge or skip like the one they may have gotten from the dry cleaners.

And it should write much longer than the giveaway model from the gas station. In fact, a Parker Arrow will write up to five miles on a single cartridge.

Of course, they'll have other things to be impressed with along the way. Like the smooth-writing tungsten carbide ball, finished to within two-millionths of an inch of perfection. The distinctive clip in 22K gold electroplate, gleaming from 24 hours of polishing and diamond milling. The lifetime guarantee, honored around the world.

That's certainly not the kind of pen they could pick up just anywhere. It shouldn't be. It's coming from you. ✦PARKER

Parker Arrow 12K gold-filled ball pen, $40. Other Arrow pens start at $15.

A FEW CAR MAKERS WHO STILL BELIEVE IN REAR WHEEL DRIVE:

Ferrari

Corvette

All 33 cars at Indy

Porsche

All Formula I Cars

Volvo

In an era when just about everyone seems to be touting front wheel drive as the greatest thing ever to come down the pike, there's one thing you should know.

Virtually every car in the world today that's famous for performance and handling uses rear wheel drive.

Of course, a Ferrari or Formula I car may not exactly fit your family's driving needs.

So why not consider a Volvo Turbo? When it comes to handling and performance, you'll find it leaves a lot of front wheel drive cars bringing up the rear.

VOLVO
A car you can believe in.

© 1982 VOLVO OF AMERICA CORPORATION

I still do.

The ring shown is available for about $2,600. Prices may vary.

The Diamond Anniversary Ring.
A band of diamonds that says you'd marry her all over again.

A diamond is forever. De Beers

133

136
ART DIRECTOR
Catherine Pelton
WRITER
Gail Litt
DESIGNER
Catherine Pelton
PHOTOGRAPHER
Gary Perweiler
CLIENT
Minton
AGENCY
Sacks & Rosen

137
ART DIRECTOR
Robert Reitzfeld
WRITER
David Altschiller
PHOTOGRAPHER
Hunter Freeman
CLIENT
Pioneer
AGENCY
Altschiller, Reitzfeld, Solin/
NCK

138
ART DIRECTOR
Su Sareen
WRITER
Ronnie Paris
PHOTOGRAPHER
Bill Carter
CLIENT
Mettoy
AGENCY
Wasey Campbell-Ewald/
London

136

Pioneer Projection TV

Shake, rattle 'n roll.

Shake it and it rattles. Shove it and it rolls.

Small discoveries to an adult, perhaps.

But matters of earth-shattering significance when you're very small.

When you look at things from the baby's point of view, you'll see the point of Babytouch.

A new generation of toys that are especially designed for very young babies.

And because Babytouch toys cost from just 99p to £3.50, they should delight a few adults too.

When a baby plays, he's not messing around. He's finding out about the world.

What 'soft' feels like. Why does red look different from blue? If I press this will it squeak?

Babytouch are in touch with how your baby feels.

So every one of our toys offers your baby something to learn. A shape. A colour. A sound. A challenge.

And every Babytouch toy is soft, hygienic and completely safe.

To you our Clutch Ball might look like any old ball.

But to a baby, it's a bright orange moving creature.

When he gets closer, he'll spot a bird. A tiny mirror. A smiling face. A flower.

When he squeezes it (and he will) he'll be thrilled to find

it responds with a squeak.

All in all, a challenge he can really get his gums into. Whether you choose the Rocking Clown (he won't fall down, and doubles as a teething ring), or Dolly

Drops (a cute little softie with a gentle squeak that won't frighten their nappies off), Mr. Fish (soft and squishy for bathtime),

the Teether Rattle with the spinning chick, or any others in the Babytouch range, you'll find the same loving attention to detail.

The same concern for safety.

In short, the same basic understanding of how your baby feels.

If you're choosing a toy for someone small, think small.

Introduce your child to the Babytouch range.

And watch him take big steps forward before he can even walk.

Babytouch

We know how your baby feels.

Consumer Magazine Black and White Campaign Including Magazine Supplements

139 GOLD

ART DIRECTORS
Roy Grace
Howard Friedman

WRITER
Irwin Warren

DESIGNERS
Roy Grace
Howard Friedman

PHOTOGRAPHERS
Michael Pateman
John Paul Endress
Larry Sillen

CLIENT
Volkswagen

AGENCY
Doyle Dane Bernbach

140

ART DIRECTOR
Nancy Rice

WRITERS
Tom McElligott
Dick Thomas

ARTISTS
Edward Sorel
Geoffrey Moss
Robert Pryor

CLIENT
ITT Life Insurance
Corporation

AGENCY
Fallon, McElligott, Rice/Mpls.

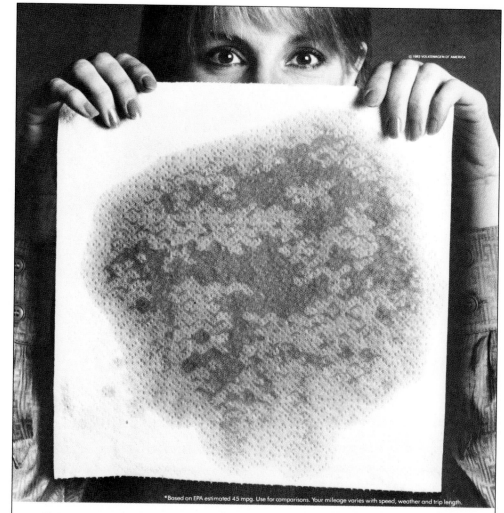

*Based on EPA estimated 45 mpg. Use for comparisons. Your mileage varies with speed, weather and trip length.

This paper towel contains enough fuel to run a Rabbit one half mile.

Astounding, isn't it?

But you probably think we're talking about some wildly advanced engine we put inside a Rabbit.

Perhaps an experiment?

Well, it's quite advanced: it's the Volkswagen Rabbit diesel.

And it makes the Rabbit the best mileage car in America.*

But it's hardly experimental.

Especially when you stop to consider the diesel's legendary reputation for durability.

Nothing else is a Volkswagen. VW

Now the question is, do you really need the best mileage car in America?

Well, some people will tell you that fuel prices will continue to drop; that gas lines are a thing of the past.

Funny about those folks who made the same predictions in 1974 and again in 1979.

A lot of them now drive Rabbits.

Is a cheaper car more expensive?

We readily admit that the Rabbit isn't the cheapest car you can buy. Or is it?

Before you run out and buy a cheap car, ask yourself a few questions.

Does a cheap car come standard with fuel injection, front-wheel drive,

and dual diagonal brakes?

Is a cheap car large enough to carry four large people without forced intimacy, yet agile enough to handle like a sports car?

Is a cheap car cheap to fix?

Or cheap when it's worth next to

nothing at trade-in time?

When you take pencil and paper and tally the real cost of owning a Rabbit versus the real cost of owning something cheaper, you'll discover the awful truth about most cheap cars. They're expensive.

Nothing else is a Volkswagen. VW

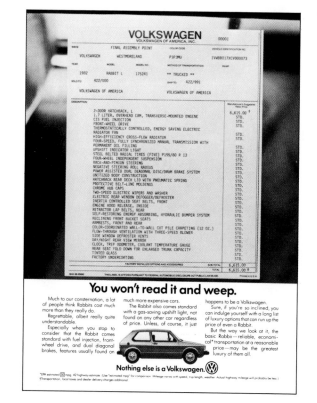

You won't read it and weep.

Much to our consternation, a lot of people think Rabbits cost much more than they really do.

Regrettable, albeit really quite understandable.

Especially when you stop to consider that the Rabbit comes standard with fuel injection, front-wheel drive, and dual diagonal brakes, features usually found on

much more expensive cars.

The Rabbit also comes standard with a gas-saving upshift light, not found on any other car regardless of price. Unless, of course, it just happens to be a Volkswagen.

Sure, if you're so inclined, you can indulge yourself with a long list of luxury options that can run up the price of even a Rabbit.

But the way we look at it, the basic Rabbit—reliable, economical* transportation at a reasonable price—may be the greatest luxury of them all.

Nothing else is a Volkswagen. VW

**Consumer Magazine
Black and White
Campaign Including
Magazine Supplements**

141 SILVER
ART DIRECTOR
Dean Hanson

WRITER
Jarl Olsen

DESIGNERS
Dean Hanson
Jarl Olsen

CLIENT
7 South 8th For Hair

AGENCY
Fallon, McElligott, Rice/Mpls.

142
ART DIRECTORS
Allen Kay
Lou Zaffos

WRITERS
Lois Korey
Dean Weller

PHOTOGRAPHERS
Larry Lapidus
Steve Steigman

CLIENT
WCBS-TV

AGENCY
Korey, Kay & Partners

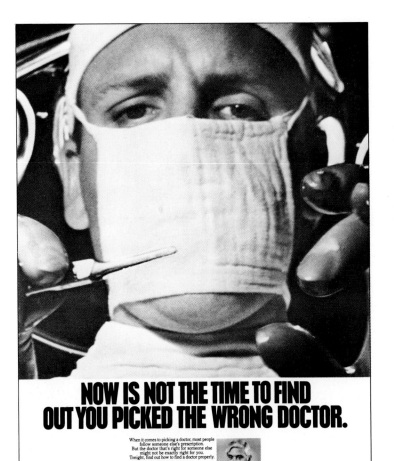

NOW IS NOT THE TIME TO FIND OUT YOU PICKED THE WRONG DOCTOR.

When it comes to picking a doctor, most people
follow someone else's prescription.
But the doctor that's right for someone else
might not be exactly right for you.
Tonight, find out how to find a doctor properly.

A 2-part Special Report by Earl Ubell.
"FINDING DR. RIGHT"
BEGINNING WEDNESDAY AT 5 AND 11.
CHANNEL ◉ 2 NEWSBREAKERS
If it concerns you, it concerns us.

SHE HAS HER MOTHER'S EYES, HER FATHER'S CHIN AND HER DOCTOR'S NOSE.

More and more men and women are accentuating the
positive and eliminating the negative through
cosmetic surgery. But before you decide to modify
your features, join us for a look at some new techniques,
the befores and afters, the successes and disasters.

A 2-Part Special Report by Betsy Ashton.
"OPERATION BEAUTY"
BEGINNING NOV. 29TH AT 6 AND 11.
CHANNEL ◉ 2 NEWSBREAKERS
If it concerns you, it concerns us.

TONIGHT WE'LL TELL YOU ABOUT PHOBIAS. IF YOU'RE NOT AFRAID TO WATCH.

There are more than 180 different types of
phobias. Tonight we'll examine some of the causes
and treatments for the millions who've become
prisoners of fear.

A 3-part Special Report by Carol Martin.
"THE PHOBIA PHENOMENON"
BEGINNING TONIGHT AT 5 AND 11.
CHANNEL ◉ 2 NEWSBREAKERS
If it concerns you, it concerns us.

**Consumer Magazine
Color Campaign
Including Magazine
Supplements**

143
ART DIRECTOR
Earl Cavanah
WRITER
Larry Cadman
PHOTOGRAPHERS
David Langley
David Bevin
Kevin Gregory
CLIENT
Volvo
AGENCY
Scali, McCabe, Sloves

144
ART DIRECTOR
Saskia Mossel
WRITER
Kirk Citron
PHOTOGRAPHER
Chuck LaMonica
CLIENT
General Foods/
Maxwell House
AGENCY
Ogilvy & Mather

IT CAN ACTUALLY MAKE 55 M.P.H. INTERESTING.

If you think that's impossible, you've never driven the Volvo Turbo.

A car whose handling equipment can turn a curve in the road or a trip to the supermarket into a driving adventure.

Its turbocharged 4-cylinder engine can dust a V-8 off the line. Automotive writers have described it as "A blast." "Spectacular." "Like cutting in an afterburner."

Maybe you think speed limits, emissions controls and government mileage requirements have made driving humdrum. But that's only because you don't own an interesting car.

THE TURBO
By Volvo.

143

Now,
it looks better
than ever.

New Maxwell House® Instant Coffee is darker. It looks richer. And that darker, richer look is just the beginning.

144

FALL IN LOVE IN 9 SECONDS FLAT.

The Volvo Turbo can hurtle you from a standing start to maximum legal speed in a mere 9 seconds.

Its turbo-charged 4-cylinder engine can blow a V-8 off the road. It has caused automotive writers to use descriptions like "Spectacular." "A blast." "Like cutting in an afterburner."

If that's the kind of driving excitement you thought had vanished with the muscle cars of the past, test drive a Volvo Turbo.

It could rekindle your love affair with the car.

THE TURBO
By Volvo.

THE WORLD'S FASTEST BAGGAGE HANDLER?

If there's a station wagon in the world that's faster than the Turbo Wagon from Volvo, it's a very well-kept secret.

The Turbo Wagon can take you from a standing start to the legal speed limit in 9.2 seconds. As *Motor Trend* puts it: "You keep hoping for a stray Saab 900 Turbo or even a BMW you can sniff out and then send scrambling to the roadside while you blow its doors in."

We assure you, a test drive in the Turbo Wagon will be very revealing.

Especially if you thought the only time a station wagon could haul was when it had something in the back.

THE TURBO WAGON
By Volvo.

Now, it smells better than ever.

New Maxwell House® Instant Coffee has even more fresh-roasted aroma. It's even more flavorful. And that's not all.

Now, it tastes better than ever.

New Maxwell House® Instant Coffee has a taste that you will love. Fresh-roasted. Flavorful. And, as always..."Good to the Last Drop."

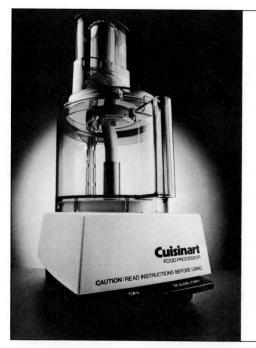

THIS YEAR, TURN PRO.

**CUISINARTS INTRODUCES THE DLC-7 PRO:
A TRULY PROFESSIONAL FOOD PROCESSOR FOR THE HOME COOK.**

Perhaps you have resisted buying a food processor, but are finally persuaded that it is truly a revolution in cooking that enables people to do more, in less time, than ever before.

Perhaps you already own an ordinary food processor, but wish you owned a better one.

Perhaps you even own one of our early models, but would like to enjoy our latest advances.

There are any number of good reasons to consider the purchase of a Cuisinart food processor this year. But the best reason is the introduction of the best machine we have ever made: the Cuisinart DLC-7 Pro.

SO PERFECTED, IT HAS BEEN U.L. LISTED FOR RESTAURANT USE.

The "Pro" has a motor so powerful and efficient, it meets the extremely rigorous requirements of the Underwriters Laboratories for restaurant use. It can knead up to 4 pounds of bread dough or, if you wish, turn out 5 batches of 3½ pounds each, one after the other,

without overheating or stalling. And it has a workbowl so large, it can chop 2 pounds of meat at one time (and do it in under 30 seconds).

The "Pro" has many important improvements over its predecessor. Especially noteworthy is our new detachable stem (see photo below) that makes disc storage easy and space saving.

In addition, the performance of our slicing disc—which was already the best on the market—has been dramatically improved. It gives you almost all perfect slices and never tears edges.

The "Pro" will accommodate the two exclusive new optional accessories: the first 8 mm. slicing disc and 3 mm. square julienne disc ever available to the home cook. Now you can effortlessly make thick, juicy slices of tomatoes, and uniform strips of just about any vegetable for stir frying, in next to no time.

These new accessories are in addition to already the most useful and extensive selection on the market. The "Pro" is, of course, equipped

with Cuisinarts exclusive Large Feed Tube, the only feed tube that lets you produce whole slices from foods as large as tomatoes, oranges, potatoes, onions. Also included as standard equipment are our superior dough blade and patented metal blade.

The "Pro" is, very simply, the finest home food processor ever made. So if you've been thinking about improving your culinary capabilities, this is the year to turn pro: the Cuisinart DLC-7 Pro.

FOR MORE INFORMATION.

One of our favorite recipes, and one that would be difficult in a lesser machine, is for a Mother's Day cake that is truly a work of culinary art. For the recipe, as well as more information about our food processors, our cookware, and our magazine, "The Pleasures of Cooking," write Cuisinarts, Inc., 411 (O) W. Putnam Ave., Greenwich, CT 06830.

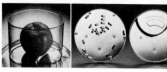

Cuisinart
Food Processor

CUISINARTS INTRODUCES THE COOKWARE THAT FINALLY AND DEFINITIVELY PUTS COPPER IN ITS PLACE.

The kind of copper cookware you are used to is the kind where the copper shows.

That's beautiful, but it's also impractical. Copper requires a protective lining (usually tin) which wears thin with use. Today, it's both time-consuming and expensive to get copper properly re-tinned. Copper also tarnishes quickly, requiring constant maintenance to keep up its appearance.

FOR THE FIRST TIME. THE ADVANTAGES WITHOUT THE DISADVANTAGES.

Cuisinarts has a different use for copper: on the inside of our stainless steel sandwich construction (stainless steel surrounding an inlay of copper). This gives you the extraordinary heat conductivity of copper, without any of its problems.

EVEN WE NEVER DREAMED OF COOKWARE THIS GOOD.

Owners of Cuisinart cookware know that our sandwich construction is not new; it is one of the features that have made our cookware famous among professional cooks for its high performance and durability. However, until this year, the inside of the sandwich was aluminum, for the simple reason that copper was ridiculously expensive. But now, as with gold, the price has dropped dramatically.

In addition, the material

The Cuisinart sandwich construction: stainless steel surrounding an inlay of copper.

The 8-piece Commercial Stainless Cookware set: 8½-quart Dutch Sauté Pan with cover, 3¾-quart Deep Saucepan with cover, 2-quart Deep Saucepan with cover, 10-quart Marmite with cover.

required for the high temperature soldering needed to form the sandwich was also incredibly expensive. Now, a new material has been invented for this process.

In short, what was once an impossible dream is now both practical and affordable.

COOKWARE FOR THE CENTURIES.

Cuisinarts Commercial Stainless Cookware is cookware whose capability and durability is

virtually unmatched in all the culinary world. It is cookware for the home cook who wants only the most professional performance.

The bottoms are perfectly flat, to give superior conduction sideways as well as upwards. This eliminates hot spots and provides constant heat over the cooking surface. And because copper conducts heat almost twice as well as aluminum, the bottoms of our new cookware do not have to be as thick.

The handles are heavy gauge stainless steel, shaped to stay cool.

Every item is designed to withstand a lifetime of rough use and retain its extraordinary beauty forever.

Our new stainless/copper sandwich construction is also available in the Cuisinart Original Stainless Cookware collection—the cookware that first made the name Cuisinart famous.

FOR MORE INFORMATION.

One of our favorite recipes (and one that is a true test of a great pan) is Crêpes Suzette. For the recipe and more information on our cookware, our food processors and magazine, "The Pleasures of Cooking," write: Cuisinarts, Inc., 411( )W. Putnam Ave., Greenwich, CT 06830.

Cuisinart
Commercial Cookware

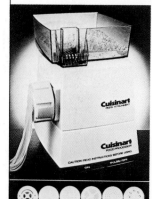

LASAGNE. FETTUCCINE. SPAGHETTI. LINGUINE. MACARONI. CUISINARTS.

Now the first name in food processors is the last word in pasta.

The Cuisinart Pasta Attachment lets you produce perfect, fresh, homemade pasta. Quickly. And effortlessly.

AT LAST, A WAY TO MAKE PASTA WORTHY OF THE NAME CUISINARTS.

Because it takes advantage of the powerful and efficient Cuisinart motor, the Cuisinart Pasta Attachment is able to produce large batches of pasta faster than most pasta machines. It kneads the dough so thoroughly, the dough actually gets warm—giving you a much higher quality final product. And because you make the pasta mixture in the bowl of the Cuisinart food processor, it's easy to be creative. For example, add some Parmesan or Romano cheese and you get an appetizing yellow color along with the delightful taste of the cheese. Or add some chopped spinach, a touch of sage—even grind up some hot chili peppers.

6 PASTA SHAPES, AND FASTER THAN MOST PASTA MACHINES.

Our Pasta Attachment kit includes 6 interchangeable discs to produce all of these pasta favorites: lasagne, fettuccine, spaghetti, linguine, macaroni, spaghettini. Any one of them can be accomplished with perfect results in less than the time recommended for most pasta machines.

The Cuisinart Pasta Attachment fits any of the models in our DLC-7 series of food processors.

FOR MORE INFORMATION.

For a selection of creative pasta recipes, as well as more information on our food processors, our cookware, and our magazine, "The Pleasures of Cooking," write: Cuisinarts, Inc., 411 (B) W. Putnam Ave., Greenwich, CT 06830.

Cuisinart
Pasta Attachment

**Consumer Magazine
Color Campaign
Including Magazine
Supplements**

147
ART DIRECTOR
Hubert Graf
WRITERS
Robert Evans
Lew Cohn
DESIGNER
Peter Fischer
CLIENT
Swissair
AGENCY
GrafDesley

148 GOLD
ART DIRECTORS
Charles Piccirillo
Gary Goldsmith
WRITERS
Ted Bell
Mike Mangano
Diane Sinnott
PHOTOGRAPHERS
Chuck LaMonica
John Paul Endress
Larry Sillen
CLIENT
General Wine & Spirits/
Chivas Regal
AGENCY
Doyle Dane Bernbach

Why isn't a better airline more expensive?

By giving more and not charging more, we have an edge over average airlines. And you have quite a buy.

Not only widebodied comfort on our big jets, but more room too. In Economy, we have one less seat per row than most other carriers. The extra space is yours.

And on Swissair, you always know where you stand – and sit – when you make a reservation. Full-fare passengers can select their favorite seat in advance.

When it's time to eat, you dine on a choice of gourmet meals served on china. Only china. Also in Economy.

In other words, we don't look upon Economy Class as a matter of doing without, but rather, of giving the most we can. Which explains why we have the greatest percentage of repeat business of all international carriers.

We depart worldwide from New York, Boston, Chicago, Toronto and Montreal. Ready? Call your travel agent or **swissair**

Big airlines may fly more passengers than Swissair. But Swissair flies passengers more often. Frequent travelers prefer to frequent Swissair.

Swissair has the highest percentage of repeat business of all international airlines.

The reason? Swiss Class. Not a gimmick – just a no nonsense attitude about giving you everything you're entitled to.

Swissair widebodies have fewer seats than most other carriers, so you have more space. When it's time to dine, you have a choice of gourmet meals served on china. And to relax, there are complimentary headsets and a choice of entertainment. All in Economy.

It doesn't cost more to go Swiss Class. Swissair has competitive fares to Switzerland and on to its entire worldwide network. So instead of asking why a better airline isn't more expensive, ask the more expensive airlines why they're not better.

We depart worldwide from New York, Boston, Chicago, Toronto and Montreal. Just call your travel agent or **swissair**

All airports accommodate airplanes. Swiss airports accommodate people too. Airplanes have needs. So do people. Happily, when you land at Zurich or Geneva, you discover that for a change, people haven't been overlooked.

If you're in a hurry, you'll thank us for having some of the fastest connecting times in Europe. And airports designed with that in mind.

If you're not in a hurry, you'll thank us for tidy shopping plazas that have every convenience imaginable – places to rest and shower, boutiques, four-star restaurants, an international pharmacy – you name it. All within a short walk.

Even your luggage will thank us. In a country "where everything works," it will arrive on the same plane you do.

Swissair departs for your two favorite airports from New York, Boston, Chicago, Toronto and Montreal, then on to the world. Just call your travel agent or **swissair**

Why settle for champagne?

Be careful! That's Chivas Regal!

$45 in Japan.
(Count your blessings.)

"Chivas Regal!...
Where do you think you are, heaven?"

Chivas Regal • 12 Years Old Worldwide • Blended Scotch Whisky • 86 Proof. General Wine & Spirits Co., N.Y.

150 GOLD

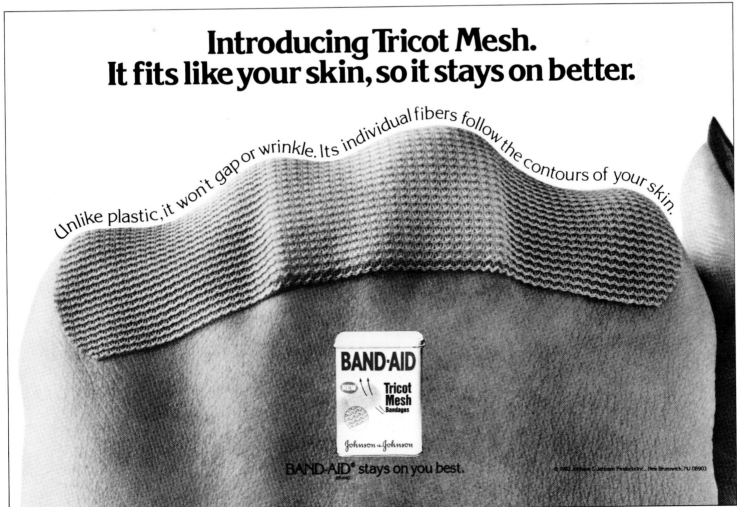

Introducing Tricot Mesh.
It fits like your skin, so it stays on better.

151 SILVER

IT'S LIKE BORROWING YOUR MOTHER'S CAR. AND JUST ABOUT AS CHEAP.

Rent a car from us and you get a good, clean, two-to-eight year old car. Nothing flashy. But as well taken care of as your mom's car.

And at just $15.95 and 100 free miles a day, it's almost as cheap as borrowing hers. Maybe even better. Because while we'll both ask you to bring it back with the gas gauge where it was when you left, we don't care how late you stay out.

Minneapolis: 333-5296   St. Paul: 644-0123

RENTING A CAR FROM THEM IS LIKE BUYING DESIGNER UNDERWEAR. YOU'RE PAYING MORE FOR SOMETHING NOBODY SEES.

You rent a Hertz or Avis car, drive it from one parking lot to another, return it and who important ever sees it?

But what you see is a bill that's about 35% higher than it has to be. Because you can rent one of our good, clean, used cars for just $15.95 and 100 free miles a day.

Why go naked and penniless? Rent-A-Wreck.

Minneapolis: 333-5296   St. Paul: 644-0123

THE DIFFERENCE BETWEEN THEIR WEEKEND RATE AND OURS IS ENOUGH TO PUT YOU TO SLEEP.

Rent a car from us for the weekend instead of Hertz or Avis and you can save enough for one night's lodging.

We're just $39.95 from anytime Friday until Monday before noon.

With 500 free miles.

Oh, they'll give you a brand new car. As opposed to our quality, clean, used car.

But would you rather have money for a nice weekend or just look like you do?

Minneapolis: 333-5296   St. Paul: 644-0123

The Grossinger's you loved when you used to drink seltzer is the Grossinger's you'll adore now that you're ordering Perrier.

The first family of hospitality

Grossinger's

The Grossinger's you loved when you used to wear sneakers is the Grossinger's you'll adore now that you're jogging in Nikes.

The first family of hospitality

Grossinger's

The Grossinger's you loved when you used to eat blintzes is the Grossinger's you'll adore now that you're nibbling on crepes.

The first family of hospitality

Grossinger's

**Consumer Magazine
Less than One Page
B/W or Color
Campaign**

154
ART DIRECTOR
Jeff Cooper

WRITER
John Burt

ARTISTS
Bob Weber
Lee Lornez

CLIENT
Pepto-Bismol

AGENCY
Benton & Bowles

155 SILVER
ART DIRECTOR
Everett F. Boykin

WRITER
Bill Teitelbaum

PHOTOGRAPHER
Jamie Cook

CLIENT
The Cooper Group

AGENCY
Howard, Merrel & Boykin/
North Carolina

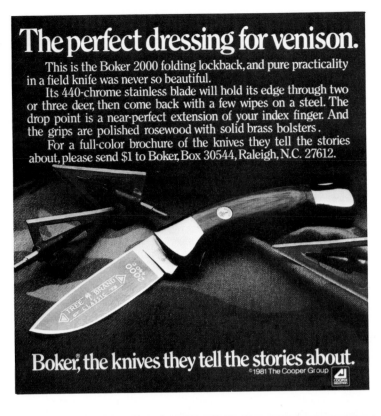
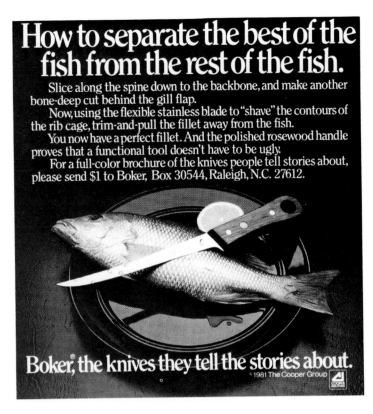
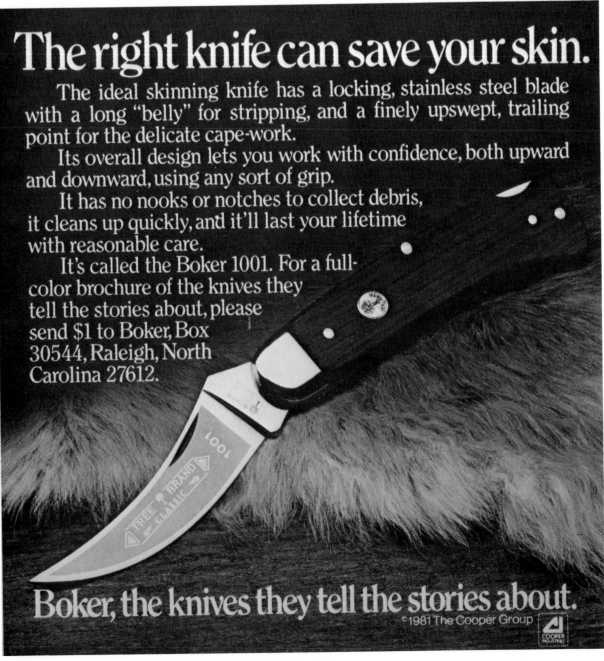

156

157

Our Chaps sport coats don't fit very well into a small ad.

But then again, neither does our clientele.

d.w. stewart's
Fashions for Tall and Big Men. In the Galleria, 69th & France, Edina. 612-920-5757

Our Damon shirts don't fit very well into a small ad.

But then again, neither does our clientele.

d.w. stewart's
Fashions for Tall and Big Men. In the Galleria, 69th & France, Edina. 612-920-5757

How to move a paragraph.

For memos or manuscripts, sales reports or book reports, a person could use the IBM Personal Computer.

Because, with the EasyWriter* software program, creating, revising and storing text is just that. Easy.

With ten function keys that help save time on repetitious tasks and "menus" that guide you along, the IBM Personal Computer can insert a clause. Delete a line. Move a paragraph from one page to another. Transfer text from file to file. Even merge words from your EasyWriter program with numbers generated by your VisiCalc‡ program.

And when you're done, a copy of the finished product can be printed out at 80 characters a second.

So if you do any kind of writing, try it on the IBM Personal Computer at your nearest authorized dealer. You'll see that the performance, quality and price are really something to write home about.

IBM

The IBM Personal Computer
A tool for modern times

How to go for the gold.

To experience the thrill of victory, a person could use the IBM Personal Computer.

With a challenging program called Microsoft Decathlon, you can compete in the world's most demanding athletic contest. Run the 100 meter dash. Clear the hurdles. Hurl the shot, discus and javelin.

Animated color graphics, music and sound effects create the excitement of real competition.

And when all ten events are completed, you can compare your score with a real, medal-winning Decathlon record.

So let the games begin. Put on your sneakers and head for your nearest authorized IBM Personal Computer dealer.

IBM

The IBM Personal Computer
A tool for modern times

JOIN THE AIR FORCE.

Anyone can join our air force. You don't need a short haircut or a lot of courage. All you need is a lot of air. That's because we've got a special fleet of toys that run on a unique engine that uses air for power. You just pump in the air and the engine does the rest. There are no batteries to run down and no expensive or messy fuel to buy. Among our top recruits are the Air Jammer Road Rammer™ that rides like the wind and the Air Jammer Cycle Scrammer™ that takes off like a bullet.

The group of high ranking Space Pets are called the Fleet Footed Floomdorm™, the High Hopping Hoondorm™ and the Stretch Legged Stoomdorm™. When you pump them up, they act as crazy as their names. So join the ranks of toy stores everywhere and enlist in the Tomy air force. And don't worry. The only active duty you'll see is your sales soaring sky-high. ©1982 Tomy Corp., 901 E. 233rd St., Carson, CA 90749. (213) 775-7585 **TOMY.**

158

We're all created equal.
After that, baby, you're on your own.

Nobody's going to hand you success on a silver platter.

If you want to make it, you'll have to make it on your own.

Your own drive, your own guts, your own energy, your own ambition.

Yes, ambition. You don't have to hide it anymore. Society's decided that now it's OK to be up-front about the drive for success.

Isn't that what the fast track is all about?

If you're one of the fast-track people, your business reading starts with FORTUNE.

After all, FORTUNE's been the magazine of business success for over 50 years.

It's the authority...the business magazine you rely on when you've *got* to be right.

It helps the movers and shakers decide how to move and what to shake. It's their

early-warning system, alerting them to opportunities and dangers up ahead.

In marketing, management, technology, the works...it's the one that gives you a vital couple of steps on the competition.

FORTUNE is the business magazine that really *can* help you make it—and keep it.

And it's the one to advertise in when you need to target the fast-track people.

**FORTUNE
How to succeed.**

159

A man who murdered his parents persuaded psychiatrists to let him live with his aunt and uncle because he loved them "like my own mother and father." Then…

...he murdered them too.

And this is just one true horror story cited by Senator Orrin Hatch in his article, "The Insanity Defense is Insane," written for the October Reader's Digest.

As criminals continue to be acquitted by reason of insanity—and as convicted killers are released from mental hospitals only to kill again—Senator Hatch says we must find a solution to this deadly problem. And he offers one.

It's Digest articles like this that help 40 million readers make sense of an often crazy world.

162 SILVER

THE FACE THAT LAUNCHED A THOUSAND SHIPMENTS

Kimberly® is a lot more than just another pretty face.

She's more like a friend, with a personality and a wardrobe just like the girls that own her.

Her clothes and accessories have a contemporary look, so they're not only cute, but realistic looking, too. Like her roller skating outfit, which comes with roller skates that really roll. She has her own school clothes, party clothes, pajamas and even jeans and tennis shoes. Many of her outfits have the same designer labels that young girls wear on their own clothes.

And Kimberly's got a face that's hard to forget, with big, bright eyes, long wavy hair and a smile that could liven up a room.

So liven up your shelves with Kimberly.

She may never launch any ships. But she'll definitely raise a lot of sales.

©1982 Tomy Corp., 901 E. 233rd St., Carson, CA 90749. (213) 775-7585 **TOMY.**

163

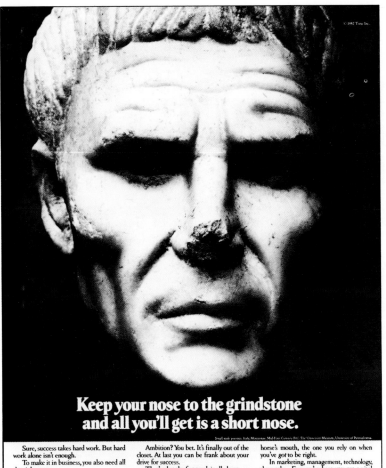

Keep your nose to the grindstone and all you'll get is a short nose.

Small male portrait, Italy, Mezzotint, Mid-First Century B.C. The University Museum, University of Pennsylvania.

Sure, success takes hard work. But hard work alone isn't enough.

To make it in business, you also need all the right moves.

You need a clear map of where you're heading, long range and short range.

You need all the smarts, guts, and ambition you can muster.

Ambition? You bet. It's finally out of the closet. At last you can be frank about your drive for success.

That's what the fast track is all about.

If *you're* running on the fast track, your business reading starts with FORTUNE.

For over 50 years, it's been the magazine of business success. It's the authority, the

horse's mouth, the one you rely on when you've *got* to be right.

In marketing, management, technology, the works...FORTUNE's where you get a vital couple of steps on the competition.

It's how to make it—and how to keep it.

So if you want to succeed with the fast-track people, put your advertising in FORTUNE.

FORTUNE
How to succeed.

164 GOLD

Only Fortrel could do more for a pair of jeans.

Some very famous names have played a big part in the success of denim jeans. And Blendship is now one of them. Put simply, it's what results when you create just the right blend of cotton and Celanese Fortrel polyester. It's also what makes a pair of jeans fit like it's your name on the back pocket instead of the manufacturer's. It's what makes them so comfortable, you'll never want to take them off. And it's what makes them hold up a lot longer than plain old-fashioned, denim jeans. Now, if you're still not sold on Blendship, we'd like to drop the name of a company who is. Levi Strauss & Co. And you know what they've done for jeans. For more information, call Celanese at (212) 719-7688. Because cotton and Fortrel is one blend that's really making a name for itself.

CELANESE

165

WE'RE ABOUT TO SHOOT SOME HOLES IN MASTER LOCK.

Practically any padlock worth its shackle can survive a bullet through the heart.
Including us. S. Parker Hardware. After all, we've been selling quality hardware to the construction trade since 1899. (If anyone knows about a product's quality, it's architects and builders.)
But the real test of how a padlock performs isn't on a firing range. It's in the stores. On the shelves. At the cash register.
This is how Parker is going to blast holes in Master Lock's market: We've created the most exciting and traffic-generating packaging in the industry—it's practically pilfer-proof.
By offering the widest variety of products in the field—50 SKU's—and counting.
By offering terrific delivery. And for ordering purposes, a convenient toll-free number. (1-800-631-1366)
By offering padlocks that are, without question, the best dollar value in the industry.
By offering you quality merchandise which can—and will—increase your gross profit margin by an average of 25%.
The result is quick turnover, fast profits.
That's how you shoot holes in a market. With sound, well-conceived business disciplines.
And, of course, giving the consumer their money's worth.
Forget rifles, machine guns or bazookas. Watch yourself, Master Lock.
Parker is ready. We're aiming. And we're about to fire.

166 SILVER

FOUR HEADS ARE BETTER THAN ONE.

J & H HARDWARE, INC.
THE AREA'S DO-IT-YOURSELF HEADQUARTERS
Complete Line of
Hand Tools
Power Tools
Plumbing Supplies
Electrical Supplies
Paint Supplies
Lawn and Garden Supplies
Housewares
Glass Products
SUMERLEA 555-2222
1447 Ringside Blvd.

J & H HARDWARE, INC.
THE AREA'S DO-IT-YOURSELF HEADQUARTERS
Complete Line of
Hand Tools
Power Tools
Plumbing Supplies
Electrical Supplies
Paint Supplies
Lawn and Garden Supplies
Housewares
Glass Products
SUMERLEA 555-2222
1447 Ringside Blvd.

J & H HARDWARE, INC.
THE AREA'S DO-IT-YOURSELF HEADQUARTERS
A Complete Line of
Match Any Color
Exterior & Interior Latex
and Gloss Paints
Stains, Varnishes
Linoleum Paints
Siding Paints
All Paint Accessories
Wood and Power Tools
SUMERLEA 555-2222
1447 Ringside Blvd.

J & H HARDWARE, INC.
THE AREA'S DO-IT-YOURSELF HEADQUARTERS
A Complete Line of
Plumbing Supplies
Pipe cut to size
Hand Tools
Power Tools
Electrical Supplies
Bathroom & Kitchen Accessories
SUMERLEA 555-2222
1447 Ringside Blvd.

HOME IMPROVEMENTS   HARDWARE-RETAIL   PAINT-RETAIL   PLUMBING SUPPLIES

Thousands of customers miss you every day.
Unless you have different ads with different headings in the Yellow Pages.
For example, hardware stores don't just sell a pound or two of hardware.
They sell glass, paint, plumbing, tools, electric supplies. Maybe even coffee pots.
But a lot of customers don't bother to think about that.
They simply open their Yellow Pages to the product or service they're looking for.
So if you're not under the right heading at the right time, you're losing customers.
That's why the odds are on your side when you take out multiple headings.
The more ads you take out, the more customers you'll bring in.
Eight out of ten people who open their Yellow Pages take action.
So, just to make sure they open their pages to your ad, call your Reuben H. Donnelley Yellow Pages Representative.
Someone who'll run the right ads in the right place at the right time.
You'll find all it takes to get more business are a few more good heads.

Bell System Yellow Pages

🔔 C&P Telephone

167

At 3M, we've got something on the ball.

Introducing the 3M Electronic Typewriters.

Actually, 3M Electronic Typewriters have a lot on the ball.

3M 200

More technology and communications know-how than today's leading electric typewriter could ever hope to have.

And then some.

Starting with a display window. So you can see your mistakes and correct them — automatically — before they're ever typed.

Add to that automatic, one-step centering and indenting. Automatic tab, margin and column setting. Automatic underscoring. Automatic decimal alignment. Automatic page numbering. Even automatic boldface type. And *reverse highlighting*.

Plus a microprocessor based memory system that automatically lets our 3M Electronic Typewriters remember exactly what you've typed. So you can make any necessary additions and corrections, then push a button and let the 3M Electronic do the typing. Automatically. Freeing up time to move on to other urgent projects.

3M 400

And instead of using a rotating ball technology, 3M Electronic Typewriters use a daisy wheel printing method.

A method that's faster. Neater. And far quieter than any electric typewriter technology.

The result is always top quality, professional looking typed documents. In less time than you ever thought possible.

Best of all, the 3M Electronic Typewriters are available in a full range of models.

That means you can get exactly the right level of sophistication you need to run your office smoothly. From our basic 3M

3M 600

200 right up to our most advanced software based 3M 800. A model that features a floppy disk data storage system.

But you don't have to take our word for it.

Why not call 800-328-1684 (in Minnesota: 800-792-1072), or send us the coupon below and see for yourself just how much

3M 800

all the 3M Electronic Typewriters have on the ball.

I want to see just how much you have on the ball. Please send me more information on the 3M Electronic Typewriters.

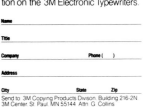

Name

Title

Company _____ Phone (   )

Address

City _____ State _____ Zip

Send to: 3M Copying Products Division: Building 216-2N
3M Center St. Paul, MN 55144 Attn: G. Collins

3M Hears You.....

3M

Juan is not enough.

They're asking for him in Aspen. They're begging for him in Boston. They're clamoring for him in California.

All over America people are thirsting for Juan Valdez, the spokesman for 100% Colombian Coffee. And it's had quite an effect on our business. In fact, the statistics show that over half the population not only likes Colombian Coffee, but they're convinced that it's the best coffee in the world.

Naturally, we're delighted with this success. However, it has posed a problem: How will we keep up with the growing demand for Juan with only one Juan?

Perhaps we should clone him.

At any rate, that's our problem, not yours. In fact, as far as you're concerned this is all to your benefit. By offering a 100% Colombian Coffee brand you can profit nicely from all our popularity. Plus you can join our promotion program and take advantage of our new trademark and sales aids to help you sell even more.

There's only one hitch. Your business could pick up so quickly that you might have to clone yourself to keep up with it all.

100% Colombian Coffee

SOMETIMES BEING IN THE RED IS GOOD FOR BUSINESS.

Red ink in your Yellow Page ads has a very noticeable effect.

It gets your ads read.

Which gets you more customers.

Because people who see your ads first usually buy from you first.

In fact, 8 out of 10 people who open their Yellow Pages take action.

And when they see your red ink ad, something happens.

Namely, more business.

But red ink isn't the only way to be outstanding.

Large display ads are a really big way to grab attention.

Because it's hard for customers to miss large ads. So it's easy for you to get big sales.

Red ink and large display ads.

Two obvious ways for your ads to stand out from the crowd.

To find out more, just call your Reuben H. Donnelley Yellow Pages representative.

Someone who'll show you some red ink that'll put your business where it belongs.

In the black.

C&P Telephone

Bell System Yellow Pages

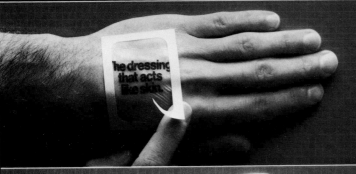

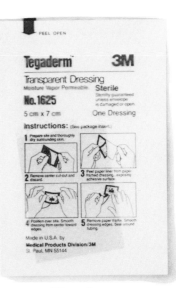

One of the ingredients in this Chef's Surprise even surprised the chef.

Maybe it's happened in your kitchen.
A wayward chunk from a metal pad clogs a drain, damages a garbage disposal, cuts your hand.
Or startles a diner at table four.
The only startling thing about our Scotch-Brite® No. 88 nylon scouring pads is how well they do their job in your full preparation kitchen.
They'll scrub those stubborn deposits off your pots and pans quicker and rinse out easier than most pot scrubbing pads.
But, because they're made of tough nylon fibers, they won't rust away. Or leave potentially harmful metal splinters anywhere in your kitchen.
And the cost?
Only half as much as most metal pads.
Call toll-free 800-328-1684, in Minnesota 800-792-1072. And we'll send you the Scotch-Brite No. 88 Extra Heavy Duty Pot 'n Pan Handler in a kit complete with three other 3M kitchen cleaning pads*.
Surprise your chef with it, before his Chef's Surprise surprises him.

Scotch-Brite is a registered trademark of 3M © 3M 1983 *Offer expires 7/31/83

Building Service and Cleaning Products Division/3M
3M hears you...

3M

173

British demand.

Danish supply.

Carlsberg

berg

Probably the best lager in the world.

174

We can't keep the lid on it. The 1982 Glow-worm Mystery Trip to [redacted] is going to be an absolute corker.

But how, you may ask, can a jaunt in [redacted] possibly surpass our scintillating safari to Las Vegas? (Who could forget that cocktail-stirring rendition of 'You'll never walk alone'? Heaven knows, we've tried.)

How can it beat Bangkok (will the elephants ever forget)?

Can it eclipse Acapulco? Will it top Tangiers? Will it better Bermuda?

Ask a stupid question. Of course it will.

And wherever we end up, be it [redacted] or even [redacted], the times of lives shall be had. The skins of chests shall be Bergasol-ed. And the opinions of installers shall be heard.

Because as usual we'll be holding the always-heated central heating forum.

Yet again we'll chew the fat about the state of the market. We'll show you what we'll be doing from our end. Then you can tell us what you think. And if previous years are anything to go by, you will. You certainly will.

Fair enough? Well then, just install a mere 105 Glow-worm boilers between May 1, 1982 and Jan. 31, 1983 and rest assured you'll soon be en route to [redacted].

And before you touch that toolbox, hear this. If you'd like to take someone with you on the greatest Mystery Trip of them all, just install 75 more boilers and he (or she) is on for it too.

In fact as long as our ticket supply lasts, you can qualify for one extra place in the sun for every 75 boilers you sell over the basic 105.

So, spanners out. Boilers in.

And we'll see you out there in [redacted].

Glow worm
THE LEADING AUTHORITY ON GAS CENTRAL HEATING AND FIRES

175

176

Trade
**Less than One Page
B/W or Color
Single**

177 SILVER
ART DIRECTOR
Stan Schofield
WRITER
Jim Parry
CLIENT
Reader's Digest
AGENCY
Posey, Parry & Quest/
Connecticut

178
ART DIRECTOR
Lila Sternglass
WRITER
Bill Hamilton
PHOTOGRAPHER
George Kanelous
CLIENT
Ladies' Home Journal
AGENCY
Rumrill-Hoyt

Car thieves are getting bolder. In Detroit, they started a taxicab company with three stolen police cars.

And in New York, one enterprising thief used his 21 stolen cars to start a rent-a-car company.

These and other stories of America's $1.7-billion-a-year stolen car racket are reported in an original article in the September Reader's Digest, an article that follows a car theft from popped ignition lock to forged vehicle identification number.

It's reporting like this—that shows 40 million readers scenes they'd never see otherwise—that makes the Digest a great vehicle.

Hey, Ogilvy, want a great American buy for the great American bar?

Your tempting ads deserve to be served up in a bright, fresh setting. The new, improved Ladies' Home Journal.

We have 25% more editorial pages than just a year ago. Filled with fascinating food, from the most sensible snack to the most fanciful dessert. Highlighted by recipes for everything from chocolate ice cream to chocolate mousse. Surrounded by involving articles and first-rate fiction.

And your richest ads will roll off our new roto presses with every calorie intact.

The new, improved Ladies' Home Journal. We'll make you look as good as a Hershey bar.

178

**Trade Any Size
B/W or Color
Campaign**

179 GOLD
ART DIRECTOR
Garry Horner
WRITER
Indra Sinha
ARTIST
Peter Brooks
PHOTOGRAPHERS
Graham Ford
John Thornton
CLIENT
Ogilvy & Mather
AGENCY
Ogilvy & Mather/London

180
ART DIRECTOR
Mark Hughes
WRITER
D.J. Webster
PHOTOGRAPHER
Larry Robins
CLIENT
Colombian Coffee
AGENCY
Doyle Dane Bernbach

They're on the road to success.

The advertising campaign for 100% Colombian Coffee has been so effective that Juan Valdez and his partner have been nominated for some prestigious awards.

Getting Juan a tuxedo for these occasions was easy enough. Finding a "6L" collar for the mule was more difficult.

But all things considered we don't mind praising them for the brilliant work they've done.

So far, Juan and his friend have boosted the awareness of Colombian Coffee to an incredible 91%. (The highest it's ever been.) And they've convinced 56% of the American population that Colombian Coffee is the best in the world.

Naturally it follows that more and more people will be asking for our delicious product. So if you're not offering 100% Colombian Coffee, the time is ripe. After all, you stand to make a lot of profits. Maybe enough to buy yourself a new wardrobe.

And that's not bad. Remember the old saying, "Clothes make the mule."

100% Colombian Coffee

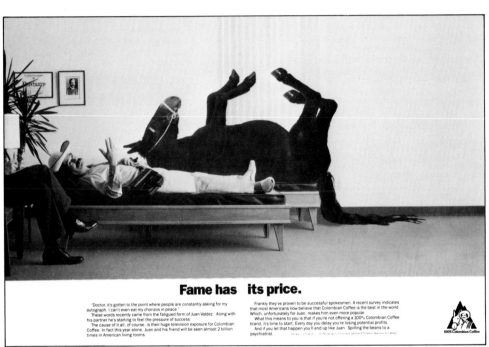

Fame has its price.

"Doctor, it's gotten to the point where people are constantly asking for my autograph. I can't even eat my chorizos in peace."

These words recently came from the fatigued form of Juan Valdez. Along with his partner he's starting to feel the pressure of success.

The cause of it all, of course, is their huge television exposure for Colombian Coffee. In fact this year alone, Juan and his friend will be seen almost 2 billion times in American living rooms.

Frankly they've proven to be successful spokesmen. A recent survey indicates that most Americans now believe that Colombian Coffee is the best in the world. Which, unfortunately for Juan, makes him even more popular.

What this means to you is that if you're not offering a 100% Colombian Coffee brand, it's time to start. Every day you delay you're losing potential profits.

And if you let that happen you'll end up like Juan. Spilling the beans to a psychiatrist.

100% Colombian Coffee

Will the popularity of Colombian Coffee go to their heads?

Nope.

Even though most Americans are convinced that Colombian Coffee is the best in the world. And even though Juan Valdez and his partner are on television all the time, success won't change them.

But their success could change you. By offering a 100% Colombian Coffee brand your sales could pick up immediately. Not to mention all of the extra profits you'll reap.

Meanwhile, Juan will remain unaffected by it all. He remarks "We like the traditional life of Colombia much better than Hollywood. So you never have to worry about us moving out to Tinseltown."

100% Colombian Coffee

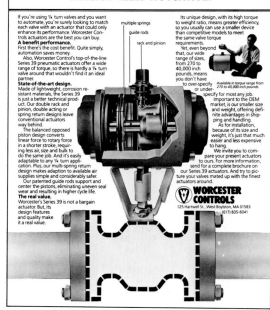
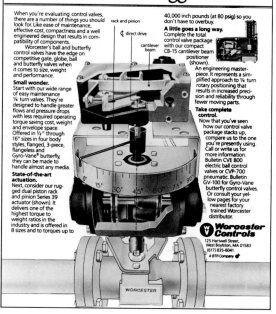

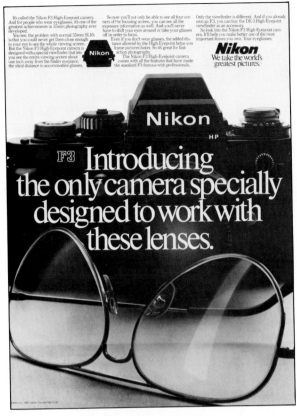

It's called the Nikon F3 High-Eyepoint camera. And for people who wear eyeglasses, it's one of the greatest achievements in 35mm photography ever developed.

You see, the problem with normal 35mm SLRs is that you could never get them close enough to your eye to see the whole viewing screen. But the Nikon F3 High-Eyepoint camera is designed with a special viewfinder that lets you see the entire viewing screen about one inch away from the finder eyepiece; the ideal distance to accommodate glasses.

So now you'll not only be able to see all four corners of the focusing screen, you can see all the exposure information as well. And you'll never have to shift your eyes around or take your glasses off in order to focus.

Even if you don't wear glasses, the added distance allowed by the High-Eyepoint helps you frame pictures faster. So it's great for fast-action photography.

The Nikon F3 High-Eyepoint camera comes with all the features that have made the standard F3 famous with professionals.

Only the viewfinder is different. And if you already own an F3, you can buy the DE-3 High-Eyepoint viewfinder as an accessory.

So look into the Nikon F3 High-Eyepoint camera. It'll help you make better use of the most important lenses you own. Your eyeglasses.

Nikon
We take the world's greatest pictures.

F3 Introducing the only camera specially designed to work with these lenses.

The Nikon FM2. For high speed and fill flash photography, no other manual even comes close.

Its maximum speed: 1/4000 sec. That's twice as fast as any 35mm SLR. Which not only gives you better fast-action shots, it lets you take outdoor photographs at wider apertures with fast film, and provides better depth of field control.

Its flash sync: 60% faster than any focal plane 35mm SLR. At 1/200 sec., the Nikon FM2 can eliminate the ghosts that haunt photographers who rely on fill flash.

To accomplish all this, Nikon developed an exclusive vertically travelling titanium shutter, and etched it with a honeycomb pattern to maintain its strength and rigidity.

So look into the Nikon FM2. For speed and handling, it just can't be beat.

Nikon
We take the world's greatest pictures.

Nikon sets two new speed records.

X200 4000

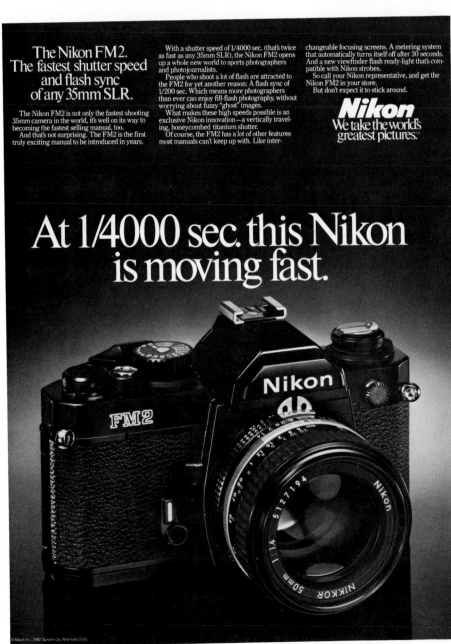

The Nikon FM2. The fastest shutter speed and flash sync of any 35mm SLR.

The Nikon FM2 is not only the fastest shooting 35mm camera in the world, it's well on its way to becoming the fastest selling manual, too.

And that's not surprising. The FM2 is the first truly exciting manual to be introduced in years.

With a shutter speed of 1/4000 sec. (that's twice as fast as any 35mm SLR), the Nikon FM2 opens up a whole new world to sports photographers and photojournalists.

People who shoot a lot of flash are attracted to the FM2 for yet another reason: A flash sync of 1/200 sec. Which means more photographers than ever can enjoy fill-flash photography, without worrying about fuzzy "ghost" images.

What makes these high speeds possible is an exclusive Nikon innovation—a vertically traveling, honeycombed titanium shutter.

Of course, the FM2 has a lot of other features most manuals can't keep up with. Like inter-

changeable focusing screens. A metering system that automatically turns itself off after 30 seconds. And a new viewfinder flash ready-light that's compatible with Nikon strobes.

So call your Nikon representative, and get the Nikon FM2 in your store.

But don't expect it to stick around.

Nikon
We take the world's greatest pictures.

At 1/4000 sec. this Nikon is moving fast.

**Trade Any Size
B/W or Color
Campaign**

185
ART DIRECTOR
Gary Walton
WRITER
Phil Wiggins
PHOTOGRAPHERS
Jerry Okel
Jack Bankhead
CLIENT
TI New World
AGENCY
TBWA/London

And then take a long look under the Sola grill, around the burners, down the sides, down the front, down the back and even underneath.
In fact, whichever way the competition, gas or electric, choose to look at it, the New World Nova has come as quite a shock.

Why we can show two fingers to the competition.

It's because both were cooked under our unique Sola grill. A grill that does something other grills can't. It grills evenly. It's a demonstration of System One's superiority. For others, look at our self-cleaning Gyroflo oven and our glass lidded hot plate. Customers are. **⑰ NEW WORLD system one**

So good-looking the competition can't stand the sight of it.

System One's elegant glass top hob is built to take anything that's splashed, spilt or even thrown at it. Underneath the style are burners sealed to the hot plate. Burners that give the fiercest of boils to the gentlest of simmers. Not even the competition can knock it. **⑰ NEW WORLD system one**

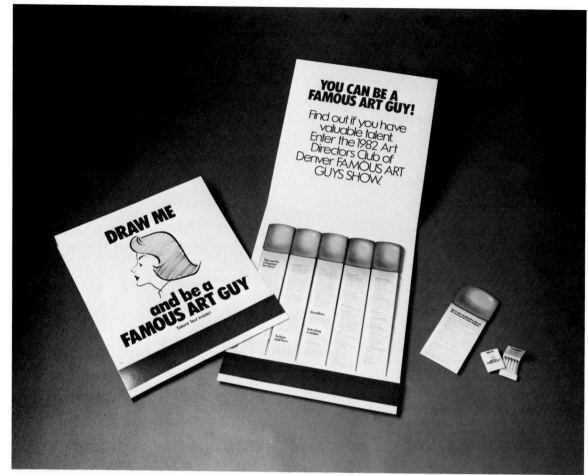

186 SILVER

188

189

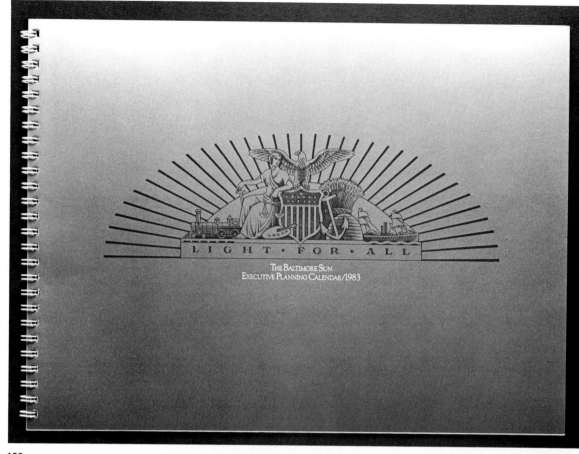

190

191 GOLD

An Introduction to Thoroughbred Horse Racing

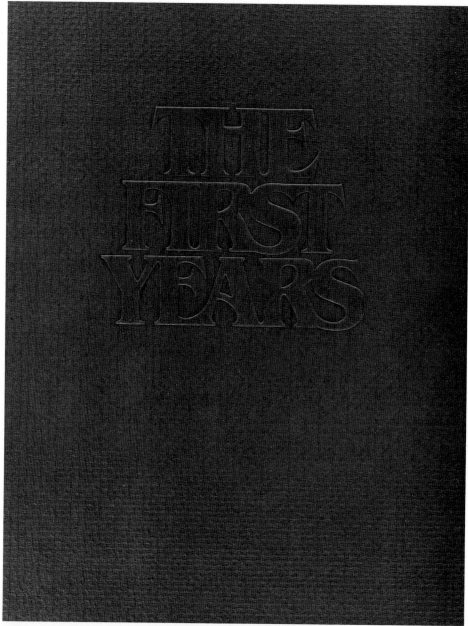

194

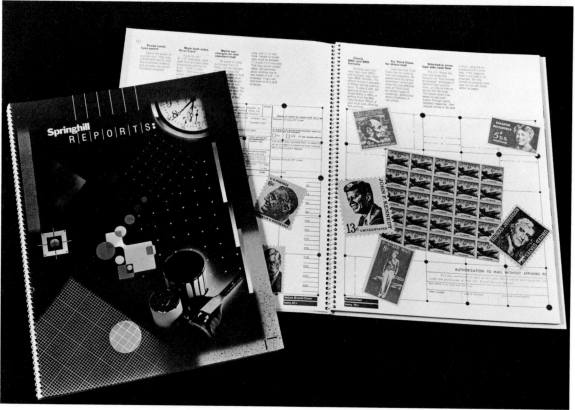

195

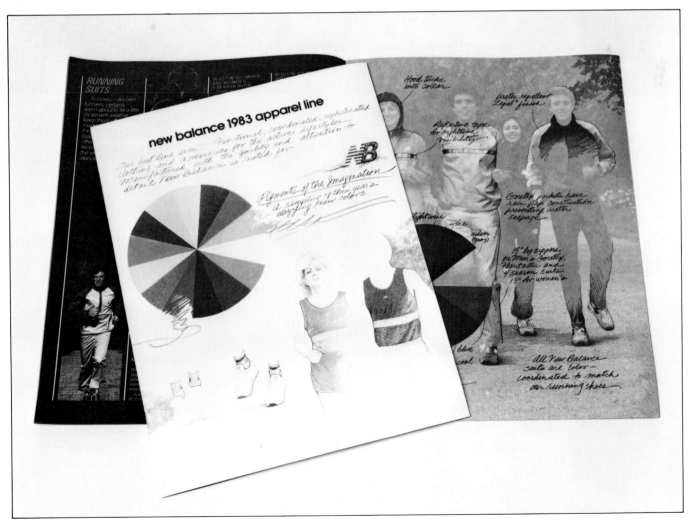

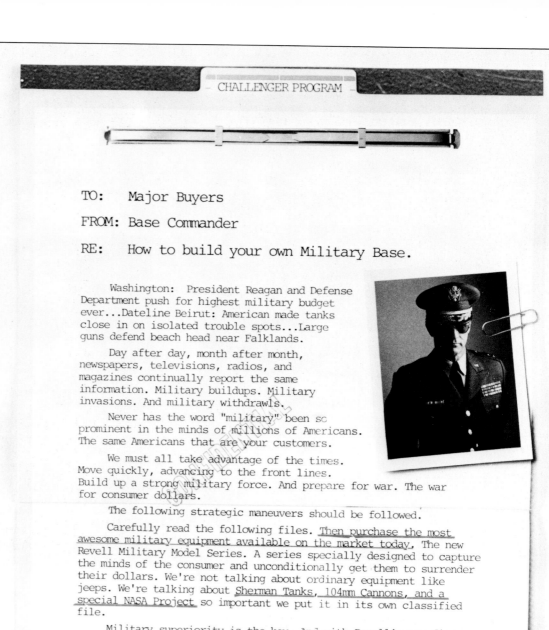

THE KINDS OF DRUGS KIDS ARE GETTING INTO.

Right now, over one-third of all kids in America use illegal drugs. In fact, one out of every 14 high school seniors is using marijuana every day.

PHARMACISTS AGAINST DRUG ABUSE

201
ART DIRECTOR
Thom LaPerle

WRITER
Stewart Nixon

DESIGNER
Thom LaPerle

ARTIST
Rick Von Holt

PHOTOGRAPHER
Tom Tracy

CLIENT
The James H. Barry Co.

AGENCY
LaPerle Associates/
San Francisco

202
ART DIRECTOR
Mark Wolf

WRITER
Ron Sackett

PHOTOGRAPHERS
Jim Marvy
Kerry Peterson

CLIENT
Harley-Davidson Motor

AGENCY
Carmichael-Lynch/Mpls.

201

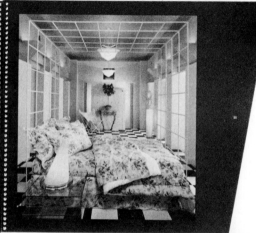

203

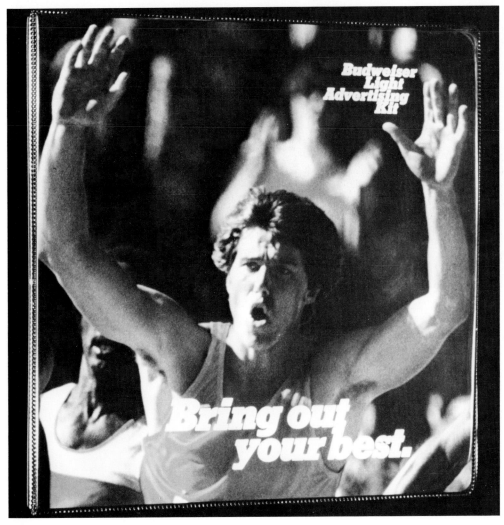

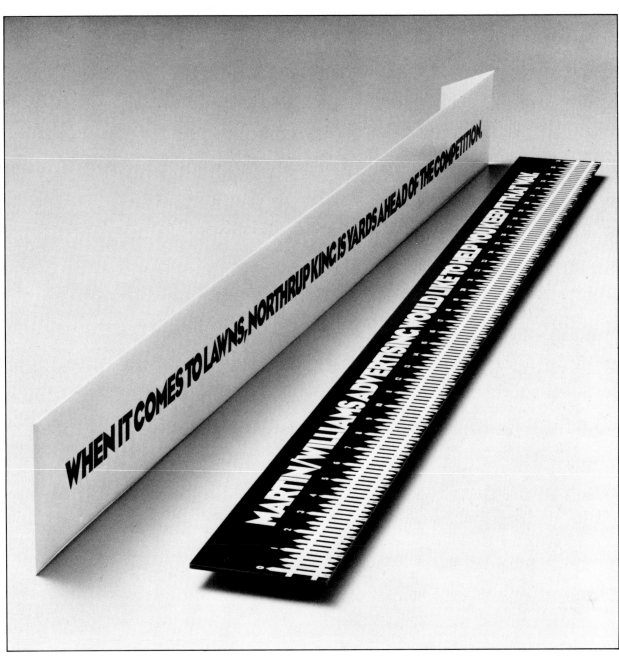

207

208

209

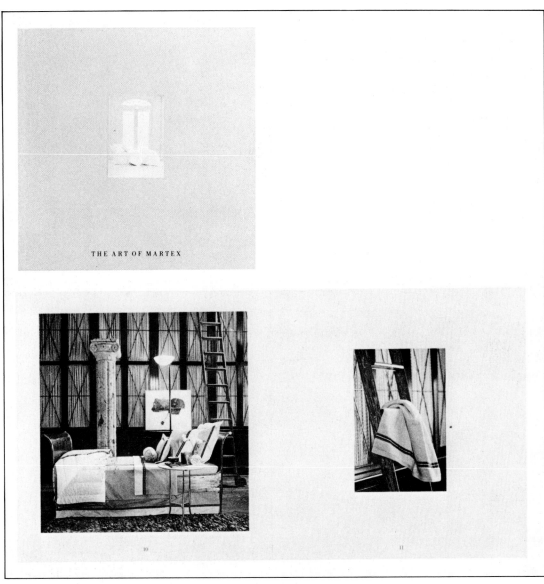

210 SILVER

211 GOLD

212
ART DIRECTOR
Rick McQuiston

WRITER
Bill Borders

DESIGNER
Ed Tajon

ARTIST
Art Farm

PHOTOGRAPHER
David Watanabe

CLIENT
Hillsboro Aviation

AGENCY
Borders, Perrin
& Norrander/Oregon

213
ART DIRECTORS
Charles Hively
Lyle Metzdorf

WRITERS
Harvey Marks
Lyle Metzdorf

DESIGNERS
Charles Hively
Lyle Metzdorf

PHOTOGRAPHER
Bill Wolfhagen

CLIENT
Metzdorf Advertising

AGENCY
Metzdorf Advertising/Houston

214 SILVER
ART DIRECTOR & WRITER
David Anderson

PHOTOGRAPHER
Dick Kaiser

CLIENT
Western Landscape
Construction

AGENCY
Ogilvy & Mather/Los Angeles

215
ART DIRECTORS
Greg Nygard
Gary Reynolds

WRITER
Jeffrey Epstein

PHOTOGRAPHER
Tony D'Orio

CLIENT
Advertising Typographers
Association

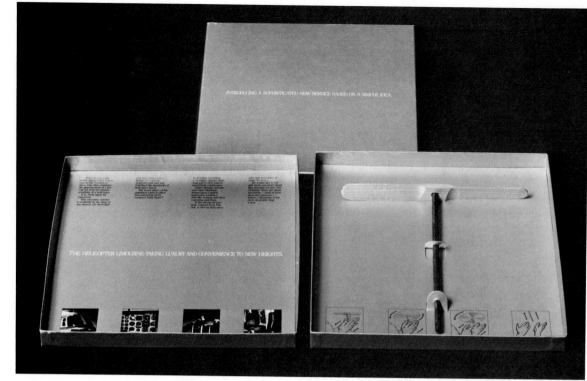

212

Guess who won more awards in
the New York Advertising Show last year?

☒ Ally & Gargano, Inc., NY   ☐ Leo Burnett Co., CHI

☐ Campbell-Ewald, DET   ☐ Marschalk, NY

☐ Cunningham & Walsh, NY   ☐ McCann-Erickson, NY

☐ Dancer Fitzgerald Sample, NY   ☐ Metzdorf Advertising, HOU

☐ DDB Group II, NY   ☐ Ogilvy & Mather, NY

☐ Doyle Dane Bernbach/West, LA   ☐ Scali, McCabe, Sloves, NY

☐ Ketchum, McLeod & Grove, NY

Chances are you didn't guess Metzdorf Advertising to be the winner over all these national agencies. That's an easy mistake to make because people tend to think of us as a Houston agency. When, in fact, we're a national agency that chooses to be headquartered in Houston.

213

WESTERN LANDSCAPE CONSTRUCTION
We're helping to build the west.

214 SILVER

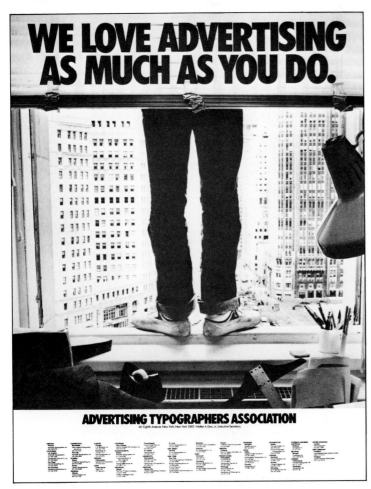

WE LOVE ADVERTISING AS MUCH AS YOU DO.

ADVERTISING TYPOGRAPHERS ASSOCIATION
461 Eighth Avenue, New York, New York 10001. Walter A. Dew, Jr. Executive Secretary

216
ART DIRECTOR
Pat Burnham
WRITER
Dick Thomas
ARTIST
Pat Burnham
CLIENT
Country Kitchen
AGENCY
Fallon McElligott Rice/Mpls.

217
ART DIRECTOR & DESIGNER
Jeneal Rohrback
ARTIST
Tom Pansini
CLIENT
ATC
AGENCY
Dailey & Associates/
Los Angeles

218
ART DIRECTORS
Peter Rauch
Anthony Angotti
WRITER
Tom Thomas
DESIGNERS
Peter Rauch
Anthony Angotti
Denise Monaco
William Hartwell
PHOTOGRAPHER
Cailor/Resnick Studio
CLIENT
BMW of North America
AGENCY
Ammirati & Puris

219
ART DIRECTOR
Ron Anderson
WRITER
Phil Hanft
ARTIST
Ron Anderson
CLIENT
MedCenter Dental Plan
AGENCY
Bozell & Jacobs/Mpls.

216

217

THE BMW LUXURY SPORTS COUPE. THE EPITOME OF TRUTH IN PACKAGING.

Don't forget to sweep up after supper.

MedCenter Plan DEN✚AL

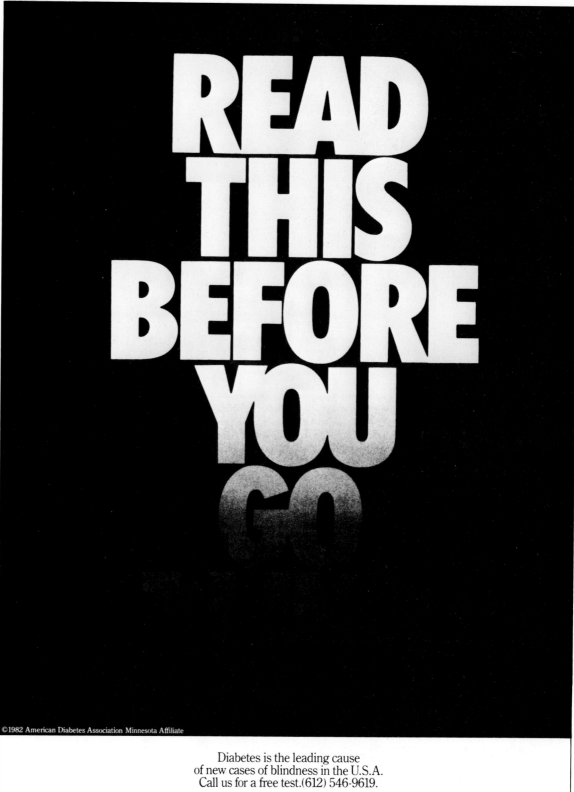

©1982 American Diabetes Association Minnesota Affiliate

Diabetes is the leading cause
of new cases of blindness in the U.S.A.
Call us for a free test.(612) 546-9619.

**American Diabetes Association
Minnesota Affiliate, Inc.**

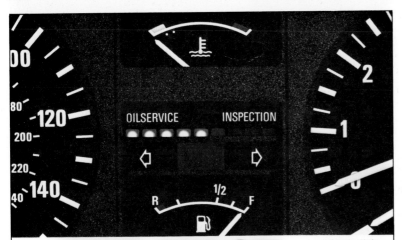

THE FIRST KNOWN EXAMPLE OF A CAR EVALUATING ITS DRIVER.

Until now, timetables for routine automobile maintenance have overlooked one important and generally unpredictable factor: the person behind the wheel.

Obviously, someone who drives mostly on crowded city streets places different stresses on a car than someone who drives mostly on uncluttered highways. Differences in driving techniques (such as how hard one accelerates) are also a significant factor.

Which is why BMW engineers have developed the Service Interval Indicator™— a computer-governed system based on the obvious fact that different people drive differently.

With the aid of electronic sensors, the Service Interval Indicator monitors individual variations in driving habits and environments—as measured by engine speeds, the number of cold starts, and miles driven.

It then processes this information, and calculates when service is actually warranted—not just dictated by an arbitrary schedule.

One of BMW's major preoccupations has always been man's interaction with machine.

And BMW's new Service Interval Indicator represents machine's latest contribution to that end.

THE ULTIMATE DRIVING MACHINE.

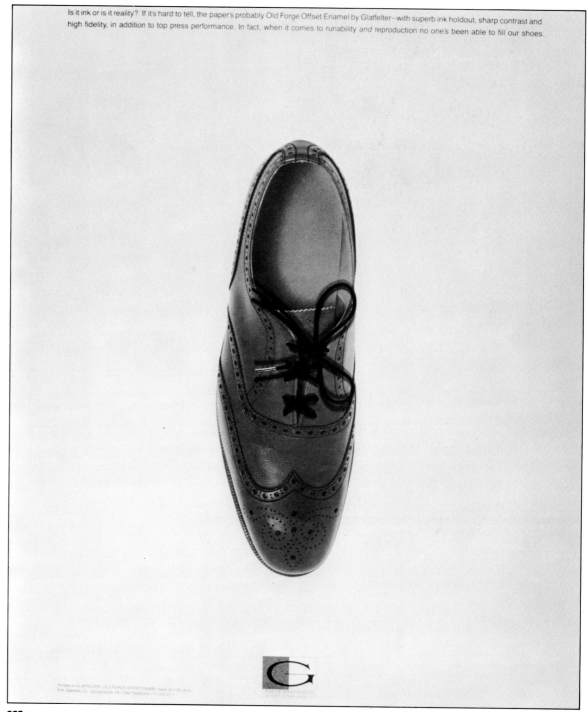

Is it ink or is it reality? If it's hard to tell, the paper's probably Old Forge Offset Enamel by Glatfelter—with superb ink holdout, sharp contrast and high fidelity, in addition to top press performance. In fact, when it comes to runability and reproduction no one's been able to fill our shoes.

223

LET THE GOVERNMENT PAY FOR SOME OF YOUR FUN. LEASE A BMW.

There are any number of cars available for leasing that may function beautifully as tax write-offs. BMW's, however, are engineered to function beautifully as cars. To provide exhilaration behind the wheel, not merely behind the calculator.

They were designed, after all, by German engineers who believe that extraordinary performance is the only rational motive for buying, or leasing, an expensive automobile.

And so, they are intended for drivers who are as fond of rounding corners and accelerating up straightaways as they are of eluding taxes. **THE ULTIMATE DRIVING MACHINE.**

224 SILVER

Holland America to Bermuda.   Wilson McLean.

225

226

227

More Headroom

American Pride Ceiling Fans

228

The Observer Guide to European Cookery starts March 28.
For 10 weeks in The Observer Magazine.

229

Outdoor
Single

230 SILVER
ART DIRECTOR
Ian Potter
WRITER
Rob Kitchen
CLIENT
Ciba Geigy
AGENCY
FCO Univas/London

231 GOLD
ART DIRECTOR
Dean Hanson
WRITER
Jarl Olson
PHOTOGRAPHER
Bettmann Archives
CLIENT
7 South 8th For Hair
AGENCY
Fallon, McElligott, Rice/Mpls.

232
ART DIRECTOR & WRITER
Noel Frankel
PHOTOGRAPHER
Steve Steigman
CLIENT
Empire State Building
AGENCY
Beber Silverstein
& Partners/Miami

230 SILVER

231 GOLD

5 states on $2.50 a day.

The Empire State Observatory offers more than the sights of New York. For the price of admission, you get four neighboring states in the bargain.

On a clear day, see the Jersey shore, the Pennsylvania Poconos, and the lakes of Connecticut and Massachusetts, shimmering in the noonday sun.

For $2.50 a day, you'll tour the countryside. And never set foot out of Manhattan.

Empire State Observatory

In the heart of midtown Manhattan at Fifth Avenue and 34th Street.
Open daily from 9:30 AM to midnight. To check visibility call, 736-3100.

233
ART DIRECTOR & DESIGNER
Denis Russell
ARTIST
Connie Saum
CLIENT
American Airlines
AGENCY
Group 2/Bozell & Jacobs/
Dallas

234
ART DIRECTORS
Brent Thomas
Tom Cordner
WRITERS
Penny Kapousouz
Brent Bouchez
DESIGNER
Amy Miyano
PHOTOGRAPHER
Mark Coppos
CLIENT
Yamaha Motor
AGENCY
Chiat/Day-Los Angeles

235
ART DIRECTOR
Tom Kelly
WRITER
Bill Borders
CLIENT
Tri-Met
AGENCY
Borders, Perrin
& Norrander/Oregon

236
ART DIRECTOR
Beth DeFuria
WRITER
Bob Nadler
CLIENT
Hertz
AGENCY
Scali, McCabe, Sloves

233

237 SILVER
ART DIRECTOR
Gordon Bennett

WRITER
Martin Puris

DESIGNERS
Gordon Bennett
Barbara Bowman

PHOTOGRAPHERS
Gilles Bensimon
Oliviero Toscani

CLIENT
Club Med

AGENCY
Ammirati & Puris

238
ART DIRECTOR
Lou Colletti

WRITER
Lee Garfinkel

PHOTOGRAPHER
Larry Robins

CLIENT
Anti-Graffiti

AGENCY
Levine, Huntley, Schmidt
& Beaver

237 SILVER

"WE GOT WHERE WE ARE BY MESSING UP OTHER FIGHTERS. NOT BY MESSING UP OUR CITY'S WALLS." JOE FRAZIER MARVIS FRAZIER

MAKE YOUR MARK IN SOCIETY. NOT ON SOCIETY.

Mayor's Task Force on Graffiti • Willard Butcher, Chairman • Edward I. Koch, Mayor • Karen Gerard, Deputy Mayor

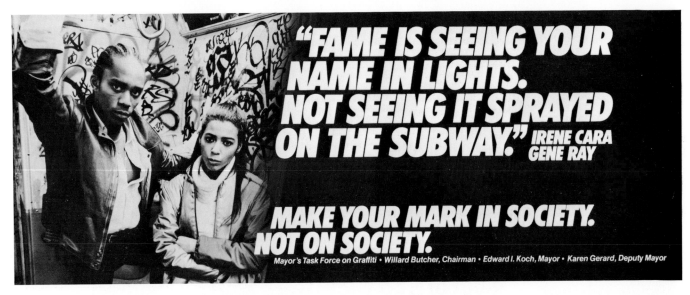

"FAME IS SEEING YOUR NAME IN LIGHTS. NOT SEEING IT SPRAYED ON THE SUBWAY." IRENE CARA GENE RAY

MAKE YOUR MARK IN SOCIETY. NOT ON SOCIETY.

Mayor's Task Force on Graffiti • Willard Butcher, Chairman • Edward I. Koch, Mayor • Karen Gerard, Deputy Mayor

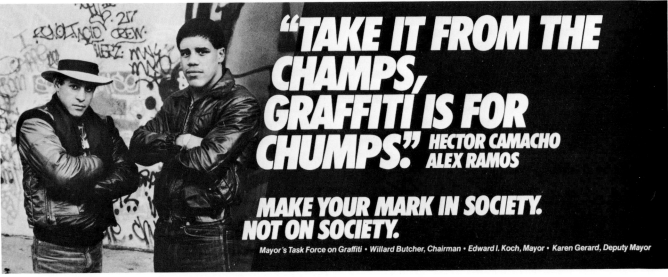

"TAKE IT FROM THE CHAMPS, GRAFFITI IS FOR CHUMPS." HECTOR CAMACHO ALEX RAMOS

MAKE YOUR MARK IN SOCIETY. NOT ON SOCIETY.

Mayor's Task Force on Graffiti • Willard Butcher, Chairman • Edward I. Koch, Mayor • Karen Gerard, Deputy Mayor

**Public Service
Newspaper or Magazine
Single**

239
ART DIRECTOR & WRITER
Diane Lozito
DESIGNER
Diane Lozito
PHOTOGRAPHER
Walter Swarthout
CLIENT
San Francisco
Child Abuse Council
AGENCY
Diane Lozito Advertising/
California

240 SILVER
ART DIRECTOR
Tana Klugherz
WRITER
Lee Garfinkel
PHOTOGRAPHER
Larry Robins
CLIENT
Planned Parenthood
of N.Y. City
AGENCY
Levine, Huntley, Schmidt
& Beaver

241
ART DIRECTOR
Chuck Marsh
WRITER
Erik Mintz
PHOTOGRAPHER
Ken Ambrose
CLIENT
The House of Seagram
AGENCY
Warwick Advertising

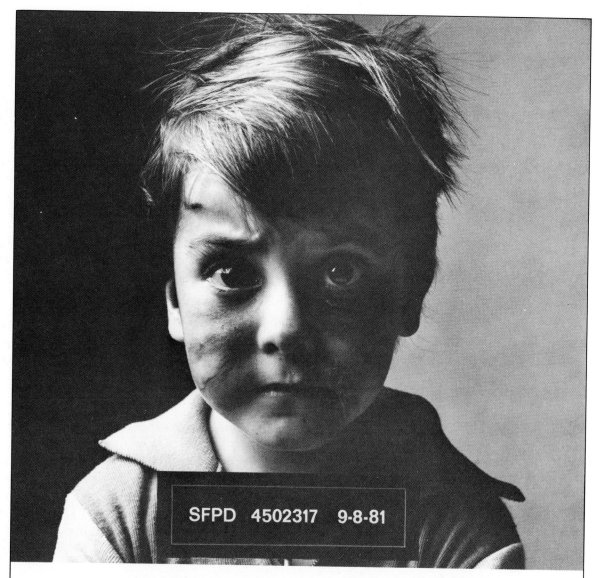

4 out of 5 convicts were abused children.

In the United Statès, an average of 80% of our prisoners were abused children. That is why we are working so hard to help these children today, before they develop into a threat to others tomorrow.

With your support, we can have a full staff of trained people available 24 hours a day. Abused children desperately need us. Please let us be there to help. Write for our free brochure, or send in your tax-deductible donation today.

San Francisco Child Abuse Council, Inc.
4093 24th Street, San Francisco, CA 94114

WHAT IF YOUR BABY IS GOING TO HAVE A BABY?

40% of all girls who turn 14 this year will become pregnant while they are still teenagers.

Each one is somebody's daughter. With her whole life in front of her.

Yet on March 10th the United States Senate Judiciary Committee took an unprecedented first step which could force a woman to bear a child. Even if she's only a child herself.

They have approved the "Hatch Amendment" to the Constitution which will now go to the Senate floor. And it may very well pass.

If this amendment becomes law, it could ultimately deny you your most fundamental personal rights: The right to have the number of children you want. When you want them. Or to have none at all.

The "Hatch Amendment" will abolish your Constitutional freedom to choose an abortion. And at the same time will allow the states and Congress to outlaw all abortion.

Even if the pregnancy is the result of rape. Or incest.

It is even possible that if you have an abortion you could be prosecuted for murder.

Backing this amendment are right-wing United States Senators who want to impose their religious beliefs on you. Your friends. Your family. Everyone.

Don't stand by silently and let the minority rule. Fill out the Planned Parenthood coupon. Give generously of your time and money. Write to your Senators. Their address is c/o The United States Senate, Washington, D.C., 20510.

Now more than ever, we must fight to keep the government from governing your private life.

The fate of safe and legal abortion lies in the balance.

JOIN PLANNED PARENTHOOD
PLANNED PARENTHOOD OF NEW YORK CITY, INC.
380 SECOND AVENUE, NEW YORK, NEW YORK 10010
212/777-2002

☐ I believe abortion is something personal, not political. Please keep me informed and add me to your mailing list.

☐ Please send me your Legislative Action Kit so I can make my voice heard.

☐ I want to keep abortion legal and wish to make a tax-deductible contribution to support Planned Parenthood's general purposes. Here is my check in the amount of $ _____

NAME _____

ADDRESS _____

CITY/STATE/ZIP _____

TELEPHONE (DAY) _____ (EVE) _____

This advertisement has been paid for with private contributions.
A copy of our financial report can be obtained from us or from the New York Department of State, Office of Charities Registration, Albany, New York 12231.
© 1982 Planned Parenthood of New York City, Inc.

ABORTION IS SOMETHING PERSONAL. NOT POLITICAL.

WHAT TO GET FOR THE PERSON WHO'S HAD EVERYTHING.

Having too much to drink is never a good idea. But if this happens to one of your guests, present him with a cab ride home. You'll be giving a gift that will insure many happy returns.

The House of Seagram

For a reprint please write Advertising Dept. TE-183, The House of Seagram, 375 Park Ave., N.Y., N.Y. 10152
© 1982 The House of Seagram

Public Service Newspaper or Magazine Single

242 GOLD
ART DIRECTOR
Tana Klugherz
WRITER
Deborah Kasher
PHOTOGRAPHER
Manuel Gonzalez
CLIENT
Planned Parenthood
of N.Y. City
AGENCY
Levine, Huntley, Schmidt
& Beaver

243
ART DIRECTOR
Jeffrey Abbott
WRITERS
Lou Schiavone
Jeffrey Abbott
DESIGNER
Jeffrey Abbott
ARTIST
Bettmann Archives
CLIENT
Friends of Bushnell Park
AGENCY
Creamer/Hartford

THE DECISION TO HAVE A BABY COULD SOON BE BETWEEN YOU, YOUR HUSBAND AND YOUR SENATOR.

For everyone who thought something like this could never happen. It has.

This week, the United States Senate will vote on two bills which could deprive you of your most fundamental personal rights: the right to have the number of children you want. When you want them. Or to have none at all.

These bills ultimately seek to outlaw all abortion. For all women.

Even if the pregnancy is the result of rape. Or incest.

Sponsoring the bills are Jesse Helms, Orrin Hatch and other right-wing U.S. Senators who will stop at nothing to impose their particular religious and personal beliefs on you. Your family. Your friends. Everyone.

And what's even more frightening, they are acting with the encouragement of President Reagan.

Don't stand by silently. Telephone and telegraph your senators today. Their address is: The United States Senate, Washington, D.C. 20510.

And fill out the Planned Parenthood coupon. Give generously of your time and money.

The fate of safe and legal abortion hangs in the balance.

JOIN PLANNED PARENTHOOD
Planned Parenthood of New York City, Inc.
380 Second Avenue, New York, N.Y. 10010
212/777-2002

☐ I believe abortion is something personal, not political. Please keep me informed and add me to your mailing list.

☐ I want to make a tax-deductible contribution to support Planned Parenthood's work. Here is my check in the amount of $_____.

NAME _____

ADDRESS _____

CITY/STATE/ZIP _____

TELEPHONE (DAY) _____ (EVE) _____

A copy of our financial report can be obtained from us or the New York Department of State, Office of Charities Registration, Albany, New York 12231
This advertisement has been paid for with private contributions
© 1982 Planned Parenthood of New York City, Inc.   NYT 8/15

ABORTION IS SOMETHING PERSONAL. NOT POLITICAL.

242 GOLD

BUSHNELL PARK.

IGNORE IT, AND MAYBE IT WILL GO AWAY.

How easily it happens. We walk through it, jog around it, eat our lunch in it, but don't really stop to look *at* it. A city park, designed like every park to be for life, is dying before our eyes.

It didn't happen overnight, either. It took years of neglect to put Bushnell Park where it is today. Criss-crossed by eroding walkways. Surrounded by benches that are falling apart. Its statuary, slowly ravaged by time, is all too frequently used as the graffiti artist's canvas. And perhaps saddest of all, the park pond, once beautiful, has become an eyesore murky with empty bottles and trash.

For all this, we can't blame anyone but ourselves—all of us who never took the time to look. Our indifference has created a situation which is almost hopeless. But not quite.

Through a group of concerned citizens named The Bushnell Park Foundation, the process of decay in Bushnell Park can be reversed. They have identified over $2 million of projects needed to revitalize Bushnell Park, such as: constructing new park benches; upgrading walkways; restoring statues; and re-creating the park pond. It will take time. It's not going to be cheap. But the problem can be solved.

The choice is clear. Open your eyes to the plight of the park and make a donation of money or time to help renew its life. Or ignore it, in which case the nation's oldest public park will continue to yield to the forces that pull at it, and it will become extinct. **IT'S COMPLETELY UP TO YOU.**

The Bushnell Park Foundation, 15 Lewis Street, Hartford, CT 06103

NAME _____

HOME ADDRESS _____

_____

HOME PHONE _____ BUSINESS PHONE _____

I want to be a friend of Bushnell Park. My tax-deductible donation for the improvement of the park is indicated below (please make checks payable to the Bushnell Park Foundation):

__ $5.00 Student or Senior Citizen
__ $10.00 Individual
__ $25.00 Family
__ $50.00 Sustaining
__ $100.00 Sponsor
__ $500.00 and over Patron

__ My donation is enclosed but I would like to know how else I can be involved in the park improvement effort. Please contact me.

For every $2 you donate, another $1 will be contributed by The Hartford Foundation for Public Giving

---

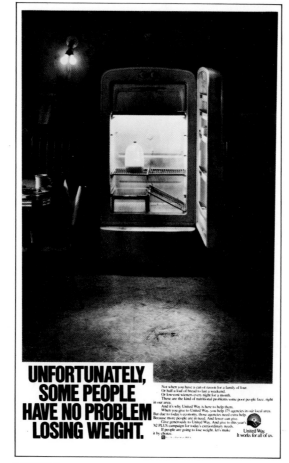

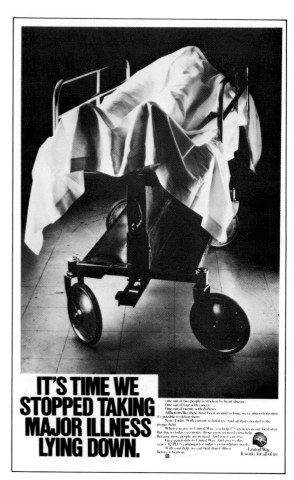

God didn't give His only begotten Son to be a spokesman for the moral majority.

If you think Jesus loves all people — even those who don't agree with Him — come and join us in a service where diversity is not only allowed, but welcomed.

The Episcopal Church

Will man destroy in six minutes what it took God six days to create?

If you think it's time Christianity raised its voice in the life and death issues of our age, come and join us in the active worship and fellowship of the Episcopal Church.

The Episcopal Church

You shouldn't have to go through channels to talk to God.

If you believe there ought to be more to God than a flickering image interrupted by commercials, join us as we worship and discover the joy of God together in the Episcopal Church.

The Episcopal Church

246
ART DIRECTOR
Myron Polenberg
WRITER
Libby Daniel
PHOTOGRAPHER
Bill Stettner
CLIENT
National Council
on Alcoholism
AGENCY
N W Ayer

247
ART DIRECTOR
Nancy Rice
WRITER
Tom McElligott
PHOTOGRAPHERS
Jim Marvy
Tom Bach
Tom Berthiaume
CLIENT
The Episcopal Ad Project
AGENCY
Fallon, McElligott, Rice/Mpls.

"I'M LIVING PROOF YOU DON'T HAVE TO DIE FOR A DRINK."

"I'm Jim Kemper Jr., Chairman of the Board of a major insurance and financial services corporation, and I'm alcoholic. I'm not alone. The facts show that there are many more like me. In fact 10% of the work force in this country is alcoholic.

"If you are in a managerial position, you have probably lost or fired many people like me. Decisions based on lack of information can be as dangerous as the disease itself. Alcoholism has nothing to do with weakness of character. It's a very complicated disease that can strike anyone who drinks, whether you work on an assembly line, in the mailroom, or the executive suite. And it can be fatal, if not treated.

"Most companies don't know how to deal with this disease. But it's much easier than you think. That's why the National Council on Alcoholism has written a manual so you can set up an "Employee Alcoholism Program," within your company to protect your people, as well as your investment in them. These programs work. I haven't had a drink in 28 years. Who knows, the next person you help may be your next Chairman of the Board."

To: THE NATIONAL COUNCIL ON ALCOHOLISM, 733 Third Avenue, New York, New York 10017
I am enclosing $6.00 for the National Council on Alcoholism's manual that will show me how to set up an Employee Alcoholism Program within my company.

My name is _____
My address is _____

246

If Jesus fed the multitudes with five loaves and two fishes, why can't the government do it with $800 billion?

If you think it's right to help people in distress, come and join us in an atmosphere where compassion toward people and the worship of God come together in joy and fellowship.
The Episcopal Church

247

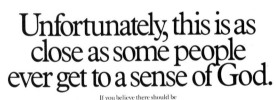
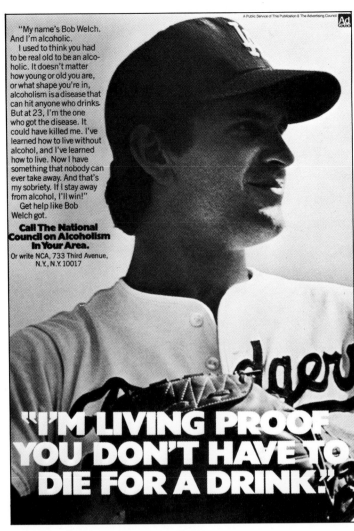

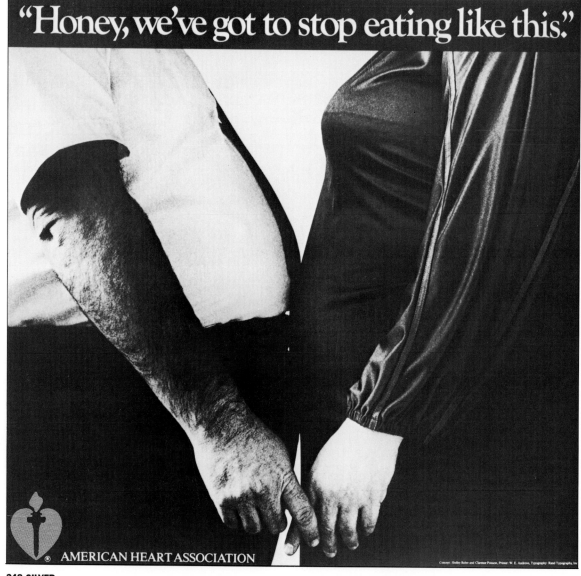

"Honey, we've got to stop eating like this."

AMERICAN HEART ASSOCIATION

Concept: Shelley Buber and Clarence Poisson, Printer: W. E. Andrews, Typography: Rand Typography, Inc.

248 SILVER

How much would you bid for this?

The world's oldest, most experienced auction house announces Sotheby's Arcade Auctions, specially created to enable you to buy and sell moderately valuable decorative arts. Each Arcade Auction, held for a two-day period every two weeks, will offer approximately 1,500 lots, valued from $50 to $5000.

A fascinating range and diversity of furniture, rugs, silver, porcelain and other decorative works of art make Sotheby's Arcade Auctions an attractive way to buy. 1,500 lots comprising approximately 10,000 items will be auctioned every two weeks in newly designed luxurious space at our York Avenue galleries.

The name of Sotheby's will benefit everything you choose to sell. Your consignments will enjoy expo-

American Banjo-Clock. Est. $600-800.

Gothic Revival Style Armchair. Est. $400-600.

sure to unprecedented numbers of serious and affluent buyers. With Sotheby's Arcade Auctions, turnover will be fast and efficient. It is only about four weeks from consignment to sale and two weeks to payment.

American Duck Decoy (one of three). Est. $200-300.

Come July 15th and 16th to York Avenue at 72nd Street, first floor for Sotheby's new Arcade Auction. For dealers, it's an efficient new way to turn inventory. For collectors of every level, it's an exciting way to find what you want and sell what you don't. Visit the exhibitions starting Friday July 10th. Catalogues are available *at the galleries only.* For more information call 212/472-3577 or write: Sotheby's Arcade Auctions, 1334 York Avenue, New York, N.Y. 10021.

Art Nouveau Stained Glass Lamp. Est. $1500-2000.

SOTHEBY'S

Sotheby's Arcade Auctions.
Every two weeks $50 to $5000.

YOU DON'T STAY THE LEADER OF A BUSINESS JUST BY INVENTING THE BUSINESS.

DuMont invented the first commercial television set. Duryea introduced the first automobile. And Hurley, the first washing machine.

Obviously, inventing a business is no guarantee that a company will keep leading that business.

Like these companies, Xerox also invented a business. Unlike them, we're still leading our business.

There's a simple reason: we never stopped inventing. Just as our original 914 was the most advanced copier in 1959, our 9500 is the most advanced today.

The 9500 performs more different tasks than any duplicator ever made. It reduces. It sorts. It collates. It even makes the best looking copies in the business.

And it does all this nearly twice as fast as the next fastest machine on the market. Two copies per second.

We also invented the 8200. It does just about any job you could ever ask of a copier. All at the touch of a few buttons. And it gives you blacker blacks, whiter whites and truer grays than any copier that's gone before.

Then there's the 5600. It's the first and only copier that automatically makes two-sided copies from two-sided originals. It has microcomputer diagnostics like the 8200 and 9500. It has a special document handler to deliver completely collated sets. And it has a very loyal following.

A recent independent survey asked people if they would replace

1932 DuMont introduces the first commercial television set.

their 5600 with any other brand of copier. Not one would.

You see, you become the DuMont of a business by inventing the business.

You become the Xerox of a business by going on and reinventing

it. Year after year after year.

For more information, call 800-828-6210, operator 100, or your local Xerox sales office.

XEROX

*In New York State, call 800-462-6432

XEROX,® 914, 9500 and 5600 are trademarks of XEROX CORPORATION.

PRO CRAS TINATION

MAY BE A BIGGER RISK THAN POLLUTION.

While you may consider your reasons valid for putting off pollution liability coverage, kindly consider the growing list of EPA and Justice Department lawsuits.

A company in Pennsylvania is sued for gradually contaminating groundwater that leached into the Delaware River. Clean-up costs: $67,000.

A company in New Jersey is sued retroactive to 1973. Penalty: $500,000 put in escrow as assurance that remedial actions will be completed.

A company in Indiana is made to reimburse the government $860,000, plus interest, in clean-up costs because of a gradual leakage of chemicals.

Etc., etc., etc. The figures for this growing list (now, by the way, up to 50 suits a year) belong to EPA and the Justice Department, not us.

What's more, even obeying today's environmental laws is no guarantee against a future catastrophe.

At the AIG Companies, we consider the problem of accidental pollution, whether gradual or sudden, so crucial, we've set up a special department to handle it.

AIG's Pollution Legal Liability Department. A department with the capability and the experience that have already established it as a major force in pollution insurance.

A department staffed with people who are authorities on every aspect of pollution, to help with

all the ins and outs of the many changing legal standards.

It is this experience that enables us to offer virtually the most comprehensive pollution insurance available, on a very practical, cost-efficient basis. For whatever kind of accidental pollution–gradual or sudden. Whether it be for a small chain of gas stations or multi-million dollar chemical plants. Against loss from personal injury, property damage, and even legal defense costs.

Incidentally, for over 60 years, AIG companies have seen to it that clients have received optimum protection for things like hurricanes, fires, floods, employee fraud and political upheavals.

Today you'll find AIG Companies leading the way to insuring global risks, energy risks, and all types of property and casualty risks, to mention just a few.

For more information about our pollution policy, contact AIG, Dept. A, 70 Pine St., NY, NY, 10270.

However, may we gently urge you not to procrastinate. This is the one time when time may not be on your side.

ONCE AGAIN THE ANSWER IS AIG.

THE AIG COMPANIES: American International Underwriters, American Home Assurance Co., Commerce and Industry Insurance Co., National Union Fire Insurance Company of Pittsburgh, Pa., American International Life Assurance Co., North American Managers, New Hampshire Insurance Co., and over 250 other companies operating around the world to meet your insurance needs.

249 SILVER

250 GOLD

251

How much would you bid for this?

The world's oldest, most experienced auction house announces Sotheby's Arcade Auctions, specially created to enable you to buy and sell moderately valuable decorative arts. Each Arcade Auction, held for a two-day period every two weeks, will offer approximately 1,500 lots, valued from $50 to $5000.

A fascinating range and diversity of furniture, rugs, silver, porcelain and other decorative works of art make Sotheby's Arcade Auctions an attractive way to buy. 1,500 lots comprising approximately 10,000 items will be auctioned every two weeks in newly designed luxurious space at our York Avenue galleries.

The name of Sotheby's will benefit everything you choose to sell. Your consignments will enjoy exposure to unprecedented numbers of serious and affluent buyers. With Sotheby's Arcade Auctions, turnover will be fast and efficient. It is only about four weeks from consignment to sale and two weeks to payment.

Come July 15th and 16th to York Avenue at 72nd Street, first floor for Sotheby's new Arcade Auction. For dealers, it's an efficient new way to turn inventory. For collectors of every level, it's an exciting way to find what you want and sell what you don't. Visit the exhibitions starting Friday July 10th. Catalogues are available *at the galleries only.* For more information call 212/472-3577 or write: Sotheby's Arcade Auctions, 1334 York Avenue, New York, N.Y. 10021.

SOTHEBY'S

Sotheby's Arcade Auctions.
Every two weeks $50 to $5000.

How much would you bid for this?

The world's oldest, most experienced auction house announces Sotheby's Arcade Auctions. This new auction service is specially created to enable you to buy and sell moderately valuable decorative arts. Every week over 800 lots comprising approximately 5000 items are auctioned at values from $100 to $5000. For buyers and sellers of every level, Sotheby's Arcade Auctions are an exciting way to find what you want and sell what you don't.

A fascinating range and diversity of furniture, rugs, silver, porcelain, and other decorative works of art are included from consignors all over the country.

Our policy is a minimum consignment of $300 including no more than three items. Exhibitions and auctions are held in newly designed, luxurious space at our York Avenue galleries. Your consignments will enjoy exposure to unprecedented numbers of serious and affluent buyers. The name of Sotheby's will benefit everything you choose to sell and, with Sotheby's Arcade Auctions, turnover will be fast and efficient. It is only about four weeks from consignment to sale and two weeks to payment.

Come every Wednesday to Sotheby's Arcade Auctions at York Avenue and 72nd Street. Exhibition galleries are open Saturday, Sunday afternoon, Monday until 8 p.m. and Tuesday until 3 p.m. Our shipping department is open Saturdays too. Catalogues are available *at the galleries only.* For more information call 212/472-3577 or write: Sotheby's Arcade Auctions, 1334 York Avenue, New York 10021. **SOTHEBY'S**

Sotheby's Arcade Auctions.
Every week $100 to $5000.

How much would you bid for this?

American Renaissance Walnut Bureau. 19th C. Est $600-800

Introducing Sotheby's Arcade Auctions.
The world's oldest, most experienced auction house, announces Sotheby's Arcade Auctions, specially created to enable you to buy and sell moderately valuable decorative arts. Each Arcade Auction, held for a two day period every two weeks, will offer approximately 1500 lots, valued from $50 to $5000.

A fascinating range and diversity of furniture, rugs, silver, porcelain and other decorative works of art make Sotheby's Arcade Auctions an attractive way to buy. 1,500 lots comprising approximately

Japanese 19th C. Est $1200-1500

10,000 items will be auctioned every two weeks in newly designed luxurious space at our York Avenue galleries.

Miniature Inlaid Table. 19th C. Est $100-150

The name of Sotheby's will benefit everything you choose to sell. Your consignments will enjoy exposure to unprecedented numbers of serious and affluent buyers. With the Arcade Auctions, turnover will be fast and efficient. It is only about four weeks from consignment to sale and two weeks to payment.

Come June 17th and 18th to York Avenue at 72nd Street, first floor for the first of Sotheby's new Arcade Auctions. For dealers, they're an efficient new way to turn inventory. For collectors of every level, they're an exciting way to find what you want and sell what you don't. Visit the exhibitions daily starting Saturday June 13th. Catalogues are available at the exhibitions only. For more information call 212/472-3577 or write Sotheby's Arcade Auctions, 1334 York Avenue, New York N.Y. 10021. **SOTHEBY'S**

Austrian Painted Faience Figure Est $300-500

Sotheby's Arcade Auctions.
Every two weeks $50 to $5000.

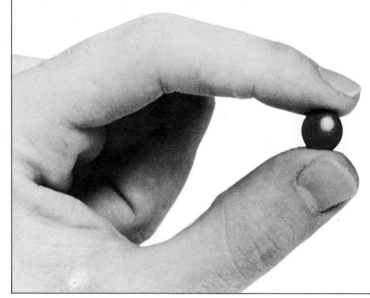

TAKE THIS PILL AND NOTHING WILL HAPPEN.

Absolutely nothing.
The pill is Control, the first birth control pill for men. Control provides total protection in a safe and effective way, a promise, that until now, no other male contraceptive could make.
Control is an idea that was conceived over twenty years ago and took twenty-five million dollars and the testing of two thousand men to make it a reality.
With a doctor's prescription, taken daily, Control is all the contraception you will ever need.
So take Control and take contraception into your own hands.
Simple. Effective.

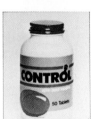

CONTROL
The first Birth Control Pill for Men
The only time it won't work is when you don't take it.

254 SILVER

Congratulations. You're about to become a father.

This man isn't smiling. And he won't be passing out cigars either. For him, and many men like him, the prospect of fatherhood is nothing to celebrate. Because all too often, the news comes as a complete surprise. Unplanned and unexpected. And suddenly, decisions have to be made. Decisions that could affect the rest of your life.

Should you consider marriage? In all likelihood, you're probably not emotionally nor financially ready to support a family. Abortion is another possibility. Or should you keep the child and then put it up for adoption? The responsibility of making these decisions can be overwhelming and more than a little frightening.

But these crises can be avoided if you take the necessary precautions to prevent pregnancy. Unfortunately, with any birth control method, there is always a risk involved. Not one has been proven 100 per cent effective.

Until now.

Because, after over twenty years of testing and twenty-five million dollars in research, we are proud to introduce a revolutionary step in contraception. Control.

Control is the first birth control pill developed specifically for men. It is a tablet, taken daily and available by doctor's prescription only, and for the past five years has been tested among two thousand men across America. With astonishing results. Control has been proven to be 100 per cent effective with no harmful side effects.

100 per cent effective. Think about it. No more anxious moments. No more sleepless nights worrying about "what if...". No more surprises. Because with Control, you decide if and when you're ready to become a father.

Because fatherhood isn't for everyone.

255

Half safe is like a little pregnant

100% Birth Control
A pill for men only

TRAMLIN
100% Sure, 100% Safe

256

MEN HAVE BABIES TOO.

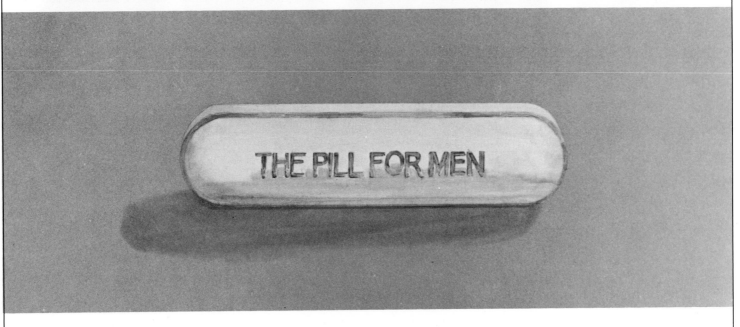

Finally, a convenient contraceptive for men. The Pill For Men from Johnson & Turturro Laboratories. It's 100% effective, it's risk-free and it's going to revolutionize the course of future relationships.

By introducing freedom. For both you and your partner. From both the fear of pregnancy and the risk of harmful side effects associated with other contraceptives. Freedom to have sex when you want. And to have a family when you want. Because The Pill For Men in no way interferes with a man's ability to father.

We're sure. After 20 years and over 25 million dollars in research, Johnson & Turturro found a way to allow each man to regulate his own fertility. And we backed that up with five years of testing more than two thousand men all across the United States.

So, if you and your partner are tired of the innaccuracies and restrictions associated with other forms of birth control, ask your doctor about Johnson & Turturro's 100% effective contraceptive in a daily tablet, The Pill For Men.

Because the method you're using is now obsolete.

Introducing The Pill For Men. A new fact of life.

After 20 years of research, 5 years of testing, and over 25 million dollars, we've come up with something really big.

The first birth control pill for men.
It's one, small, daily way of letting men share
some of the responsibility that women have assumed for years.
And it's worry-free. In national studies the pill has been proven
100% safe, 100% effective, and is now available by a doctor's prescription.
Show how much you care about your relationship.
Because a little can say a lot.

BCM. The Birth Control Pill for Men. Provided by one of America's most respected pharmaceutical companies.

4

1983 Radio Finalists

Radio Finalists

259

DICK: It's just, I never counted on my daughter marrying a "Slime Bucket".

BERT: Okay...

DICK: That is the name of your punk rock group, isn't it?

BERT: Yeah, wanna hear our latest song, "Hit Me With A Tire Iron, Baby"?

DICK: Maybe later. First, young man, can you support my Judy?

BERT: Whaddaya mean?

DICK: Well, what about your retirement? You're not going to be a "Slime Bucket" all your life!

BERT: Oh, that's taken care of, sir. I just opened an individual retirement account at Astoria Federal Savings. You should look into it!

DICK: Not me, I've got Social Security and a pension plan...

BERT: So have I!

DICK: The "Slime Buckets" have a pension plan?

BERT: Doesn't everybody? But with the cost of everything going up, I ask, will it be enough?

DICK: Excuse me?

BERT: Judy and I can put up to 4,000 dollars a year in a high interest, tax deferred IRA savings account at Astoria Federal.

DICK: You know, I can't believe you make enough money at this music thing to need an IRA tax shelter from Astoria Federal.

BERT: Well, last year, not counting T-shirts, dolls and posters, our net was about a half a million dollars...

DICK: Judy! Your future husband's here! (SINGS) *Hit Me With A Tire Iron, Baby......*

260

ANNCR: Whether you're 12, or 18, or 15 going on 21, it's your turn to play face invaders, like it or not. Yes, the pimples are coming, or the pimples are here. It's science...not fiction...but you can beat the odds out of them by using the force in the field.

By using Oxy 5. Which contains benzoyl peroxide, the most effective acne-pimple medication you can buy without a prescription.

More science...In an American Druggist survey of pharmacists, Oxy 5, yes incredible Oxy 5, was recommended almost 5 to 1 over the leading competitor.

So don't let pimples blow your Friday night date. Even the score with Oxy 5, or for stubborn acne get 10% benzoyl peroxide in Maximum Strength Oxy 10, or new Oxy Cover.

Why play games with your pimples, when you can...

Oxy 5 (SFX: BLAST), Oxy 10 (SFX: BLAST), Oxy Cover (SFX: BLAST) Them.

261

YOUNG GUY'S VOICE OVER WEST INDIAN MUSIC)

Dear Mum. Barbados is everything I imagined. I am writing to you from an amazing beach. This morning I met Ingrid. Ingrid is from Germany and is with me at the moment on the sand. She is rubbing a suntan oil called Tropical Blend all over her berah...berah...beautiful...long... thighs. Ingrid says Tropical Blend gives her a deep, dark almost native tan. She says her Tropical Blend is the new Piña Colada fragrance. You know, like the tropical drink. Ingrid has just asked me if I'd like to teruh...teruh...taste the taste of Piña...Piña...ah...ah...

(JINGLE COMES UP FULL)

See the pretty girl (with the handsome man)
They got the tropical moon, (they kiss and hold hands)
They got the tropical blend, (they got the chocolate tan)
They got their tropical friend, Tropical Blend.

262

LEAD VOCAL: *The cold black night surrounds me*
I've never been so alone.
Can't wait to get that ticket
And leave this town for home.

BACKGROUND VOCALS: *Going' home on a Greyhound.*

LEAD VOCAL: *It may be miles to where I'm going*

BACKGROUND VOCALS: *I'm feelin' good inside.*

LEAD VOCAL: *Feels like I'm almost there.*

BACKGROUND VOCALS: *Goin' home on a Greyhound.*

LEAD VOCAL: *Already seeing friendly faces.*

BACKGROUND VOCALS: *I think I'm gonna like this ride.*

LEAD VOCAL: *Yes, I think I'm gonna like this ride.*

BACKGROUND VOCALS: *Goin' home on a Greyhound.*

LEAD VOCAL: *I'm goin' home.*

BACKGROUND VOCALS: *I'm feelin' good inside.*

LEAD VOCAL: *Goin' home.*

BACKGROUND VOCALS: *Goin' home on a Greyhound.*

LEAD VOCAL: *On Greyhound, they make you feel at home*
While they take you there.

263

(SFX: CARS SHIFTING THROUGH GEARS SPEEDING BY)

ANNCR: In Germany, a Porsche 928 costs around 85-thousand Deutsche marks. Or 37-thousand dollars. A BMW Coupe goes for 82-thousand marks. And a Mercedes-Benz 380 Sedan can run as high as 90-thousand marks.

(SFX: LAST CAR RUSHES BY)

ANNCR: For ten years, who have the owners of these superbly engineered cars trusted to wash them more than anyone else? Us, Hot Springs Auto Wash. In fact, we wash almost two million cars a year in Germany. Using the most sophisticated technology available, we designed a car wash that not only does a thorough job, it does a careful job. After all, when a car costs a small fortune just to drive off the showroom floor, we think it should look like new for many miles down the road.

Hot Springs Auto Wash, now in America.

Exterior wash, five and a half marks...err (corrects himself), two dollars and ninety cents.

264

ANNCR: This year, billions of bugs will lose their lives on the nation's highways. Chances are, a lot of them will end up on the front of your car. And if you don't get them off, they'll come back to haunt you.

(SFX: MUSIC AND SOUND EFFECTS UNDER)

ANNCR: You see, as bugs decompose, they give off a strong acid that actually eats away at your car's chrome and paint...making it dull. The hotter the weather, the faster the acid is made.

But there is a brighter side to all of this: come to Hot Springs Auto Wash. We've developed a way to completely remove bugs before they kill your car's finish.

In fact, Hot Springs is the only car wash to make this guarantee: If you find as much as one single little mosquito on your car after we've washed and dried it, we'll give you your two dollars and ninety cents back.

(SFX: MUSIC AND SFX OUT)

ANNCR: Next time, we'll talk to you about the problem with birds.

(SFX: BIRDS CHIRPING)

265

ANNCR: Your car is 93 million miles away from the sun. That seems like a reasonably safe distance. But is it? Well, consider this...

(SFX: MUSIC AND SOUND EFFECTS)

ANNCR: On an average summer day, the sun's rays can heat a car's surface to over 200 degrees Fahrenheit. Just imagine what that's doing to your car's paint.

Fortunately, there is something you can do about the sun...come to Hot Springs Auto Wash. We've developed a special protectant for your car. It's called Polysilicone Weatherguard. And it costs only five dollars. Used monthly, Poly-silicone Weatherguard forms an extremely hard shell that keeps the sun's damaging ultraviolet rays out, and the paint's natural oils in.

The result is a car that looks like new, long after the new car smell is gone.
Hot Springs Auto Wash. We're like no other car wash you've ever seen before.

Oh, and when you're here, remind us to tell you what Polysilicone Weatherguard can do for your car when the sun doesn't shine.

(SFX: CLAP OF THUNDER, SOUND OF RAIN...FADE OUT)

266

(MUSIC UNDER)

VO: When you think about it, a mother is truly a remarkable individual. As skilled in medicine...

MOTHER: Here, let me kiss it, and make it better.

VO: As she is talented in engineering...

MOTHER: You'd forget your head, if it wasn't screwed on.

VO: Mothers know all about marine biology...

MOTHER: Don't worry, there are plenty of other fish in the sea.

VO: Economics...

MOTHER: Money doesn't grow on trees you know.

VO: Even anatomy...

MOTHER: You keep pushing on your nose like that and it'll get stuck that way.

VO: But most amazing, mothers can see into the future...

MOTHER: Someday, you'll thank me.

VO: This Mother's Day, show her how right she really was. With something special. Really special. From Zell Brothers. It doesn't have to cost a fortune. Zell Brothers has terrific gifts and jewelry in every price range. It's just, that when you get something at Zell Brothers, you know it's the best. A gift so exceptional, it might result in a truly rare situation...

MOTHER: I...I...I just don't know what to say, it's so...so...

VO TAG: ZELL BROTHERS. Morrison at Park, Washington Square, and Clackamas Town Center.

267

CHORAL SINGERS: *Ho hum, ho hum, ho hum...*

ANNCR: The ho hum Christmas gift. It's found at department stores everywhere.

SALESWOMAN: Now Honey, ah, what about this nice, safe little gift.

CHORAL SINGERS: *Ho hum, ho hum, ho hum.........*

SALESWOMAN: Or maybe this predictable belt? Absolutely everybody's wearing it!

CHORAL SINGERS: *Ho hum, ho hum, ho hum...*

ANNCR: Ho hum is the one thing St. Anthony Main is not. We're a place that makes looking as much fun as giving. Our gifts are memorable, intriguing, one-of-a-kind. Gifts with a certain ho ho!

CHORAL SINGERS: *Ho ho, ho ho, ho ho...*

ANNCR: Christmas at St. Anthony Main. More ho ho's, less ho hum's.

268

BERT: Son, I'm afraid you can't live at home anymore.

DICK: Why, Dad?

BERT: You're 37 years old!

DICK: Oh boy...

BERT: And you're the Governor of this State. It just doesn't look right...

DICK: But nobody makes Tuna Surprise like Mom!

BERT: Norman!

DICK: Besides, it's too expensive to move!

BERT: Call Jartran

DICK: Is that the Lieutenant Governor?

BERT: Jartran Truck Rental!

DICK: I don't know...

BERT: Well, all Jartran vans are late models with automatic transmission, radio, power steering, power brakes, good gas mileage...

DICK: But, I'm not really handy...

BERT: You mean like when your mother has to cut your meat?

DICK: You chose an extreme example, Dad.

BERT: Jartran gives you a complete guide that tells you how to pack and wrap everything.

DICK: Wow!

BERT: Plus a 24 hour toll free number to call if you need road service for your van, truck, or trailer.

DICK: Lemme think about it.

BERT: Hey, what would the taxpayers say if you told them you saved *up to 50%* of the cost of a van line move?

BERT: OK

DICK: You dial, I'm not...

BERT: Handy, I know—

ANNCR: Jartran. The professional moving system for the amateur mover. Check the Yellow Pages under "Truck Rental and Leasing" for your nearest Jartran dealer.

269

(SFX: THROUGHOUT THE COMMERCIAL, WE HEAR THE CONSTANT NOISE OF HAMMERING AND SAWING IN THE DISTANCE.)

AUSTRALIAN HOUSEWIFE, RESIGNED VOICE: Artistically, my Gary is a bit of a disaster. He's just designed his own tool shed. It's a cross between early Gothic and late Hansel and Gretel.

Worst of all, he's built it with Hardiplank. Hardiplank can't warp, rot, split or burn, so it'll last for ages.

Just like the Japanese carport, the Polynesian inspired bungalow, the Cape Cod attic, and the Bavarian playroom.

270

(SFX: THROUGHOUT THE COMMERCIAL WE CAN HEAR THE CONSTANT NOISE OF HAMMERING AND SAWING IN THE DISTANCE.)

AUSTRALIAN HOUSEWIFE, RESIGNED VOICE: There are grass widows, football widows, racing widows. I am a Hardiplank widow.

Since Gary found out how easy it is to build with Hardiplank, I hardly see him.

It began with the new garden fence. Then came the nursery. Closely followed by the new doghouse and the garage. Now it's the barbecue shelter.

Thanks to Gary and Hardiplank, we've got everything we need...except a baby, a dog, a car and a barbecue.

271

ANNCR: This is a match.

(SFX: MATCH BEING LIT. CRACKLING SOUNDS AS FLAMES GET HIGHER. INCREASE CRACKLING SOUNDS UNDER ANNCR.)

ANNCR: If you were to light it and drop it on a newspaper on a sofa, the flames would be two feet high in 25 seconds; the temperature at the ceiling would be 100° Fahrenheit.

(SFX: ADD TO CRACKLING SOUNDS A FIRE SIREN APPROACHING FROM DISTANCE. INCREASE SIREN SOUND UNDER ANNCR.)

ANNCR: In less than one and one-half minutes, the ceiling temperature would be 800 degrees; in a little over two minutes, 1200 degrees. If you were in the room at this point, you would be consumed by flames. But it wouldn't matter. You would already be dead from smoke and gas inhalation, a victim of one of the most misunderstood killers in America today—fire.

(SFX: OUT)

ANNCR: Diana Williams and WBTV News at 11:00 take a new look at fire this week in a revealing three-part series entitled "Fire: the New Alarm." It's about arson—for fun and profit. And it's about the growing number of fires in public buildings and fires in the home. Watch "Fire: the New Alarm" this week on WBTV News at 11:00.

272

(MUSIC: WHEN JOHNNY COMES MARCHING HOME AGAIN.)

ANNCR: In World War II, American soldiers returned home heros to confetti and ticker tape parades.

(SFX: WAR DEMONSTRATORS.)

ANNCR: In the Vietnam War, they came home to another kind of parade.

(MUSIC: WHEN JOHNNY COMES MARCHING HOME AGAIN.)

ANNCR: In World War II, soldiers were called patriots.

(SFX: WAR DEMONSTRATORS.)

ANNCR: In the Vietnam War, they were called baby killers.

(MUSIC: WHEN JOHNNY COMES MARCHING HOME AGAIN.)

ANNCR: In World War II, a soldier seemed to know who the enemy was.

(SFX: WAR DEMONSTRATORS.)

ANNCR: In the Vietnam War, it was sometimes hard to tell.

(MUSIC: WHEN JOHNNY COMES MARCHING HOME AGAIN.)

ANNCR: In World War II, soldiers came home and found jobs and became leaders in their communities.

(SFX: WAR DEMONSTRATORS.)

ANNCR: In the Vietnamese War, they came home and looked for jobs and wondered why. What did the Vietnamese War do to the people who fought in it, and why are many of them still fighting it? That's the subject of a three-part series entitled "The Vietnam Hangover" this week on WBTV News at 6:00. See it. And maybe you'll see why all the casualties of Vietnam haven't been counted yet.

(SFX: OUT)

273

(MUSIC)

WILLARD: Hey, Rafert

RAFERT: What ya need, Willard?

WILLARD: How come the radio don't work?

RAFERT: I don't know. What ya want the radio to work fer?

WILLARD: Well, we're goin' to be on it here pretty quick.

RAFERT: Oh, that's right.

WILLARD: Maybe I give it a little shake...

RAFERT: Oh, don't shake it, don't shake it. I've got a better idea.

WILLARD: What's that?

RAFERT: Why don't you plug it in?

WILLARD: Oh...ya.

RAFERT: (LAUGH)

(ANNCR. COPY)

(MUSIC)

WILLARD: Hey, Rafert, come in here, it's done!

RAFERT: What 'ya need phew...what are ya doin' in here.

WILLARD: Oh, I'm makin' up a batch of my Willard famous super duper hot horseradish sauce.

RAFERT: Aw...not again, you do that every fall. Lord! Nobody goin' to eat that stuff! I tried it last year and couldn't get my mouth to work for 5 days.

WILLARD: Oh, no. It's better this year. I changed the recipe.

RAFERT: What'd you do?

WILLARD: I added another half gallon of tobaski sauce and 4 ballbearings.

RAFERT: 4 ballbearings! What in the world are you puttin' ballbearings in the horseradish fer?

WILLARD: Tell when it's done! When they disappear, it's done!

RAFERT: Well, I ain't tastin' none.

WILLARD: Oh...here...I'll taste a little bit for you, show you it won't hurt you. Come on...here... watch this.

WILLARD: (TASTING SOUND)

RAFERT: You didn't even make a face!

WILLARD: Perfect! It's beautiful! It's delicate! It's wonderful! It's perfect! Ya gotta taste this, Rafert.

RAFERT: Well, maybe just a little bit.

WILLARD: Here...go ahead.

RAFERT: Oh...

WILLARD: Good! Huh?

RAFERT: Hm...

WILLARD: Need more wusti-sushti sauce?

RAFERT: Hm...Um...

WILLARD: Your goin' out on the porch?

RAFERT: Um...Hum...

WILLARD: Oh!...

RAFERT: Ah......!!!!!!!!!!!

WILLARD: Oh, PERFECT BATCH! (LAUGH)

(MUSIC)

Willard & Rafert have been brought to you today by your Paymaster dealer.

274
WRITER
David Metcalf

CLIENT
Maxell

AGENCY PRODUCER
Dane Johnson

AGENCY
Scali, McCabe, Sloves

275
WRITER
David Metcalf

CLIENT
Maxell

AGENCY PRODUCER
Dane Johnson

AGENCY
Scali, McCabe, Sloves

276
WRITER
Naomi Schwartz

CLIENT
Eastman Kodak

AGENCY PRODUCER
Ellen Linhart

AGENCY
J. Walter Thompson

277
WRITERS
Brian Sitts
Bonnie Berkowitz

CLIENT
Burger King

AGENCY PRODUCER
Gary Bass

AGENCY
J. Walter Thompson

278
WRITERS
Linda Kaplan
Robin Schwarz

CLIENT
Toys "R" Us

AGENCY PRODUCER
David Schneiderman

AGENCY
J. Walter Thompson

279
WRITERS
Linda Kaplan
Arthur Linowitz

CLIENT
Burger King

AGENCY PRODUCER
Meredith Wright

AGENCY
J. Walter Thompson

280
WRITERS
Ann Winn
Garrett Brown

CLIENT
Molson Golden Beer

AGENCY PRODUCERS
Gene Novak
Bill Hamilton

AGENCY
Rumrill-Hoyt

274

(SFX: ELECTRONIC EFFECTS THROUGHOUT.)

NEW WAVE VOICE: New wave should not be recorded on punk tape. And a cassette is the perfect place to hide punk workmanship. Something you won't find in a Maxell cassette. So don't get stuck with a punk tape, get Maxell tape. It's worth it.

275

(MUSIC: RIDE OF THE VALKYRIES FIVE SECONDS CLEAR THEN THROUGHOUT.)

VO: Even after five hundred plays...Maxell high fidelity tape...still delivers...High fidelity.

NEIGHBOR: Hey you in there...

(SFX: THUMP! THUMP!)

NEIGHBOR: Give me a break.

VO: Because at Maxell we make tape to standards that are 60% higher than the industry calls for. Precision engineered tape that retains the clarity you recorded long after ordinary tapes have worn themselves out.

(SFX: THUMP! THUMP! THUMP!)

NEIGHBOR: How many times you gonna play that thing?

VO: So try Maxell. And play, after play, after play, the only noticeable thing you'll wear down...

NEIGHBOR: Please...I can't take it anymore...

VO: Is your neighbors.

NEIGHBOR: I beg of you.

(SFX: MUSIC UP. THUMP! THUMP! THUMP!)

VO: Maxell. It's worth it.

276

BUD: Hey pallie, what's dis?

LOU: This is the *Disc*.

BUD: Dat's what I said. What's dis?

LOU: The *Disc*.

BUD: Dis is the dis?

LOU: This is the *Disc* film that goes into the new Kodak *Disc* camera.

BUD: Dis camera is a dis camera. What's dat?

LOU: A Disc camera. It's the new camera from Kodak that anybody can use.

BUD: Yeah? Even me?

LOU: Of course...just press this button and the Kodak *Disc* camera does it all. It reads the light...

BUD: Dis camera can read?

LOU: The light. It knows exactly when to flash. And it can flash again in 1⅓ seconds.

BUD: Oh, dat's fast.

LOU: No, that's the *Disc* camera. It even advances the film automatically.

BUD: You mean dat camera does all dis?

LOU: No...the *Disc* camera does all that.

BUD: Dat's what I said. But what's dis camera called?

LOU: It's the Kodak *Disc* camera.

BUD: Right...but if dat camera is dis camera, than what's dis camera called?

LOU: The Kodak *Disc* camera.

BUD: Oh...

277

ANNCR: Did you know when you buy a regular burger at McDonald's, they make it with twenty percent less meat than the regular burger you get at Burger King?

GIRL: They do?

GIRL: Holy bananas!

BOY: Holy cow!

BOY: I didn't know.

GIRL: Am I allowed to tell anybody this?

ANNCR: It's true. Before cooking, McDonald's regular hamburger has twenty percent less meat than the regular burger at Burger King. (Difference is less after cooking.) Why would McDonald's do that?

BOY: I don't know.

BOY: Cause they want people to be skinny!

BOY: I am so *angry* about that!

ANNCR: Now that you know there's more meat in a regular Burger King burger, how do you feel about Burger King?

GIRL: I just guess Burger King cares more.

BOY: I love Burger King.

BOY: A burger at Burger King is so delicious, they're so good!

BOY: I get so hungry I can eat a cow.

SINGERS: *Aren't you hungry*
Aren't you hungry
Aren't you hungry for Burger King now?

278

SINGERS: *I don't want to grow up*
I'm a Toys "R" Us kid
There's a million toys at Toys "R" Us
That I can play with

BOY: Toys "R" Us is terrific.

BOY: There's a lot of toys here.

BOY: Thousands.

GIRL: Toys "R" Us has everything.

GIRL: They don't sell fruits.

GIRL: Just toys.

BOY: And record players.

SINGERS: *I don't want to grow up*
I'm a Toys "R" Us kid
They got the best for so much less
You'll really flip your lid

BOY: Things are less expensive and I like the toys.

GIRL: Spectacular.

GIRL: Terrific.

BOY: This is really a great place.

SINGERS: *From bikes to trains to video games*
It's the biggest toy store there is.

BOY: Kids think it's fun because there's toys in it.

BOY: It's so big I think it's the only one that great.

SINGERS: *I don't want to grow up*
cause baby if I did
I couldn't be a Toys "R" Us kid

BOY: I've been coming here for a long, long time since I was little.

SINGERS: *I wanna be a Toys "R" Us kid*

BOY: I love you Toys "R" Us, I mean it.

279

(AREN'T YOU HUNGRY 50's DOO-WOP STYLE SINGING)

ANNCR: Remember how hungry you were for your first flame-broiled burger at Burger King?

(AREN'T YOU HUNGRY BEATLES STYLE "YEAH, YEAH, YEAH")

ANNCR: Then the years rolled by and you tried your first Burger King Double Cheeseburger. And it was groovy.

(AREN'T YOU HUNGRY 70's DISCO-STYLE)

ANNCR: And remember when you dug into your first Double Whopper? Yeah, you sure were hungry then!

(DISCO SEGUES TO CONTEMPORARY ROCK)

ANNCR: And now, (BACON) when you're hungrier than ever. (BACON) Burger King introduces the new Bacon Double Cheeseburger.

SINGERS: *Aren't you hungry?*

ANNCR: Two juicy flame-broiled burgers.

SINGERS: *Aren't you hungry?*

ANNCR: Thick, rich, melted cheese

SINGERS: *Aren't you hungry?*

ANNCR: Topped with lean, sizzlin' crispy bacon. The new Bacon Double Cheeseburger at Burger King
I'm tellin' ya, there's never been a better time to be hungry.

(DOO-WOP A CAPELLA STYLE)
Wish we had the Bacon Double Cheeseburger back then. Ooh-wee-ooh-wee-ooh.

280

WOMAN: Excuse me, is this stool taken?

MAN: Ah, no, help yourself.

WOMAN: Oh good. Do you mind if I sit here? No? Thanks.

MAN: Would you pass me the peanuts?

WOMAN: Sure.
Oh, Oh! I'm terribly sorry. Oh, I have ruined that tie and it's so beautiful too. Let me wipe it off. Ah, that's a very interesting cologne you're wearing.

MAN: What? It's beer.

WOMAN: (LAUGHING) Oh I'm sorry, let me buy you another one, please.

MAN: No that's all right, I'll just suck my tie.

WOMAN: Let me make it up to you. How about a Molson Golden?

MAN: Molson Golden?

WOMAN: Ya, imported from Canada. It's excellent, crisp, clear. You'll really love it.

MAN: Ah ya, ya.

WOMAN: You will?

MAN: Are you trying to pick me up?

WOMAN: (LAUGHING) The thought never entered my mind.

MAN: Well, think.

ANNCR: Molson Golden, smooth and easy. That's Canadian for great taste. Molson Golden, imported by Martlet Importing Co., Great Neck, N.Y.

MAN: Well! You're not doing a very good job of this.

WOMAN: I know, let me start over. Is this stool taken?
(LAUGHING)

MAN: (LAUGHING) Hold the peanuts.

Consumer Radio Single

281
WRITERS
Ann Winn
Garrett Brown
CLIENT
Molson Golden Beer
AGENCY PRODUCERS
Gene Novak
Bill Hamilton
AGENCY
Rumrill-Hoyt

282 SILVER
WRITERS
John Cleese
Lynn Stiles
CLIENT
Callard & Bowser/USA
AGENCY PRODUCER
Robert L. Dein
AGENCY
Lord, Geller, Federico,
Einstein

283
WRITER
Lee Garfinkel
CLIENT
The Entertainment Channel
AGENCY PRODUCER
Rachel Novak
AGENCY
Levine, Huntley, Schmidt
& Beaver

284
WRITER
Lee Garfinkel
CLIENT
The Entertainment Channel
AGENCY PRODUCER
Rachel Novak
AGENCY
Levine, Huntley, Schmidt
& Beaver

285
WRITER
Barry Dickson
CLIENT
Savin
AGENCY PRODUCER
Barry Dickson
AGENCY
Sklar-Lenett Associates

286
WRITERS
Ann Winn
Garrett Brown
CLIENT
Molson Golden Beer
AGENCY PRODUCERS
Gene Novak
Bill Hamilton
AGENCY
Rumrill-Hoyt

287
WRITER
Jack Supple
CLIENT
Oak Grove Dairy
AGENCY PRODUCER
Jack Supple
AGENCY
Carmichael-Lynch/Mpls.

288
WRITER
D.J. Webster
CLIENT
Speedy Muffler
AGENCY PRODUCER
Michael E. Doran
AGENCY
Doyle Dane Bernbach

281

MAN: Oh Miss!

WOMAN: Ya?

MAN: Any bones broken?

WOMAN: No, I'm fine, I'm fine I'm just having a hard time getting down.

MAN: We know, we've been watching you for an hour from the lodge.

WOMAN: Ya, well, these moguls, they're just too much, and look at this slope.

MAN: This is the expert slope. How many lumps do you have?

WOMAN: It is! Three.

MAN: I mean, you have fallen down more than anyone I have ever seen.

WOMAN: Ya, I was considering taking off my skis and rolling down, but really, I want to get back to the lodge.

MAN: It's getting dark. It's 4:30. Please get in the snowcab. We'll drive you back down. I'll buy you a beer.

WOMAN: This is so embarrassing!

MAN: I'll buy you a Molson Golden.

WOMAN: No, I can, I can...

MAN: You can tell them you rescued me.

WOMAN: Ah, a Molson Golden.

MAN: C'mon, cool, clear, crisp and clean. Imported from Canada.

WOMAN: Sounds good, not a bad idea.

MAN: But I recommend you never go.

ANNCR: Molson Golden. Smooth and easy. That's Canadian for great taste. Molson Golden, imported by Martlet Importing Co., Great Neck, N.Y.

WOMAN: What is it you think I'm doing wrong?

MAN: I think you have only one problem with skiing.

WOMAN: What's that?

MAN: Gravity.

282 SILVER

Hallo there. Look, apparently last time I was on the radio, talking about this frightfully good rather sophisticated English candy, when I said the name of the people who make this candy, which is Callard and Bowser, I didn't say Callard and Bowser terribly clearly and so all you good American persons have been going into Supermarkets and Drugstores asking for Bollard and Trouser, and Callous and Grocer, Gizzard and Powder, so let's get the name straight, shall we, it's Callard and Bowser. Cal-lard... Cal as in *Cal*vin Coolidge and lard as in Jess Wil*lard* and Bowser, that's Bow as in the *Bau*haus, or better still Mutiny on the *Bou*nty and - ser, as in Pan*zer* Division. So if you want to try the best most sophisticated and upper class candy we make in England, it's quite simple, all you have to do is think of *Cal*vin Coolidge and Jess Wil*lard*, *and* as in Hans Christian *And*ersen and then the *Bau*haus or Mutiny on the *Bou*nty and a Pan*zer* Division, Callard and Bowser. It may take a little time to get hold of but I think you'll find it's worth it.

283

ANNCR: Since television is the world's most powerful form of communication, let's look at how network executives might decide what this awesome technology should communicate.

EXEC 1: We need a show about a single mother who moves her two kids to the city from the country.

EXEC 2: Sounds complicated.

EXEC 3: Not enough realism.

EXEC 4: Realism isn't good for ratings.

EXEC 1: I have a *big* idea, make it a divorced uncle with two nieces and a talking chimp.

EXEC 2: Chimps are out.

EXEC 3: Chimps don't appeal to women 14-85.

EXEC 4: Chimps aren't good for ratings.

EXEC 1: How about a single parent with nine kids who can't pay the mortgage.

EXEC 2&3: That's a great idea for a comedy.

EXEC 4: Great ideas aren't good for ratings.

EXEC 1: Make it a summer replacement for a miniseries.

EXEC 2: Sounds like a spinoff.

EXEC 3: Can we spinoff a spinoff?

EXEC 4: Spinoffs of spinoffs aren't good for ratings.

ANNCR: For people who aren't satisfied with the level of television, we introduce a new pay television network, The Entertainment Channel. Commercial-free, quality programming you won't see anywhere else. The Entertainment Channel. When you've outgrown ordinary television like...

EXEC 1: A variety show about an undercover cop posing as a foreign exchange student hosting a game show...

284

ANNCR: Over the years, television has given us a lot of programming. Unfortunately, it hasn't given us a lot of different programming.

VOICE #1: (QUICKLY) Ironside was a cop who couldn't walk, Longstreet was a cop who couldn't see, Columbo was a cop who couldn't stop eating.

VOICE #2: (QUICKLY) Then there were shows like Alice, Hazel, Benson, Phyllis, Flipper...

VOICE #3: ...M Squad, Racket Squad, Mod Squad, Rat Patrol, Highway Patrol, the FBI, Today's FBI, Hawaiian Eye, Hawaii Five-O, Harry-O, Adam 12 and Surfside Six.

VOICE #4: (QUICKLY) Plus—Life With Father, Bachelor Father, Father Knows Best, The Courtship of Eddie's Father.

VOICE #1: (QUICKLY) And on Bewitched *she* made objects disappear. My Favorite Martian—he made *objects* disappear. I Dream of Jeannie—she made objects *disappear*.

VOICE #2: (QUICKLY) And a series of miniseries, maxi series, limited series, summer series, semi-series...

ANNCR: If all this sounds familiar, it is. That's why we're introducing a new pay television network, The Entertainment Channel. Commercial-free, quality programming you won't see anywhere else. The Entertainment Channel. When you've outgrown ordinary television like...

VOICE #4: (QUICKLY) Love Boat, Love of Life, Joannie Loves Chachi, Bridget Loves Bernie.

285

OPERATOR: That's Savin, ma'm. Booth 90. (CLICK) (RING) Office Equipment Show. Switchboard.

CALLER 1: I'm looking for the copiers with interest-free leases.

OPR.: That's the Savin booth. (CLICK) (RING) Equipment Show.

CALLER 2: I heard someone's offering free supplies and service with their copiers.

OPR.: Savin. (CLICK) (RING) Show.

CALLER 3: Someone's leasing a copier for only $89 a month?

OPR.: (GETTING ANGRY) Savin. (CLICK) (RING) Show.

CALLER 4: Is there an interest-free...

OPR.: Savin! (CLICK) (RING)

CALLER 5: Uh...

OPR.: (FREAKING OUT) Savin! All right! Savin! Who's leasing copiers interest free? Savin! Who also has other deals that include free supplies? Savin! Who has a copier that's only $89 a month? Savin! Whatever you're asking, the answer is Savin. Who was 16th president of the United States? Abraham Savin!! OK! Savin, *Savin*!

286

PILOT: We'll be flying at 35 thousand feet...

WOMAN: Can I get you something?

MAN: Um, I'd like a beer.

WOMAN: O.K.

MAN: Molson Golden.

WOMAN: Ah, Um, I'm afraid we don't serve Molson Golden in main cabin.

MAN: Really, well you do serve it in First Class. I have seen the bottles go by, the smiling faces...

WOMAN: Oh ya, I know.

MAN: I mean that's really what I want, that's my brand.

WOMAN: I understand Molson Golden is really good but I don't have it.

MAN: Crisp, clean taste, clear, fresh, imported daily from Canada.

WOMAN: Right, I know.

MAN: How can you force a passenger to do without Molson Golden?

WOMAN: I am sorry, but why didn't you buy a ticket in First Class?

MAN: Had I known, I certainly would have. Do you think you could just sort of sneak up there, sneak back one?

WOMAN: If I bring one back, everyone will want one.

MAN: How about putting it in a bag?

WOMAN: Ah, I don't have a bag.

MAN: Ah well, you could use this bag.

WOMAN: Ah, (LAUGHING) all right.

ANNCR: Molson Golden, smooth and easy. That's Canadian for great taste. Molson Golden, imported by Martlet Importing Co., Great Neck, N.Y.

MAN: Thank you.

WOMAN: You know this is the first time I ever brought one of these back to a passenger.

MAN: That's great. You got an opener?

WOMAN: Sorry, we only have openers in First Class.

MAN: What!

(LAUGHING...)

287

FRAN: The Oak Grove Dairy in Norwood, Minnnesota, will soon celebrate its 50th Anniversary. Ort Paulson knows that one thing has surely changed over the years—bringing home milk in the carton is considerably easier than bringing home milk...in the cow.

(SFX: WIND BLOWING ON MICROPHONE, BIRDS CHIRPING IN FIELD)

ORT: I'm out in this field to help call the cows home. Lot of times they put the cattle out to pasture for the day and you've got to call them in. So here we go.

(CALLING) Come-Boss! Come-Boss! Come-Boss!

(LONG PAUSE; NOTHING HAPPENS)

(LOUDER) COME-BOSS! COME-BOSS! COME-BOSS!

(STILL NOTHING)

FRAN: (CHUCKLES) Bring home a carton of fresh Oak Grove Dairy milk. It's like bringing home the cows, only easier. Oak Grove Dairy. After 50 years, they really know their cows.

ORT: Here, one's moving...she stopped now. Awww, come-Boss, come-Boss, come-Boss (FADE)

288

GUY: Hi, I need my muffler fixed in a hurry, so I came to you guys at Speedy Muffler King. Now, how fast are your mechanics?

(SFX: WOOSH.........)

GUY: That's pretty fast.

SPM: Yes, Sir.

GUY: What???

SPM: Yes, Sir.

GUY: Hey, don't tell me that you guys at Speedy are so quick you even talk fast?

SPM: Yes, Sir, you got it!

GUY: (LAUGHING) Now, before you work on my car, I want to know if you have a *guaranteed estimate*.

SPM: (GIBBERISH)

GUY: What????...

SPM: Right!

GUY: Oh, you guarantee that my price will never be more than my written estimate.

SPM: That's what I said...

GUY: If you have to do any extra work, you'll do it for free.

SPM: Right!

GUY: Wow!! Okay, *give me an estimate*.

SPM: Here!!!

GUY: You're done. (LAUGHING)

SPM: Yes, Sir.

GUY: Okay. Now go to work on my muffler.

(SFX: WOOOSH.........)

GUY: You're done again.

SPM: Yes, Sir.

GUY: You guys are too much.

SPM: I know, I know!!

GUY: Hey, you know I could use a cup of coffee...

GUY: It's instant!!! (LAUGHING)

SPM: LAUGHING

289

ANNCR: Betty Camastro?

BETTY: Yes!

ANNCR: This is your vacation. Yesterday while you were trying on bikinis in Florida, your life back home was changing.

BETTY: What??

ANNCR: Your brother Rick, the best carpenter in Chicago...

BETTY: He's very good...

ANNCR: Hit himself in the head with a hammer.

BETTY: Oh no!!!

ANNCR: And was taken to a special hospital.

BETTY: Where??

ANNCR: In Bolivia.

BETTY: What!!!!

ANNCR: Even though he was unconscious it would've been nice to call.

BETTY: I don't speak Bolivian.

ANNCR: And then there's your dog!

BETTY: Oh no!!

ANNCR: He missed you so much that he left Chicago to find you, and was last seen in Montreal.

(SFX: DOG BARKING...)

ANNCR: You could've called, Betty. If your dog could've just heard your voice it would've been enough.

BETTY: Oh no, no...

ANNCR: General Telephone just wants to remind you that while you're on vacation call home—to let everyone know what a wonderful time you're having and to make sure that everything's just the way you left it.

290

Hallo... Um... look there's some frightfully good rather sophisticated English candy now being sold in the US of A, it's terribly popular among the upper classes here in England so please do try some. It's called Callard and Bowser candy and it's butterscotch and toffee and toffee comes in seven exciting new flavours, Raspberry, Aubergine, Smoky Passionfruit, Mackerel, Pork and Prune, Lamb and Banana, and the flavour of the month Leather, Tangerine and Raccoon, a new taste sensation... I'm sorry those aren't the flavours at all, I made them up, it was a cheap trick to catch your attention, and I'm very ashamed of myself because the real flavours are perfectly sensible and quite delicious, and rather sophisticated because Callard and Bowser candy isn't quite as sweet as ordinary candy, so it appeals to rather sophisticated, urbane, educated people who wouldn't like silly publicity stunts about Leather Tangerine and Raccoon flavoured toffee at all. So please forgive me; completely ignore this commercial. Forget all about it and simply try some of Callard and Bowser's candy and I promise not to be naughty again.

291

(SFX: RESTAURANT SOUNDS IN BACKGROUND)

ANNCR: Fellow came in the other day and said,

INDIANA FELLOW: I've been hearing about this Pagliai's Pizza all the way to Indiana.

ANNCR: I've been hearing about this Pagliai's Pizza all the way to Indiana.

INDIANA FELLOW: They say you aren't fast...

ANNCR: They say you aren't fast...

INDIANA FELLOW: Just how long *does* it take to get one?

ANNCR: Just how long *does* it take to get one? We said, twenty minutes. And he said...

INDIANA FELLOW: All right, I'll try it. Put me one on.

ANNCR: All right, I'll try it. Put me one on... and we did. We told him that what most folks mean is that we aren't a fast food pizza operation. What we are is a genuine, home owned, home operated pizza parlour.

INDIANA FELLOW: Yeah, well, I've never really been in one of those...

ANNCR: He said he'd never really been in one of those... and we told him he'd taste the difference...

INDIANA FELLOW: Great!

ANNCR: And he did...

INDIANA FELLOW: Hey, I hear you make the crust, the sauce, *everything* right here in this kitchen every day.

ANNCR: He said he heard we make the crust, the sauce, *everything* right here in this kitchen every day... which we do... but, like we told him, the cooking never enters your mind. All that's important is that anytime you come into Pagliai's you're only twenty minutes away from the best pizza in the State of Kentucky...

INDIANA FELLOW: Betcha nobody ever complains about those twenty minutes, huh?

ANNCR: He asked if anybody ever complains about those twenty minutes...

INDIANA FELLOW: Hey, 20 minutes... what's that?

ANNCR: We told him nobody in their right mind has complained about it yet...

INDIANA FELLOW: Well, let me tell you, it was worth every minute of it...

ANNCR: 753-2975

(FADE SFX.)

292

ANNCR: The BMW 320i has always been engineered to outperform conventional status symbols. But last year, it also outperformed what is arguably the most coveted status symbol of them all—the dollar.

According to the U.S. Bureau of Labor Statistics, the dollar retained 91.1% of its value last year. But according to the National Automobile Dealers Association's Used-Car Guide, the BMW 320i retained an astonishing 97.7% of its value.

In fact, the 320i has outperformed the dollar, not to mention most status symbols of the 4-wheeled variety, in every year of its existence.

The BMW 320i.

A better value for your money.

And maybe even a better value *than* money.

293

EDITH: (SINGING TO HERSELF) LaLaLaLa...

(SFX: CAR DOOR OPEN AND CLOSE. RRRRRRR OF CAR NOT STARTING.)

EDITH: Oh dear.

(SFX: RRRRRRR.)

EDITH: Oh dear, oh dear.

VO: This week, at Montgomery Ward Auto Centers, the Getaway 48 battery is on sale for just $47.97 with trade-in.

(SFX: RRRRRRR.)

EDITH: Oh dear, oh dear, oh dear.

VO: The sale lasts only till Saturday, and it's your chance to save $12 on a Montgomery Ward's Getaway 48 battery in sizes to fit practically any car, U.S. or import.

(SFX: DIALING A PAY TELEPHONE. AS NUMBERS BEEP, WE HEAR THE LADY MUMBLING TO HERSELF.)

EDITH: Oh dear, oh dear, oh dear, oh dear.

VO: And if you come to Montgomery Ward by Saturday, you'll get free installation, and a free check of your electrical system, in addition to the $12 savings.

(SFX: PHONE RING.)

HAROLD (ON PHONE): Hello?

EDITH: Oh, dear?

VO: The Getaway 48. On sale for just $47.97 with trade-in through Saturday at Montgomery Ward Auto Centers.
Where you can buy your next car battery in the best way possible...On Sale.

294 GOLD

Hallo, have you heard about this rather unusual English candy which has a more sophisticated kind of taste than regular candy, not quite as sweet but a very fine classy sort of taste, and it's made by an English firm called Callard and Bowser and it really is jolly good. In fact, the truth is, it's jolly, jolly good, and you'll like it, and as I say it *is* English so please buy it because we need the money in England at the moment, I mean we're all as poor as church mice now, servants are unbelievably expensive and our industry's practically disappeared, about all we make is muffins and cricket bats and really good candy and half the cricket bats come from Hong Kong, so please, do us a favour and just try this Callard and Bowser candy, its rather sophisticated taste and I'm sure you'll approve of it and after all, I mean we did fight on your side in the War and we always let you beat us at golf and incidentally, let's not forget you pinched our language, if we hadn't forgotten to copyright that you'd be paying us the most amazing royalties every week so instead please buy Callard and Bowser's rather sophisticated English candy and help England back on its feet, frankly I think it's the least you can do.

295

ANNCR: The best pizza in the State of Kentucky. Step #6, *Roll Call.* Who drives those seven delivery vehicles that deliver 120 pizzas all over town every night? Well, call 753-2975 and order your Pagliai's Pizza and you might find it delivered...

DELIVERY BOY #1: (INTERRUPTS) Hot!

ANNCR: ...by a fellow named Charlie "Flat Out" Vella...

DELIVERY BOY #2: (MAKES SOUNDS LIKE A '55 CHEVY REVVING UP, DRIVING OFF AND CONTINUING THROUGH ENTIRE SPOT.)

DELIVERY BOY #3: (MAKES SOUNDS LIKE A SAAB, 2-CYCLE, NO MUFFLER, CONTINUING THROUGHOUT SPOT.)

ANNCR: ...or Clark "Screech" Sheeks...

DELIVERY BOY #4: (MAKES SOUNDS LIKE A MASERATI GHIBLI-5TH GEAR — FLAT OUT)

ANNCR: ...or "Jim Wheelie"...

DELIVERY BOY #1: (INTERRUPTS) That's Tim.

ANNCR: (CHUCKLES) That's Tim...

DELIVERY BOY #5: (MAKES SOUND LIKE '62 CORVETTE OVERTAKING THE MASERATI.)

ANNCR: ...or "Hot Rod" Harrison...

DELIVERY BOY #6: (MAKES SOUNDS LIKE GMC PICKUP WITH BLOWN HEAD GASKET HAVING TROUBLE GETTING STARTED THROUGHOUT SPOT.)

ANNCR: ...or "Blitz Fritz"...

DELIVERY BOY #7: (MAKES SOUNDS LIKE 1953 NASH RAMBLER— SORT OF A WHEEZING SOUND.)

ANNCR: ...or "Lightnin' Rude"...

DELIVERY BOY #8: (MAKES SOUNDS LIKE '67 CHEVY LAYING DOWN RUBBER IN 2ND GEAR.)

ANNCR: ...or "Mad Mark"...

DELIVERY BOY #9: (MAKES SOUNDS LIKE 1926 JOHN DEERE PICKUP IN A HARD PULL.)

DELIVERY BOY #4: (MASERATI DOWN-SHIFTS TO 3RD GEAR COMING INTO A CURVE.)

ANNCR: ...or "Freeway" Hatcher...

DELIVERY BOY #10: (MAKES SOUNDS LIKE DATSUN 240 Z CHANGING GEARS TO PASS THE PICKUP.)

ANNCR: ...or "No Stall" Paul...all driving the best pizza in the State of Kentucky to your door any hour from 4 p.m. till 1 a.m.

DELIVERY BOY #1: (INTERRUPTS AGAIN) 2 a.m. on weekends!

ANNCR: All right, 2 a.m. on weekends...Look for 'em...

(SFX: ALL DELIVERY BOYS INTERRUPT WITH CAR SOUNDS GETTING LOUDER...DOWN SHIFTING...UP SHIFTING)

ANNCR: Look for 'em...

(SFX: CAR SOUNDS GET LOUDER)

ANNCR: LOOK for 'em within about 40 minutes from the time...

(SFX: CAR SOUNDS GET EVEN LOUDER...TIRES SCREECHING...ENGINES SCREAMING)

ANNCR: (Laughs) Yeah, I go through this all the time...Look for 'em within about 40 minutes from the time you call Pagliai's...

(SFX: IT NOW SOUNDS LIKE A RACETRACK)

ANNCR: ...753-2975. Oh, and do try to have the right change...

(SFX: CARS BEGIN TO BACKFIRE)

ANNCR: We let this bunch carry pizza...not money. Pagliai's, 753-

(SFX: ALL CARS BACKFIRE, SQUEAL TIRES, ETC.)

ANNCR: ...2975.

296
WRITER
Carol Lloyd
CLIENT
Carlton & United Breweries
AGENCY PRODUCER
Carol Lloyd
AGENCY
George Patterson (Brisbane)
PTY. LTD./Australia

297
WRITER
Paul Wilson
CLIENT
Amatil PTY. LTD.
Stud Cola
AGENCY PRODUCER
Paul Wilson
AGENCY
Monahan Dayman Adams
(NSW) PTY. LTD./Australia

298
WRITERS
Jack Foster
Bill Bartley
CLIENT
Atlantic Richfield
AGENCY PRODUCER
Pat Garvin
AGENCY
Foote, Cone & Belding/Honig-
Los Angeles

299
WRITER
Kerry Feuerman
CLIENT
Hot Springs Auto Wash
AGENCY PRODUCER
Kerry Feuerman
AGENCY
Siddall, Matus & Coughter/
Virginia

300
WRITERS
Tom McElligott
Mal Sharpe
CLIENT
Pontillos Pizzeria
AGENCY PRODUCER
Tom McElligott
AGENCY
Fallon, McElligott, Rice/Mpls.

301
WRITERS
Martin Greenhouse
Joel Greenhouse
Susan Borneman
CLIENT
WNEW
AGENCY PRODUCER
Martin Greenhouse
AGENCY
Berenter Greenhouse Elgort

302
WRITER
David Ham
CLIENT
Northside Bank (San Antonio)
AGENCY PRODUCER
David Ham
AGENCY
Reed Ham Jackson/Texas

296

UNISON MALE VOCAL: *It's - the -*
Rippa Bewdy Bonza Bottla Brisbane Bitter
Beer Sale
Buy a stack and save a packet
Sockin' down a cold ale
Crack a trout - don't hang about
We'll put you on the right trail
Rippa Bewdy Bonza Bottla Brisbane Bitter
Beer Sale.

MALE VOICE (1): Hey Frank! - can you give us a
lift down the pub?

MALE VOICE (2): Sure mate - something wrong with
your car?

VOICE (1): No, but there's this Rippa Bewdy Bonza
Bottla Brisbane Bitter Beer Sale on, ya see, and
me and the blokes thought we'd pick up a few
bottles while they're going cheap - should just
about fit in yours. . . .

VOICE (2): Bewdy! - hop in!

(SFX: AIR BRAKE RELEASE, SEMI ROARS OFF)

MALE VOCAL (1): Rippa!

MALE VOCAL (2): Bewdy!

MALE VOCAL (3): Bonza!

MALE VOCAL (4): Bottla!

UNISON: Brisbane Bitter Beer Sale!

VOICE (3): *On now!*

VOICE (1): . . . A man 'ud be a mug to miss it!

297

(SFX: MUSIC IN. IT BEGINS IN AN ALMOST-ROMANTIC MOOD.)

MACKA: (UNUSUALLY SUBDUED)
I'd cross the hottest desert
Without a pair of shades.

MAXINE: Oh Macka.

MACKA: *And crawl a mile on broken glass*
And rusty razor blades.

MAXINE: Isn't he a dreamboat?

MACKA: *I'd climb a nest of soldier ants completely*
in the (nudd).

MAXINE: I love it when he talks like that.

MACKA: *I'd even swap old Maxine here,*
For a drink of that new Stud.

MAXINE: Stud?

LYRIC: *Gimme a Stud*
Gimme a Stud
The ban is over, so somebody gimme a Stud.
(MUSIC CONTINUES)

MACKA: It's drinking time again, people! Stud Cola's
back.

MAXINE: How could you talk about swapping me,
Macka? How could you?

LYRIC: *Gimme a Stud.*
Gimme a Stud
Let's get drinking so somebody gimme a Stud.
(MUSIC CONTINUES)

MACKA: Drink like there's no tomorrow people.
Nothing in the world tastes better than an ice
cold Stud Cola.

MAXINE: What about me, Macka? What about me?

LYRIC: (LAST PHRASE BUILDS)
Give 'er a Stud!

298

INTERVR: Yes, you're a 4-cylinder 3-year old car. . . tell
me what's wrong.

CAR: I can't get star-star-star-star-started in the
morning.

INTERVR: Hmmnn. Sounds to me like your owner's
been gambling with tune-ups.

CAR: He sure-sure-sure-sure-sure has.

INTERVR: Well, introducing MP&G Tune-Up Centers.
They take the gamble out of tuning your car.

CAR: Ha-ha-ha-ha-ha, how?

INTERVR: With a guarantee from ARCO. ARCO
guarantees you'll like your MP&G Tune-Up or
ARCO will return your money.

CAR: AR-AR-AR-AR-AR . . .

INTERVR: (Interrupting and irritated) Yes, ARCO.
And the suggested price is only $45.95 for a
4-cylinder car, including parts, labor, and taxes.
So you see, you don't have to gamble with
tune-ups anymore.

CAR: Th-th-th-th-th-th-thanks.

INTERVR: Nurse, get in here quickly.

LIVE ANNCR: ARCO MP&G Tune-Up Centers.

299

ANNCR: This year, billions of bugs will lose their lives
on the nation's highways. Chances are, a lot of
them will end up on the front of your car. And if
you don't get them off, they'll come back to
haunt you.

(SFX: MUSIC AND SOUND EFFECTS UNDER)

ANNCR: You see, as bugs decompose, they give off a
strong acid that actually eats away at your car's
chrome and paint. . . making it dull. The hotter
the weather, the faster the acid is made.

But there is a brighter side to all of this: come to
Hot Springs Auto Wash. We've developed a
way to completely remove bugs before they kill
your car's finish.

In fact, Hot Springs is the only car wash to make
this guarantee: If you find as much as one
single little mosquito on your car after we've
washed and dried it, we'll give you your two
dollars and ninety cents back.

(SFX: MUSIC AND SFX OUT)

ANNCR: Next time, we'll talk to you about the
problem with birds.

(SFX: BIRDS CHIRPING)

300

MAL: From Rome, Italy, we're really here. This is Mal Sharpe. I'm at a huge outdoor market and I'm trying to get some Romans to eat some Pontillo's pizza.

FIRST MALE VO: Ma come e fatta.

FEMALE INTERPRETER: What kind of stuff is this?, he says.

MAL: This is the best pizza in the world.

FIRST MALE VO: Questa pizza qui e schifosa.

FEMALE INTERPRETER: He said... that in Naples they make the best pizza in the world.

MAL: He's never had pizza from Minnesota. Now, look, your friend over here is making the O.K. sign.

SECOND MALE VO: E buona.

MAL: E buona. Si, e buona.

FEMALE INTERPRETER: He will try.

MAL: He's gonna try it. You gotta grow up in... people are honking. We're almost getting run over here now as a little orange car is getting us out of the way. Now, he is eating it here. Now, how is it?

SECOND MALE VO: 'Tis very good, this pizza.

MAL: Tell him I will take him to Minneapolis today to taste real pizza. On the airplane...

FEMALE INTERPRETER: Ti porta in America e ti fa...

SECOND MALE VO: Ma mia moglie non vuole. Vado solo io.

FEMALE INTERPRETER: His wife doesn't want him to go.

FEMALE INTERPRETER: He wants to leave his wife here.

MAL: A whole crowd around us here now. Now everybody wants Pontillo's pizza.

SECOND MALE VO: Ma che e buona.

301

(SFX: SOUND OF TELEPHONE DIALING)

MAN: Hi Marcie, this is Greg. Greg Snead. S-N-E-A-D. We met last night at the bar. Listen, I thought you and I could go out sometime. Oh, you're getting married? Tomorrow? Well, call me if it doesn't work out. (CLICK)

(DIALING SOUNDS)

Hi Vivian, this is Greg. Greg Snead. S-N-E-A-D. We met last night at the bar. Funny thing, you gave me the wrong number. It was for Con Ed, but I found you; lucky break, huh. Listen, you want to go out sometime? Oh, you're leaving the country. Tomorrow? Bon Voyage. (CLICK)

(DIALING SOUNDS)

Hello Betsy, this is Greg. Greg Snead. S-N Hello? Hello?

(DIALING SOUNDS)

VOICE: Hello, this is Dr. Ruth Westheimer, you are on the air.

ANNCR: If you're looking for advice on personal relationships tune in every Monday thru Friday morning at 9:30 to the Dr. Ruth Show on Channel 5.

SINGERS: *Your choice is 5*

302

CHORUS (SUNG): *Northside's bank is Northside Bank.*

RECEPTIONIST: Hello, Northside Bank.

CHORUS (SUNG): *Let's talk banking one-to-one.*

MAN: Yeah, uh—are you the executive vice president or the vice president or the president or...?

BANKER: No, no, I'm just Allen.

MAN: Oh, thank goodness.

CHORUS (SUNG): *Let's talk banking one-to-one.*

WOMAN: Congratulations on your new promotion.

BANKER: Thank you.

WOMAN: When should I come around to meet your replacement?

BANKER: Oh, I'll still be handling your account—if you *want* me to.

WOMAN: Wow. And you're a vice president.

CHORUS (SUNG): *Let's talk banking one-to-one.*

SECOND MAN: I got this little business, you know? Little music store, you know? But... I don't guess you're interested—it's retail...

BANKER: *Sure*, I'm interested, Jim.

SECOND MAN: You *are*?

CHORUS (SUNG): *Let's talk banking one-to-one.*

ANNCR: If your bank has changed into a big corporation, now's the time for you to change banks. Pick up the phone and call 732-7111.

CHORUS (SUNG): *We're Northside Bank.*

ANNCR: Northside Bank is a member of FDIC.

303
WRITERS
David Ham
Dirk Ronk
CLIENT
Victoria Bank & Trust
AGENCY PRODUCERS
David Ham
Dirk Ronk
AGENCY
Reed Ham Jackson/Texas

304
WRITERS
Brian Sitts
Bonnie Berkowitz
CLIENT
Burger King
AGENCY PRODUCER
Gary Bass
AGENCY
J. Walter Thompson

305 SILVER
WRITERS
Steve Sandoz
Palmer Pettersen
CLIENT
Pizza Haven
AGENCY PRODUCERS
Palmer Pettersen
Steve Sandoz
AGENCY
John Brown & Partners/
Washington

306 GOLD
WRITERS
John Cleese
Lynn Stiles
CLIENT
Callard & Bowser/USA
AGENCY PRODUCER
Robert L. Dein
AGENCY
Lord, Geller, Federico,
Einstein

307
WRITERS
Stephanie Arnold
Neil Drossman
CLIENT
Ralston Purina-Meow Mix
AGENCY PRODUCER
Rhoda Malamet
AGENCY
Drossman Yustein Clowes

308
WRITERS
Pete Mathieu
Barbara Gans Russo
John Clarkson
CLIENT
New York Air
AGENCY PRODUCER
Barbara Gans Russo
AGENCY
Mathieu, Gerfen & Bresner

303

ANNCR: The true measure of a bank is not just the good times. Fred Patterson should know.

FRED PATTERSON: Well, when that Depression hit, there didn't nobody have no money. You couldn't sell anything. So I went down there one day and I told him—I says, "Mr. Blackburn, I want to talk to you. I don't know what to do." I says, "I...I'm not gonna be able to pay y'all." "Well," he says, "how do you know?" "Well, I don't know," I says, "maybe you just better... take over." Well, he laughed about it. "Why," he says, "we don't do that." He says, "We're not a-goin' to do it." He says, "As long as you stay out there and work and try, we're gonna stay with you." He says, "we're gonna do all our customers that way." He says, "we ain't goin' to quit anybody that don't quit us."

ANNCR: That's the spirit—the genuine spirit of the Texas Crossroads. We're Victoria Bank & Trust. Member FDIC.

304

ANNCR: Did you know when you buy a regular burger at McDonald's, they make it with twenty percent less meat than the regular burger you get at Burger King?

GIRL: They do?

GIRL: Holy bananas!

BOY: Holy cow!

BOY: I didn't know.

GIRL: Am I allowed to tell anybody this?

ANNCR: It's true. Before cooking, McDonald's regular hamburger has twenty percent less meat than the regular burger at Burger King. (Difference is less after cooking.) Why would McDonald's do that?

BOY: I don't know.

BOY: Cause they want people to be skinny!

BOY: I am so *angry* about that!

ANNCR: Now that you know there's more meat in a regular Burger King burger, how do you feel about Burger King?

GIRL: I just guess Burger King cares more.

BOY: I love Burger King.

BOY: A burger at Burger King is so delicious, they're so good!

BOY: I get so hungry I can eat a cow.

SINGERS: *Aren't you hungry
Aren't you hungry
Aren't you hungry for Burger King now?*

305 SILVER

(MUSIC: PIANO INTRO TO HALLELUJAH CHORUS UP AND UNDER.)

ANNCR: And now, the 18 fresh toppings of Pizza Haven as sung by the Jalapeno Chorus.

(MUSIC: SUNG TO TUNE OF HALLELUJAH CHORUS)

LARGE CHORUS: *Jalapeno, jalapeno,
Pepperoni, pepperoni,
Green peppers and mushrooms.*

CHORUS: *Fresh tomato, delicious sausage,
With anchovies or pineapple,
We top it just for you.*

MEN: *For the best pizza you have eaten.*

CHORUS: *Salami, fresh onions,
Black olives with bacon.*

SOPRANOS: *Have your choice,*

MEN: *Extra cheese or shrimp and ham.*

SOPRANOS: *Choose your size,*

MEN: *Sauerkraut or lean ground beef.*

CHORUS: *And we shall eat for ever and ever.
Pizza Haven, pizza heaven, Pizza Haven, pizza heaven, Piz-za Hav-en.*

ANNCR: Pizza Haven *is* pizza heaven.

306 GOLD

Hallo there. Look, apparently last time I was on the radio, talking about this frightfully good rather sophisticated English candy, when I said the name of the people who make this candy, which is Callard and Bowser, I didn't say Callard and Bowser terribly clearly and so all you good American persons have been going into Supermarkets and Drugstores asking for Bollard and Trouser, and Callous and Grocer, Gizzard and Powder, so let's get the name straight, shall we, it's Callard and Bowser. Cal-lard... Cal as in *Cal*vin Coolidge and lard as Jess Wil*lard* and Bowser, that's Bow as in the *Bau*haus, or better still Mutiny on the *Bou*nty and - ser, as in Pan*zer* Division. So if you want to try the best most sophisticated and upper class candy we make in England, it's quite simple, all you have to do is think of *Cal*vin Coolidge and Jess Wil*lard, and* as in Hans Christian *And*ersen and then the *Bau*haus or Mutiny on the *Bou*nty and a pan*zer* Division, Callard and Bowser. It may take a little time to get hold of but I think you'll find it's worth it.

ANNCR: Ladies and gentlemen, we're with Professor Yustein, a man of many languages. Who has a cat of many languages.

2ND VOICE: Mais oui, I have a cat of many languages.

ANNCR: How do you account for that professor?

2ND VOICE: He just picks up languages well. He has a good ear.

ANNCR: Did he study it in school?

2ND VOICE: No, it's all self taught.

ANNCR: Well how fluent is he?

2ND VOICE: Go ahead, Petey, say something.

CAT: Meow, meow, meow, meow.

ANNCR: What did he say?

2ND VOICE: What'sa matter, you don't understand English?

ANNCR: No, I just...

2ND VOICE: All right, I'll get you off the hook. He was telling me that he's hungry and what he wants to eat.

ANNCR: I'll bet it's a hot dog, huh? Heh...heh.

2ND VOICE: Nah. He wants Meow Mix. The cat food cats ask for by name. With three delicious flavors they love. In separate bite-size morsels.

ANNCR: Oh, now could we hear him say something in French?

2ND VOICE: Mais oui, Pierre, voulez vous parlez en francais?

CAT: Meow, meow, meow, meow

ANNCR: I'll bet he's asking for Meow Mix again, huh?

2ND VOICE: You know your French.

ANNCR: Well I can understand it un peu. But I don't speak it as well as he does.

CAT: Meow, meow, meow, meow

ANNCR: I'll bet that was Italian. It's kind of easy once you get the hang of it, you know?

2ND VOICE (CHUCKLING): No that wasn't Italian. It was a dialect of Northern Spanish that's kind of similar to Italian. I can see where you could misunderstand.

VO: Meow Mix Brand Cat Food. The only cat food cats ask for by name. In any language.

SINGERS & MUSIC: ("DESTINATIONS" COMPARE NEW YORK AIR) *If you're squeezed in to Cleveland*
Like sardines in the air
If you're hassled to Detroit
When your business flies you there
If you're hustled to D.C. or Boston
And you can't reserve a seat
Or doing business in Orlando or Raleigh-Durham
And need more room for your feet
Compare New York Air, the airline that works for your business
We care, New York Air, the airline that works for your business

ANNCR (VO): (MUSIC UNDER) The best way out of New York? New York Air. From both LaGuardia and Newark...we give you more leg room and service from people who really care. Plus, free drinks and snacks on every weekday flight. Compare New York Air.

SINGERS & MUSIC: *Compare New York Air, the airline that works for your business*

Public Service
Radio Single

309
WRITERS
Dick Orkin Creative Services
CLIENT
The Church of Jesus Christ
of Latter-Day Saints
AGENCY PRODUCER
Kevin Kelly
AGENCY
Bonneville Productions/Utah

Public Service
Radio Campaign

310
WRITER
Rick Korzeniowski
CLIENT
United Way
AGENCY PRODUCERS
Mario Pellegrini
Rick Korzeniowski
AGENCY
Bozell & Jacobs/Virginia

Corporate Radio
Campaign

311
WRITERS
Jon Goward
Michael Feinberg
CLIENT
Preterm
AGENCY PRODUCER
Jon Goward
AGENCY
ClarkeGowardCarr&Fitts/
Boston

BERT: What's the problem, Norm?

DICK: Teenagers, go figure them out; I can't.

BERT: Did you ever just try talking to them?

DICK: You can't talk to teenagers.

BERT: Why not?

DICK: They don't talk like we do. They've got a lingo that juxtaposes monosyllables incomprehensively.

BERT: What?

DICK: And their values aren't like our values. No way.

BERT: Well Norm, values change.

DICK: Like I gave my older son, what's his name?

BERT: Ralph.

DICK: Ralph, a dollar allowance. Poof! It's gone in a week.

BERT: Maybe you should get ahold of a new booklet called, "How to Talk to Your Teenager."

DICK: The only way to talk to them is to shout.

BERT: It's been prepared by a team of parents and experts so a...

DICK: Or my youngest one, she doesn't think I pay attention to her.

BERT: Who?

DICK: The red-headed one. Starts with a "G" or a "J."

BERT: Nancy?

DICK: That's it. Teenagers!

BERT: Oh, you need the booklet, Norm. "How to Talk to Your Teenager."

DICK: Then there's my boy in the middle.

BERT: Oh, Norm!

DICK: That's it, oh Norm. He's girl crazy. All he thinks about is girls, girls, girls...

BERT: Didn't you?

DICK: What?

BERT: Didn't you think...

DICK: Excuse me, who's the new secretary over by the water cooler over there...

BERT: See what I mean, Norm...

ANNCR: If you're not connecting with the teen in your home, there's a new booklet every parent should have—"How to Talk to Your Teenager." It's yours free by writing to: "Talk," Salt Lake City, Utah 84150. That's "Talk," Salt Lake City, Utah 84150. Free from The Church of Jesus Christ of Latter-day Saints, the Mormons.

ANNCR: Do you believe in telepathy?

VOICE: I've had enough experiences: there is something to it.

ANNCR: I want you to think about your favorite towel. The color of your favorite towel. The radio audience and I are going to try and vibe in on your head and see whether we can guess the color of that towel.

VOICE: I've got the color.

ANNCR: You've got the towel? One, two, three—concentrate. I have the feeling you're not concentrating on the towel.

VOICE: I am.

ANNCR: You're thinking about the United Way.

VOICE: United Way?

ANNCR: You're thinking about the United Way. You're thinking, who makes up the United Way? I mean, who are the people that do it?

VOICE: No, I already know the color of the towel.

ANNCR: I want to tell you that it's over 20 million volunteers. Those are the people that make up the United Way.

VOICE: Oh, I see. Twenty million is quite a few.

ANNCR: Over 20 million. And that's the people who raise the money, help provide the services.

VOICE: Like you say, that's what makes it work.

ANNCR: Why do you still look puzzled?

VOICE: That's the way I always look. I was born with that look.

ANNCR: But do you give to the United Way?

VOICE: I certainly do.

ANNCR: Well, listen—thanks to you, it works for all of us. The United Way, O.K.? By the way, what color is your towel?

VOICE: Blue.

ANNCR: I thought it was orange.

VOICE: Oh boy!

VOICE 1: Goodnight bloody Peoria! I love you!

(SFX: RUN OFF STAGE, CHEERING IN BACKGROUND)

VOICE 2: Hey Jack!

VOICE 1: Not now Brian, me and the band are gonna go pick-up some honeys and trash the hotel.

VOICE 2: Jack, I got a letter here—you know a girl named "Sherry" from New Jersey?

VOICE 1: Don't believe I've had the pleasure yet.

VOICE 2: Well, that's not what her lawyer says. Look Jack, this is the second paternity suit this month. And as your manager I think it's high time you did something about it!

VOICE 1: What are you drivin' at?!

VOICE 2: A vasectomy.

VOICE 1: A vahootamy?

VOICE 2: A vasectomy is where they . . . (WHISPER)

VOICE 1: Yow? Not with me you don't! I happen to like women!

VOICE 2: Hey, you'll still be the same 'ol Jack, because the only thing it'll keep you from doing is getting any more of these bloody paternity suits.

VOICE 1: Well, if I do it, can I get a tighter pair of pants?

VO: If you're a rich, famous rock star faced with one paternity suit too many, and you're absolutely sure you don't want to have children, a vasectomy may be just the thing to make sure you never will. This message from Preterm, the most experienced Reproductive Health Care Center in the Northeast.

1983 Television Finalists

Television Finalists

**Consumer Television
60 Seconds Single**

312
ART DIRECTOR
Nick Gisonde
WRITER
Jeane Bice
CLIENT
Miller Brewing/Lite Beer
DIRECTOR
Bob Giraldi
PRODUCTION CO.
Giraldi Productions
AGENCY PRODUCER
Marc Mayhew
AGENCY
Backer & Spielvogel

313
ART DIRECTOR
Bob Steigelman
WRITER
Charlie Breen
CLIENT
Miller Brewing/High Life
DIRECTOR
Don Guy
PRODUCTION CO.
Dennis/Guy/Hirsch
AGENCY PRODUCER
Sally Smith
AGENCY
Backer & Spielvogel

312

JONES: Decon's my name, bowling's my game.

MADDEN: Gutter Ball! Gutter Ball!

SNELL (VO): How you going to score that?

MARTIN: Come on, three strikes you're out.

HEINSOHN: But we just won another round of Lite Beer from Miller.

AUERBACH: Well, Lite sure tastes great!

YELLOWS: Less Filling!!!!!

REDS: Tastes Great!!!!!

POWELL: Hold it! Hold it, Jim.

TEAMS: You're going the wrong way.

POWELL: There it is down there.

MIZERAK: Eight Ball in the pocket.

BUTKUS: Hey Bubba, this ball doesn't have any holes in it.

SMITH: Now it does.

MEREDITH: The score is all even.

NITSCHKE: Last frame. Who's up?

CARTER: Rodney...

CROWD: Rodney?????????

CARTER: Got to be a mistake.

DANGERFIELD: Hey you're kidding. It's a piece of cake.

DAVIDSON: All we need is one pin Rodney.

(VO): Lite Beer from Miller.
Everything you always wanted in a beer.
And less.

MADDEN: I didn't get my turn yet. I'm gonna break this tie.

313

(SFX: STREET NOISES.)

1ST GUY: Hey, hey here comes, Tiny...

2ND GUY: Yes, here he is ladies and gentlemen, the up and coming...

ANNCR: One inch farther that's how far he wants to throw it today. And tomorrow an inch farther than that.

Because he's got a dream that says some day he's gonna throw that 161 lb. piece of iron farther...

S.P. (VO): Ugh.

ANNCR: than any other man in the summer games.

1ST GUY: You're not gonna win any gold medals doin' that, man.

2ND GUY: Shhh, Shhh.

(MUSIC UP)

ANNCR: In the past it probably would have been just a dream but today he just might become as good as he believes he can be...

S.P. (VO): Ugh.

ANNCR: Because today he can go to the U.S. Olympic Training Center in Colorado Springs. And maybe on a summer day in 1984... He'll go up against the best in the world and he'll throw it...one inch farther.

(CHANT UNDER: USA, USA, USA.)

ANNCR: This American Dream was brought to you by Miller High Life...

The sponsor of the U.S. Olympic Training Center.

314 SILVER
ART DIRECTORS
Mark Nussbaum
Bob Lenz
WRITER
Barry Lisee
CLIENT
Miller Brewing/High Life
DIRECTOR
Joe Hanwright
PRODUCTION CO.
Larkin Productions
AGENCY PRODUCER
Barry Lisee
AGENCY
Backer & Spielvogel

315
ART DIRECTOR
Alan Sprules
WRITER
Roger Proulx
CLIENT
Peugeot Motors of America
DIRECTOR
Gerard Hameline
PRODUCTION CO.
1/33 Productions/Paris
AGENCY PRODUCER
Bernard Wesson
AGENCY
Ogilvy & Mather

316
ART DIRECTOR
Lee Clow
WRITER
Steve Hayden
CLIENT
Apple Computer Inc.
DIRECTOR
Leslie Dector
PRODUCTION CO.
Associates & Toback
AGENCY PRODUCERS
Richard O'Neill
Rosalinde Estes
AGENCY
Chiat/Day-Los Angeles

314 SILVER

(MUSIC UNDER)

(VO): 'Round here, well I guess we take work about as serious as anybody else. But I'll tell you somethin' boys, come sundown ain't nobody more serious about havin' a good time.

(MUSIC IN): *Welcome to Miller Time. It's all yours, and it's all mine. Bring your thirsty self right here, you've got the time we've got the beer for what you had in mind. Welcome to Miller Time.*

(VO): The best beer for the best time of the day. Miller High Life.

(MUSIC): *Bring your thirsty self right here, you've got the time, we've got the beer for what you have in mind. Oh-oh; Welcome, you know you're welcome, welcome, everybody's welcome. Welcome to Miller Time. Yours and mine.*

315

(SFX: NATURAL THROUGHOUT MUSIC BEGINS, OVER SFX.)

ANNCR (VO): Before there was Peugeot 505...there was testing.

The handbrake...on, off...40,000 times.

Turn signals...left, right...50,000 times.

The Peugeot shock absorbers...

designed to endure for 60,000 miles...

tested...

tested again.

The Peugeot doors...open, shut...100,000 times.

Clutch pedal...in, out...one million times.

Testing...

testing...

more testing.

Peugeot has little tolerance for poorly made cars.

Plant Manager, Stuttgart, Germany.

Head Chef, Paris, France.

Little Kid, Dayton, Ohio.

(SFX: AMBIENT SOUND THROUGHOUT.)

(MUSIC THROUGHOUT.)

CHINESE::
   Apple Computer.
   (Thank you for coming. This is my Apple
   computer.)

GERMAN:: Produktion Kontrolle ohne den Apfel?
   Unmöglich!
   (Production control without the Apple?
   Impossible!)

JAMAICAN: My Apple is my manager.

DICK CAVETT (VO): There are more people in more
   places doing more things with Apples than with
   any other personal computer in the world.

CHILDREN: Estamos estudiando con la Apple.
   (We're studying with an Apple.)

SANTA: (CHUCKLES)

MANAGER: My Apple has a great head for statistics.
   It sure makes my job easier.

(SFX: CRACK OF BAT AND CROWD ROAR.)

ROCK MUSICIAN: Man, we never travel without the
   Apple.

CHEF: Sans mon Apple, je deviendrais fou!
   (Without my Apple, I'd go crazy!)

MECHANIC: La mia Apple non sbaglia mai. Lui
   sbaglia.
   (My Apple never makes mistakes. He does.)

CAVETT (VO): And of all those people using Apples,
   most had never touched a computer before.

KID: This is my Apple.

CAVETT (VO): Apple.

(SFX: CRUNCH.)

CAVETT (VO): The most personal computer.

317
ART DIRECTOR
Amil Gargano
WRITER
Ron Berger
CLIENT
Calvin Klein
DIRECTOR
Adrian Lyne
PRODUCTION CO.
Jennie
AGENCY PRODUCER
Janine Marjollet
AGENCY
Ally & Gargano

318
ART DIRECTOR
Terrance Iles
WRITER
William Lower
CLIENT
Ralston Purina (Canada)
DIRECTOR
Ousama Rawi
PRODUCTION CO.
Rawifilm Canada
AGENCY PRODUCER
Nicole Tardif   ns
AGENCY
Scali, McCabe, Sloves/Canada

319
ART DIRECTOR
Terrance Iles
WRITER
William Lower
CLIENT
Ralston Purina (Canada)
DIRECTOR
Ousama Rawi
PRODUCTION CO.
Rawifilm Canada
AGENCY PRODUCER
Nicole Tardif
AGENCY
Scali, McCabe, Sloves/Canada

317

(MUSIC AND SFX PEOPLE BREATHING THROUGHOUT)

ANNCR (VO): There's a fitness craze in America...that takes a lot of different shapes and forms.

Today, over 55 million people do some kind of exercise regularly.

Well, for all those people who struggle to stay in shape there's now a reward.

A great new collection of active wear from Calvin Klein.

Because why go to all the trouble of staying in shape if you can't show it off?

318

(SFX: MUSIC UNDER)

GIRL: Mommy, will Charlie live forever?

MOTHER: No, dear, Charlie can't live *forever*.

GIRL: Well, how long will he live?

MOTHER: Oh, Charlie's going to live a long, long time.

GIRL: But how long Mommy?

ANNCR (VO): For over half a century, Ralston Purina has done extensive research on nutrition, searching to find ways to help dogs live longer lives. And we've succeeded. With Purina Dog Chow.

GIRL (CALLING): Charlie! Come on!

ANNCR (VO): Because every nutritional discovery in the world that can help dogs live longer, goes into Purina Dog Chow.

There's nothing better for your dog.

GIRL: I love you Charlie.

(VO): Purina Dog Chow. Helping dogs live longer lives.

319

(SFX: MUSIC UNDER)

BOY: Dad?

DAD: Uh-huh.

BOY: How old is Danny Boy?

DAD: Oh, he's almost as old as you are.

BOY: That old?

DAD: Yeah, that old.

BOY: Dad?

DAD: Uh-huh.

BOY: How old will he get?

DAD (KINDLY): Oh, he's gonna be with us a long, long time, son.

ANNCR (VO): For over half a century, Ralston Purina has done extensive research on nutrition, searching to find ways to help dogs live longer lives. And we've succeeded. With Purina Dog Chow.

BOY: Come on, Danny Boy! Come on!

ANNCR (VO): Because every nutritional discovery in the world, that can help dogs live longer, goes into Purina Dog Chow.

There's nothing better for your dog.

BOY: Danny Boy, you're terrific.

ANNCR (VO): Purina Dog Chow. Helping dogs live longer lives.

320 GOLD
ART DIRECTOR
Dave Davis
WRITER
Bob Meury
CLIENT
Sony Corporation-
Betamax Components
DIRECTOR
Gary Princz
PRODUCTION CO.
EUE Productions
AGENCY PRODUCERS
Lois Rice
Bruce Giuriceo
AGENCY
Backer & Spielvogel

321
ART DIRECTOR
Jerry Box
WRITER
Jim Copacino
CLIENT
Alaska Airlines
DIRECTOR
Joe Sedelmaier
PRODUCTION CO.
Sedelmaier Films
AGENCY PRODUCER
Virginia Pellegrino
AGENCY
Chiat/Day/Livingston-Seattle

322
ART DIRECTOR
Don Slater
WRITER
Adam Hanft
CLIENT
Satellite News Channel
DIRECTOR
Mark Ross
PRODUCTION CO.
Mark Ross Films
AGENCY PRODUCER
Robin Dobson
AGENCY
Slater Hanft Martin

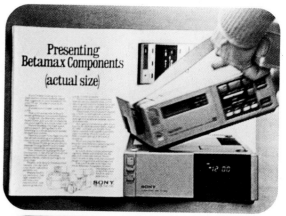

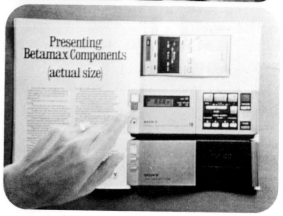

320 GOLD

ANNCR: Have you seen the latest ad for Sony
    Betamax Components? There they are. Actual
    size.

I can't believe it. They look so real. Oh. They are
real! This is terrific.

And look. A wireless remote control that does
just about everything. Let's see. Umm. Reverse,
whoh... whoh. And forward. In almost any
speed you want. Boy, that was fast. Umm, I'd
better put it back.

And Betamax Components are so compact and
lightweight, you can take the recorder anywhere
to shoot your own movies. This could be my big
chance!

Let's see. What else is there to play with. Oh, a
coupon. Oh, there's the Sony Trinicon Color
Camera. It gives you instant replay right
through the eyepiece... There's even an offer for
free tapes. Mmm... I think I'll keep the
coupon.

The Sony Betamax Component System.

You know what?

I think I'll keep the whole thing.

321

(SFX: MUSIC UNDER.)

ANNCR: For centuries, mankind dreamed of flying.

Now mankind wonders why.

After all, just getting to your plane can be a trip in itself...

With seats that cramp your style...

And food that's hard to swallow.

Fortunately, there's Alaska Airlines.
With close-in gates...

...roomy seating...

...And our special Gold Coast service.

So next trip, fly Alaska Airlines

And fly with a happy face.

322

ANNCR (VO): Introducing Satellite News Channel.
We're the Non-Stop News Machine.
A whole new way to get the news on cable TV and only on cable.
So even when you shut our news off...it never stops.

It never stops because for the first time someone is there live...with all news, all the time.

It never stops because it's there 24 hours a day...7 days a week.

It never stops because any time you tune in you get filled in—with a complete, updated news report in a swift 18 minutes.

And it never stops because the Non-Stop News Machine is powered by non-stop people—the largest newsgathering team in television—cable, or otherwise.

The world doesn't stop.
And now the news doesn't stop.
On Satellite News Channel.
The Non-stop News Machine.
Give Us 18 Minutes. We'll Give You the World.

323
ART DIRECTOR
Brent Thomas

WRITER
Penny Kapousouz

CLIENT
Pioneer Electronics

DIRECTORS
Bill Bratkowski
Brent Thomas
Mark Coppos

PRODUCTION CO.
Director's Consortium

AGENCY PRODUCER
Morty Baran

AGENCY
Chiat/Day-Los Angeles

324
ART DIRECTOR
Manfred Knuth

WRITER
Richard Fowler

CLIENT
Rowntree Hoadley Ltd./
Kit Kat

DIRECTOR
John Marles

PRODUCTION CO.
The Midnight Movie Co.

AGENCY PRODUCER
Ruth Frenkl

AGENCY
Ogilvy & Mather/Australia

325
ART DIRECTORS
Tom Mabley
Bob Tore

WRITER
Arlene Jaffe

CLIENT
IBM

DIRECTOR
Dick Loew

PRODUCTION CO.
Gomes Loew

AGENCY PRODUCER
Robert L. Dein

AGENCY
Lord, Geller, Federico
Einstein

323

(MUSIC: ROSSINI'S OVERTURE TO THE BARBER OF SEVILLE.
MUSIC STOPS.)

ANNCR (VO): At Pioneer, we make 210 different
products...that only do one thing...make
music.

Pioneer. Because the music matters.

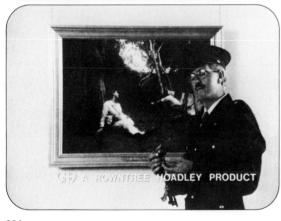

324

(SFX: DOOR SLAMMING, ECHOING FOOTSTEPS, DEAD SILENCE)

MAN (STRETCHING): Aah!...Mmm!...What a day!...

WOMAN: I think we deserve a break

MAN: Let's have a KIT KAT!

MVO: When you have a break...(SFX: SNAP)
Have a KIT KAT...
crisp...(SFX: SNAP) light...
wafer biscuit...
covered in milk chocolate...
That's KIT KAT!...(SFX: SNAP)

MAN: Cor...a lot of people in today.

(SFX: KEYS JANGLING)

MAN: SHH!

MVO: Have a break (SFX: SNAP)
Have a KIT KAT.

325

(MUSIC)

GARY MERRILL (VO): If you run a small business profits can get squeezed when inventory doesn't match up with production. What can help is a visit to an IBM Personal Computer dealer. Once you've explained the kind of help you need, a computer expert will show you the system that's right for you...show you how simple it is to get started...and how IBM's easy-to-follow instructions and library of business and management software can help you solve your problems and give you a tool for modern times. The IBM Personal Computer...not only can it help you plan ahead, it'll balance your books and give you more time to make dough. And the cost? That's the icing on the cake. Your own IBM Personal Computer. Try it at a store near you.

Consumer Television
60 Seconds Campaign

326 SILVER

ART DIRECTORS
Lee Gleason
Ralph Love

WRITERS
David Lamb
Larry Simon
David Klehr

CLIENT
Anheuser-Busch/
Budweiser Light

DIRECTOR
Joe Pytka

PRODUCTION CO.
Levine Pytka

AGENCY PRODUCERS
David Lamb
Gary Conway

AGENCY
Needham, Harper & Steers/
Chicago

327

ART DIRECTOR
Amil Gargano

WRITER
Ron Berger

CLIENT
Calvin Klein

DIRECTOR
Adrian Lyne

PRODUCTION CO.
Jennie

AGENCY PRODUCER
Janine Marjollet

AGENCY
Ally & Gargano

328 GOLD

ART DIRECTORS
Mark Nussbaum
Bob Lenz
Gerald Pfiffner
Jim Anderson

WRITERS
Barry Lisee
Gerald Pfiffner

CLIENT
Miller Brewing/High Life

DIRECTORS
Joe Hanwright
Steve Horn
Joe Pytka

PRODUCTION COS.
Larkin Productions
Steve Horn Productions
Levine Pytka

AGENCY PRODUCERS
Barry Lisee
Andy Cornelius
Tom Dakin

AGENCY
Backer & Spielvogel

329

ART DIRECTOR
Dennis Merritt

WRITER
Charlie Thomas

CLIENT
Southwest Savings and Loan

DIRECTOR
Kent Wilson

PRODUCTION CO.
Raintree

AGENCY PRODUCER
Charlie Thomas

AGENCY
Winters Franceschi Callahan/
Phoenix

326 SILVER

(MUSIC)

GOALIE (VO): You can protect everything but your
ego. "Cause they know how it hurts."

SINGERS: *Bring out your best.*

GOALIE: And they'll go for it again.

ANNCR (VO): The best never comes easy. That's why
there's nothing else like it. Budweiser Light.

SINGERS: *Bring out your best*
You've got to reach deep inside.
Bring out your best
Budweiser Light
Bring out your best
Budweiser Light.

ANNCR (VO): The best. You've found it in yourself and
now you've found it in the beer you drink

SINGERS: *BUDWEISER*
BUDWEISER LIGHT.

327

(SOFT MUSIC UNDER THROUGHOUT)

ANNCR (VO): For a lot of people staying in shape has
become a labor of love.

In fact today, over 55 million people do some kind
of exercise regularly.

Well, for all those people who work hard at
staying in shape, and succeed, Calvin Klein
introduces a great new collection of active wear.
Because why go to all the trouble of staying in
shape, if you can't show it off?

328 GOLD

(MUSIC UNDER)

(VO): 'Round here, well I guess we take work about as serious as anybody else. But I'll tell you somethin' boys, come sundown ain't nobody more serious about havin' a good time.

(MUSIC IN): *Welcome to Miller Time. It's all yours, and it's all mine. Bring your thirsty self right here, you've got the time we've got the beer for what you had in mind. Welcome to Miller Time.*

(VO): The best beer for the best time of the day. Miller High Life.

(MUSIC): *Bring your thirsty self right here, you've got the time, we've got the beer for what you have in mind. Oh-oh; Welcome, you know you're welcome, welcome, everybody's welcome. Welcome to Miller Time. Yours and mine.*

329

(MUSIC UP, THEN UNDER)

CARLOS (VO): It's called the White Dove of the Desert. You can see it for miles, and the closer you get the better it looks.

ANNCR (VO): Carlos Elmer is a photographer and author who's spent his life telling the story of the Southwest.

CARLOS: I was raised in Arizona. I've always been fascinated by the many forms and textures here. Sometimes you can move your camera just a few inches and find a completely different picture.

ANNCR (VO): At Southwest Savings, we think someone like Carlos should get as much out of life as he puts into it. That's why our Prime-Time Investment is guaranteed to pay even more interest than the money fund average.

CARLOS (VO/OC): I like things that are done right. In the same spirit of excellence as this church. That's number one in my book.

ANNCR (VO): Doing things right, that's the Southwest way.

330
ART DIRECTOR
Robert Wilvers
WRITER
Robert Wilvers
CLIENT
Miles Laboratories
DIRECTOR
Stan Dragoti
PRODUCTION CO.
EUE Productions
AGENCY PRODUCER
Mary Kaplun
AGENCY
Wells, Rich, Greene

331
ART DIRECTOR
Bob Musachio
WRITER
Steve Katcher
CLIENT
Sharp
DIRECTOR
Frank Stiefel
PRODUCTION CO.
Michael Ulick Productions
AGENCY PRODUCER
Nancy Braunstein
AGENCY
Rosenfeld, Sirowitz & Lawson

332
ART DIRECTOR
Dave Davis
WRITER
Robert Tamburri
CLIENT
Miller Brewing/Lite Beer
DIRECTOR
Steve Horn
PRODUCTION CO.
Steve Horn Productions
AGENCY PRODUCER
Marc Mayhew
AGENCY
Backer & Spielvogel

330

ANNCR (VO): It's been another one of those days, and
you're facing the longest walk of your life...
To the Alka-Seltzer waiting inside the medicine
cabinet.
But is it?
You gamble it's there to relieve your acid
indigestion with headache.
Will America's home remedy be home?

MAN (HUMBLY): You're here.

ANNCR (VO): Nothing's more soothing
Nothing works better than Alka-Seltzer.

331

VO: Sharp introduces the SF-825 copier.

MAN: Hold it, I'm here to demonstrate how the SF-825 reduces two ways or enlarges.

WOMAN: Really.

FACE (VO GETS SMALLER): Make a small copy of me.

(VO GETS SMALLER): . . . even smaller.

(VO GETS BIGGER): Or an enlargement up to 120%.

FACE (WITH EMPHASIS): Sharp's SF-825 has 44 diagnostic features.

WOMAN: I love the copier . . . and you're cute too.

FACE: Hey, don't forget your original.

From Sharp Minds Come Sharp Products.

332

BOOG: You know there's nothing like gettin' together for a nice friendly game of cards.
Jim brings the cards.

VO: Uh oh!

BOOG: Mickey brings the doll.

VO: (WHISTLE.)

MICKEY: Thanks doll.

LEE: (GIGGLES.)

BOOG: And I bring the beer—Lite Beer from Miller. Lite tastes great, it's got a third less calories than their regular beer and it's less filling. And you don't want to get filled up when you're dealing with these guys.

BOOG: 'Kay Numa, cut the cards.

NUMA: Ummm.

BOOG: Oh no!

NUMA: EEyaahhhhhh!!!!!

(SFX: GENERAL COMMOTION.)

ANNCR: Lite Beer from Miller. Everything you always wanted in a beer. And less.

LEE: (GIGGLE.)

333
ART DIRECTOR
Nick Gisonde
WRITERS
Jeane Bice
Charlie Breen
CLIENT
Miller Brewing/Lite Beer
DIRECTOR
Bob Giraldi
PRODUCTION CO.
Giraldi Productions
AGENCY PRODUCER
Marc Mayhew
AGENCY
Backer & Spielvogel

334
ART DIRECTOR
Rich Martel
WRITER
Al Merrin
CLIENT
General Electric
DIRECTOR
Joe Sedelmaier
PRODUCTION CO.
Sedelmaier Films
AGENCY PRODUCER
Nancy Iannicelli
AGENCY
BBDO

335 SILVER (TIE)
ART DIRECTOR
Cindy Perego
WRITER
Tom McNeer
CLIENT
Jartran
DIRECTOR
Joe Sedelmaier
PRODUCTION CO.
Sedelmaier Films
AGENCY PRODUCERS
Tom McNeer
Cindy Perego
AGENCY
Bozell & Jacobs/Atlanta

336
ART DIRECTOR
John Cruickshank
WRITER
George Anketell
CLIENT
Canadian General Electric
DIRECTOR
Ousami Rawi
PRODUCTION CO.
Aisha Film Co.
AGENCY PRODUCER
Audrey Telfer
AGENCY
MacLaren Advertising/Toronto

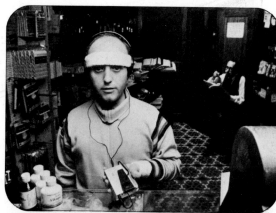

333

(MARIACHIS PLAYING UNDER.)

CARLOS: My American friends introduced me to my
favorite beer, Lite Beer from Miller.
Now I'm introducing them to my favorite food.
With Nachos the best thing about Lite is it
tastes great.

TOMMY: Not bad!

CARLOS: With enchiladas the best thing is it's got a
third less calories than their regular beer.

CARLOS: With Burritos the best thing is it's less
filling.

TOMMY: Carlos, what's this?

(SFX: CRUNCH)

CARLOS: And with Jalapeno peppers the best thing
about Lite is... it's *cold*!

TOMMY: OOH, hah, oh, oh, oh...

ANNCR: Lite Beer from Miller
Everything you always wanted in a beer.
And less.

(MARIACHIS' VO: SINGING & PLAYING.)

334

MAN: Uh, batteries.

CLERK #1: Batteries.

CLERK #2: Batteries.

(SFX: CASH REGISTER)

ANNCR (VO): Buying batteries...

MAN: Batteries.

CLERK #1: Batteries.

CLERK #2: Batteries.

(SFX: CASH REGISTER)

ANNCR (VO): can be an expensive habit.

MAN: Uh, batteries.

CLERK #1: Batteries.

CLERK #2: Batteries.

(SFX: CASH REGISTER)

ANNCR (VO): Unless you buy GE Rechargeables.
They cost more. But they can be recharged
over and over up to 4 years. Just two
GE Rechargeables, used 10 hours a week,
can outlive all these alkaline batteries.

MAN: Uh, cottonballs.

CLERK #1: Cottonballs?

CLERK #2: Cottonballs.
GE Rechargeables. You can recharge them over
and over, (SFX: CASH REGISTER) but we only charge
you once.

335 SILVER (TIE)

CLARA: Ed, it's time to take the rabbits to the pet store. I better rent a trailer.

ANNCR (VO): A lot of folks call Jartran when their business expands faster than expected.

CLARA: Ed, I think we need a truck.

ANNCR (VO): You see, most Jartran trucks have automatic transmission. And they all have a low price.

CLARA: Ed, I think we need a bigger truck. (PAUSE) Ed...

ANNCR (VO): So when you need a truck for your business or your family, just call your Jartran dealer. And he'll hop right to it.

336

MAN (LIP SYNC): Me and Eloise couldn't get along without this CGE Air Cleaner. See, Eloise doesn't like cigar smoke, hates the smell of boiled cabbage. Soo ...

(SFX: CLICK OF MACHINE TURNING ON AND HUM OF MOTOR AND FAN.)

MAN: Smoke and smells in here
Fresh clean air out here
Works good
Matter of fact...the CGE Air Cleaner and Deodorizer is the only thing that keeps Eloise and me together.
Isn't it, my little flower?

(TURNS UP MACHINE)

(SFX: CLICK AND INCREASED HUM OF FAN AT HIGHER SPEED.)

MUSIC & SINGERS: *G.E. We bring good things to life.*

337
ART DIRECTOR
David Nathanson
WRITER
Peter Falkner
CLIENT
Atari
DIRECTOR
Michael Ulick
PRODUCTION CO.
Michael Ulick Productions
AGENCY PRODUCER
Janice Stolar
AGENCY
Doyle Dane Bernbach

338
ART DIRECTOR
Joe Del Vecchio
WRITER
Peter Bregman
CLIENT
GTE
DIRECTOR
Mark Story
PRODUCTION CO.
Pfeifer Story
AGENCY PRODUCER
Jim Callan
AGENCY
Doyle Dane Bernbach

339
ART DIRECTOR
Lester Feldman
WRITER
Michael Mangano
CLIENT
GTE
DIRECTOR
Norman Toback
PRODUCTION CO.
Associates & Toback
AGENCY PRODUCER
Stuart Raffel
AGENCY
Doyle Dane Bernbach

340
ART DIRECTOR
Ted Shaine
WRITER
Irwin Warren
CLIENT
Volkswagen
DIRECTOR
Steve Horn
PRODUCTION CO.
Steve Horn Productions
AGENCY PRODUCER
Susan Calhoun
AGENCY
Doyle Dane Bernbach

337

ATARI DEALER (CHEERFULLY): Hi, listen, I've got this great Atari calendar offer. It starts November fifteenth.

(SFX: PULSING, THREATENING SOUNDS OF SPACE INVADERS)
And it's...er...not going to last long. Just buy any Atari game system and you can get this free Atari calendar. It's beautiful! And it's got twenty-five dollars worth of coupons. You'll save five dollars off games like...er...Space Invaders, Yar's Revenge...and Bezerk!
But hurry! On December thirty-first...it's all over!

(SFX: MUSIC OUT)

338

VO: Sooner or later, everybody gets something from somebody in Florida.

GIRL: Cute.

VO: ...one of the nicest and least expensive gifts you can send your family and friends back home to show them what a great time you're having is your voice.
So when you get a chance, call home.

MAN: Hellooo?

VOICE: Hiya, Charlie! Didja get 'em?

MAN: Yeah...Fred. They're really...swell.

339

(SFX: PHONE RINGS)

MOM: Hello.

SON (OVER TELEPHONE): Hello, Mom?

MOM: Who's this?

SON: Your son... Phillip.

MOM: Son? I don't have a son. A son calls his mother.

SON: Ma, listen I'm...

MOM (TO FATHER, INTERRUPTING SON): Fred, do you remember having a son?

SON: I've been busy, Ma.

MOM: Too busy to call your mother?

SON: Mother? What mother? I don't have a mother. Remember?

(MOM'S VOICE GOES UNDER)

ANNCR (VO): A long distance call can cost so little... and mean so much.

MOM: Are you eating all right? You sound thin.

340

VO: Did you know that there is an inexpensive, fuel efficient car engineered in Germany, that is so fast, so sure footed and possessing such remarkable brakes that you could very well look forward to seeing these signs as long as you own this one.
The Volkswagen Rabbit.
It expects the unexpected.

341
ART DIRECTOR
Sam Scali
WRITER
Ed McCabe
CLIENT
Perdue
DIRECTOR
Norman Griner
PRODUCTION CO.
Griner/Cuesta
AGENCY PRODUCER
Carol Singer
AGENCY
Scali, McCabe, Sloves

342
ART DIRECTOR
Earl Cavanah
WRITER
Larry Cadman
CLIENT
Volvo
DIRECTOR
Lee Lacey
PRODUCTION CO.
N. Lee Lacey
AGENCY PRODUCER
Dane Johnson
AGENCY
Scali, McCabe, Sloves

343
ART DIRECTOR
Sam Scali
WRITER
Ed McCabe
CLIENT
Perdue
DIRECTOR
Henry Sandbank
PRODUCTION CO.
Sandbank Films
AGENCY PRODUCER
Carol Singer
AGENCY
Scali, McCabe, Sloves

344
ART DIRECTOR
Cathie Campbell
WRITER
Geoffrey Frost
CLIENT
Wind Song-Prince
Matchabelli
DIRECTOR
John Danza
PRODUCTION CO.
Birbrower/Danza
Productions
AGENCY PRODUCER
Dane Johnson
AGENCY
Scali, McCabe, Sloves

341

ANNCR (VO): Perdue Fresh Cornish Game Hens...the gourmet meal so easy to prepare you can do it in less than an hour.
Try Perdue Fresh Cornish Game Hens.

(SFX: DOORBELL RING)
And spend more time with your guests.

342

ANNCR: At this year's Geneva Auto Show, an amazing new car was introduced. The Volvo 760 GLE. The Italians absolutely adored it. The French loved it. Even the Japanese liked it. Only one group seemed unimpressed. The Germans. But when you consider that this new Volvo is more aerodynamic than their Porsche 928...costs thousands less than their Mercedes...and can outmaneuver their Audi...the German reaction isn't surprising.

343

ANNCR: Perdue says...

FRANK PERDUE: Don't buy a chicken.
When you want lamb chops you don't buy one of these do you? Unless you're making a sweater at the same time.
So why buy a whole chicken?
Buy Perdue Prime Parts and get only the parts you like best.
Perdue Prime Parts are the *only* ones good enough to be called Prime.
So don't buy a chicken.
Buy the best a chicken has to offer.

344

(MUSIC: INSTRUMENTAL INTRO UNDER)

(SFX: RESTAURANT SOUNDS)

WOMAN 1: Did you tell Richard you'd be here?

WOMAN 2: No.

WOMAN 1: Well, he's here.

WOMAN 2: Oh, waiter...

(MUSIC: WINDSONG THEME)

WOMAN 2: Give it to the gentleman right over there.

(MUSIC)

SINGER: *...I can't seem to forget you...*
...Your Windsong stays on my mind...

ANNCR (VO): Windsong Perfume by Prince Matchabelli.

345
ART DIRECTOR
Sam Scali
WRITER
Michael Robertson
CLIENT
American Can Co.
DIRECTOR
Bill Hudson
PRODUCTION CO.
Bill Hudson Films
AGENCY PRODUCER
David Perry
AGENCY
Scali, McCabe, Sloves

346
ART DIRECTOR
Michael Tesch
WRITER
Patrick Kelly
CLIENT
Federal Express
DIRECTOR
Patrick Kelly
PRODUCTION COS.
Hampton Road Films
Kelly Pictures
AGENCY PRODUCER
Maureen Kearns
AGENCY
Ally & Gargano

347
ART DIRECTOR
Tod Seisser
WRITER
Jay Taub
CLIENT
Chemical Bank
DIRECTOR
George Gomes
PRODUCTION CO.
Gomes Loew
AGENCY PRODUCER
Linda Tesa
AGENCY
Della Femina, Travisano
& Partners

348
ART DIRECTOR
Amil Gargano
WRITER
Ron Berger
CLIENT
Calvin Klein
DIRECTOR
Adrian Lyne
PRODUCTION CO.
Jennie
AGENCY PRODUCER
Janine Marjollet
AGENCY
Ally & Gargano

345

(SFX: CRASH! MUSIC UNDER.)

MOM (VO): Jenny! Did you knock over this vase? Jenny!

ANNCR (VO): Northern Bathroom Tissue is quilted for extra softness. It's so soft... you can actually see it.

MOM (VO): Jenny! Come here, Jenny!

ANNCR (VO): But mostly, you can *feel* it.

346

FEEMER: Schtoolum, do you know how to get this big package to Seattle overnight?

SCHTOOLUM: Gee I don't know, Feemer, let's go up and bounce it off Boomer.

(SFX: ELEVATOR)

BOOMER: Gosh, I don't know fellas, let's go up and run it by Rizzo.

RIZZO: Let's parade it by Pooperman.

POOPERMAN: Let's waltz it by Wimpus.

WIMPUS: Let's dance it by Dolt.

ANNCR (VO): If more people knew that Federal Express handles great big packages even up to 70 pounds, it sure would save everybody a whole lot of trouble.

347

ANNCR: Chemical Bank now offers . . . Rosenfeld
Luggage.
Sure it's made of heavy duty nylon, but it's
also . . . beautiful. And practical. And we're giving
it away. Invest $5,000 in one of Chemical's high
interest C.D.'s and a three-piece set of designer
luggage is yours. So come into Chemical Bank.
And claim your baggage. Certain C.D.'s require
larger minimum deposits. Additional information
about deposits, eligibility qualifications and
restrictions available at any branch. Substantial
interest penalties for early withdrawal. Member
FDIC. Offer may be withdrawn without notice.

348

(SFX: PEOPLE BREATHING THROUGHOUT THE SPOT, MUSIC
BEGINS)

ANNCR (VO): There's a fitness craze in America . . . that
takes a lot of different shapes and forms.
Today, over 55 million people do some kind of
exercise regularly.

(MUSIC)

ANNCR (VO): Well, for all those people who struggle
to stay in shape. There's now a reward.
A great new line of active wear from Calvin Klein.
Because why go to all the trouble of staying in
shape, if you can't show it off?

(MUSIC ENDS)

349
ART DIRECTOR
Stan Block
WRITER
Frank DiGiacomo
CLIENT
WNBC Radio
DIRECTOR
Mark Story
PRODUCTION CO.
Pfeifer Story
AGENCY PRODUCER
Linda Tesa
AGENCY
Della Femina, Travisano
& Partners

350
ART DIRECTOR
Amil Gargano
WRITER
Ron Berger
CLIENT
Calvin Klein
DIRECTOR
Adrian Lyne
PRODUCTION CO.
Jennie
AGENCY PRODUCER
Janine Marjollet
AGENCY
Ally & Gargano

351
ART DIRECTOR
Barry Vetere
WRITER
Tom Messner
CLIENT
Commodore
DIRECTOR
Mike Cuesta
PRODUCTION CO.
Griner/Cuesta
AGENCY PRODUCER
Bob Van Buren
AGENCY
Ally & Gargano

352
ART DIRECTOR
Stan Block
WRITER
Frank DiGiacomo
CLIENT
WNBC-Radio
DIRECTOR
Mark Story
PRODUCTION CO.
Pfeifer Story
AGENCY PRODUCER
Linda Tesa
AGENCY
Della Femina, Travisano
& Partners

349

ANNCR (VO): We asked people about Howard Stern's
return to N.Y. as afternoon D.J. on WNBC
radio.

COUNSELOR: After 33 years of camping, I can
truthfully say, Howard Stern is the only boy I
never liked.

WOMAN: Papa, Howard's coming home.

MAN: Not to this home.

WOMAN: A disc jockey on WNBC, I knew that boy
would never amount to anything.

IMUS: Folks, don't pay any attention to those people.
Howard Stern is as normal as I am.

ANNCR: Listen to the return of Howard Stern.
66 WNBC.

350

ANNCR (VO): Over 55 million people in America today
work very hard at something besides their jobs.
And that's staying in shape.
If you're one of those people who struggles to
stay in shape, well, thanks to Calvin Klein, the
virtues have never been quite so evident.
Calvin Klein introduces Active Wear.

351

(SFX: GAME)

ANNCR (VO): There are two kinds of teenagers today. One strives to rack up 30,000,000 points on video games.

(MUSIC UNDER)
The other finds it challenging to invent his own game.

(SFX: GAME)
One depends on somebody else's imagination.

(MUSIC UNDER)
The other on his own.

(SFX: GAME)
One owns a video game machine.

(MUSIC UNDER)
The other has a Commodore
VIC 20 Home Computer.
But they do have one thing in common.
Some day, both will be trying to get into college.

(MUSIC OUT)

352

VO: Imus as the Rev. Billy Sol Hargus.

IMUS: Friends. You have made 66 WNBC—New York's #1 radio station. But we need your support to continue our noble work of playing all the most popular songs and giving out more prizes all day long.
Remember, you ain't got a prayer—if you ain't got that ratings share.
66 WNBC AAA-M
New York's #1 radio station.

353
ART DIRECTOR
Amil Gargano
WRITER
Ron Berger
CLIENT
Calvin Klein
DIRECTOR
Adrian Lyne
PRODUCTION CO.
Jennie
AGENCY PRODUCER
Janine Marjollet
AGENCY
Ally & Gargano

354 SILVER (TIE)
ART DIRECTOR
George Euringer
WRITER
Tom Messner
CLIENT
MCI
DIRECTOR
Bob Giraldi
PRODUCTION CO.
Giraldi Productions
AGENCY PRODUCER
Jerry Haynes
AGENCY
Ally & Gargano

355
ART DIRECTOR
Tony DeGregorio
WRITER
Ken Schulman
CLIENT
Sony Trinitron
DIRECTOR
Bob Gaffney
PRODUCTION CO.
Bob Gaffney Productions
AGENCY PRODUCER
Dick Standridge
AGENCY
McCann-Erickson

356
ART DIRECTOR
Barry Vetere
WRITER
Tom Messner
CLIENT
Commodore
DIRECTOR
Mike Cuesta
PRODUCTION CO.
Griner/Cuesta
AGENCY PRODUCER
Bob Van Buren
AGENCY
Ally & Gargano

353

(SFX: NATURAL SOUND EFFECTS THROUGHOUT. AN
   UPBEAT MUSICAL RHYTHM BEGINS.)

ANNCR (VO): Keeping fit has become an American
   passion.
   Today, over 55 million people have taken the
   plunge. Exercising regularly. To keep their
   bodies fit.

(SFX: SOUND EFFECTS AND MUSIC CONTINUE.)
   Well, for all those people who keep their bodies
   in shape, Calvin Klein brings you something
   beautiful... to slip those bodies into.
   Calvin Klein Active Wear.

354 SILVER (TIE)

(MUSIC UNDER)

MAN: Have you been talking to our son on long
   distance again?

WOMAN: (NODS AND WHIMPERS)

MAN: Did he tell you how much he loves you?

WOMAN: (NODS AND WHIMPERS)

MAN: Did he tell you how well he's doing in school?

WOMAN: (NODS AND WHIMPERS AND CRIES)

MAN: All those things are wonderful. What on earth
   are you crying for?

WOMAN: Did you see our long distance bill?

(MUSIC)

ANNCR (VO): If your long distance bills are too much,
   call MCI. Sure, reach out and touch someone.
   Just do it for a whole lot less.

355

ANNCR (VO): Paulatuk, the Arctic Circle
The winters can be ten months long and fifty degrees below.
So people stay home and watch a lot of TV.
Maybe that's why the Tatkiak family chose the only TV to win an Emmy for its beautiful picture.
The Sony Trinitron.
But maybe the Tatkiaks chose a Sony because the nearest TV repairman is two-hundred and fifty miles away.

356

MAN: Do do do do, hut hut hut... (CONT. UNDER ANNCR)

ANNCR (VO): There are those who worry that video game playing can become obsessive.
At Commodore, while we think that's a little extreme, increasing your game scores may not always increase your I.Q.

(MUSIC UNDER)
So Commodore's games come in a different package: A full-fledged computer, the VIC 20, that allows your mind to expand into the thousands of things a computer can do... In addition to playing games.

357
ART DIRECTORS
Peter Hirsch
Mike Withers

WRITER
Hy Abady

CLIENT
AAMCO Transmissions

DIRECTOR
Joe Sedelmaier

PRODUCTION CO.
Sedelmaier Films

AGENCY PRODUCER
Frank DiSalvo

AGENCY
Calet, Hirsch, Kurnit
& Spector

358
ART DIRECTOR
Dennis Hodgson

WRITER
Pat Dennis

CLIENT
McCulloch Corp.

DIRECTOR
Amanda Eggers

PRODUCTION CO.
Eggers Films

AGENCY PRODUCER
Vicki Blucher

AGENCY
Benton & Bowles/Los Angeles

359
ART DIRECTOR
Brent Thomas

WRITER
Dave Butler

CLIENT
Yamaha Motor Corp.

DIRECTORS
Adrian Lyne
Paul Esposito

PRODUCTION CO.
Jennie

AGENCY PRODUCER
Richard O'Neill

AGENCY
Chiat/Day-Los Angeles

360
ART DIRECTOR
Jeff Roll

WRITER
Bill Hamilton

CLIENT
Wienerschnitzel

DIRECTOR
Jim Hinton

PRODUCTION CO.
Wilson-Griak/Mpls.

AGENCY PRODUCER
Morty Baran

AGENCY
Chiat/Day-Los Angeles

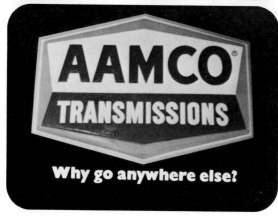

357

MAN: Sure, we're experts. Transmissions, carburetors, what have you.

VO: A lot of places claim to be transmission experts.

MAN: Sure, we're experts. We've been fixing transmissions for close to a month and a half now. Good month and a half.

MAN #1: Sure, we're experts. Why, we've fixed this gentleman's transmission eighteen times, alone.

MAN #2: Nineteen.

MAN #1: Nineteen, nineteen.

VO: Take your car to the real transmission experts. The place that only fixes transmissions and fixes more of them than anyone. AAMCO.

(BEEP-BEEP) Why go anywhere else?

358

TELLER: Oh, you wanted to make a deposit?

BARNEY: You bet. $30.

BILLY: Yeah. It's our McCulloch rebate money.

TELLER: McCulloch? You mean McCulloch chain saws?

BILLY: Yeah. With McCulloch's rebates you can save up to $30.

BARNEY: On gas and electric saws.

TELLER: What do beavers need a chain saw for?

BARNEY/BILLY: We're building a lakehouse.

TELLER: Lakehouse?

BILLY: With a fireplace.

BARNEY: And a hot tub.

TELLER: A hot tub? Sounds romantic.

BARNEY: Say, anyone ever tell you you have great teeth?

BILLY: I think she likes you, Barney.

ANNCR: Get a McCulloch with Chain Brake and get a rebate at your local McCulloch dealer.

359

(SFX: ALL EFFECTS ARE SLIGHTLY LOUDER THAN NORMAL.)

(MUSIC: VOICES AND INSTRUMENTS PLAY THROUGHOUT IN A HUMMED MANNER.)

ANNCR (VO): The Yamaha Virago gives you a V-Twin engine, monoshock suspension, shaft drive... and the satisfaction of knowing that while the others are off following the crowd... you're not.

360

MUSIC: ORIGINAL THROUGHOUT.

SINGERS: *Wienerschnitzel, Wienerschnitzel, Wienerschnitzel, Wienerschnitzel, Wienerschnitzel, Weldon P. Wienerschnitzel Hot Dogs!*

361
ART DIRECTOR
Gary Geyer
WRITER
Peter Murphy
CLIENT
Stroh's Beer
DIRECTOR
Bob Giraldi
PRODUCTION CO.
Giraldi Productions
AGENCY PRODUCER
Paula Dwoskin
AGENCY
The Marschalk Company

362
ART DIRECTOR
Ron Travisano
WRITER
Lew Sherwood
CLIENT
Beech-Nut
DIRECTOR
Bruce Nadel
PRODUCTION CO.
Nadel Film Consortium
AGENCY PRODUCER
Peter Yahr
AGENCY
Sherwood & Schneider

363
ART DIRECTOR & WRITER
Joe LaRosa
CLIENT
Great Waters of France/Perrier
DIRECTOR
R.O. Blechman
PRODUCTION CO.
The Ink Tank
AGENCY PRODUCER
Susan Fehlinger
AGENCY
Waring & LaRosa

364
ART DIRECTOR
Ron Travisano
WRITER
Jerry Della Femina
CLIENT
Airborne Freight
DIRECTOR
Ralph DeVito
PRODUCTION CO.
Ralph DeVito Productions
AGENCY PRODUCER
Dominique Bigar
AGENCY
Della Femina, Travisano
& Partners

361

FIRST MAN: Where are you going?

SECOND MAN: To get a Stroh's

FIRST MAN: That's a 200 mile hike through heavy snow.

SECOND MAN: I know.

FIRST MAN: If you think of it, get two.

SONG: *From one beer lover to another—Stroh's*

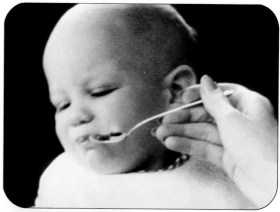

GOOD NUTRITION THAT TASTES GOOD.

362

ANNCR: What good is good nutrition if it doesn't taste good? Because if food doesn't have the taste babies like . . . they could miss getting the nutrition they need. BEECH-NUT, with over 50 years of experience, knows how to make food with the taste babies like and the nutrition they need.
Without adding artificial flavorings or preservatives. And no other Baby Food is more nutritious than delicious BEECH-NUT.

BEECH-NUT. Good nutrition that tastes good.

BABY: Ahhhhhhhhhhhh.

363

(SFX: MUSIC THROUGHOUT.)

CAVEMAN: Eh?

(SFX: SLURPS...KISS SOUND.)

CAVEMAN: C'est magnifique! Un miracle!

ANNCR (VO): Sparkling, refreshing Perrier.
Created by the earth when it was new.
Perrier, Earth's First Soft Drink.

(SFX: SLURP.)

364

VO: Airborne presents the nightmare of shipping
with the wrong air express company.

MAN: Hello. My package is three hours late.

VO: This is your late arriving package nightmare.
And Airborne doesn't ever want it to happen to you.
That's why we're always shooting for 100% on–time
delivery. In fact these days we're making most of
our deliveries before 10:30 a.m.

AIRBORNE OVERNIGHT. We're shooting for
100% on–time delivery.

365
ART DIRECTOR
Ron Travisano
WRITER
Jerry Della Femina
CLIENT
Airborne Freight
DIRECTOR
Ralph DeVito
PRODUCTION CO.
Ralph DeVito Productions
AGENCY PRODUCER
Dominique Bigar
AGENCY
Della Femina, Travisano
& Partners

366
ART DIRECTOR
Andrew Nairn
WRITER
Alan Wooding
CLIENT
Amatil Ltd.
DIRECTOR
Peter Cherry
PRODUCTION CO.
MacDonald, Ibbetson, Cherry
AGENCY PRODUCERS
Andrew Nairn
Alan Wooding
AGENCY
Doyle Dane Bernbach/
Australia

367
ART DIRECTOR
Steve Rosenhaus
WRITER
David Leddick
CLIENT
Revlon
DIRECTOR
Ed Vorkapich
PRODUCTION CO.
Lipson Film Associates
AGENCY PRODUCER
John Greene
AGENCY
Grey Advertising

368
ART DIRECTOR
Steve Rosenhaus
WRITER
David Leddick
CLIENT
Timex
DIRECTOR
Don Cohen
PRODUCTION CO.
Iris Films
AGENCY PRODUCER
John Greene
AGENCY
Grey Advertising

365

SPOKESMAN: Your boss said the deal and your job
depended on this getting to Chicago by twelve noon.
Well, your package didn't make it on time. It wound
up in Package Never-Never Land.

VO: Airborne is working day and night to make
sure your packages aren't delayed in package
Never-Never Land. So, while our competition boasts
about 95% on-time delivery, Airborne is shooting
for 100%.

DELIVERER: This one's going to be late for
Des Moines.

VO: Airborne Overnight. We're shooting for 100%.

366

(MUSIC: THREAD OF MT. FRANKLIN THEME, VERY SOFT
UNDER.)

FARMER (THOUGHT VOICE OVER): I've been livin' near
Mount Franklin most o' my life.

(SFX: WHISTLES TO DOG.)

FARMER TVO: Y'git a lot o' rain here. There's
mineral water all round here under the mountain.
Local people'd collect it in their billies where it
soaked out. Now there's other people comin' up for it.

VO: G'Day

(SFX: WATER.)

FARMER TVO: I've known there was mineral
water under Mount Franklin for forty years. City
people were a bit slower catchin' on.

(SFX: BIRDS.)

(MUSIC: OUT.)

367

FEMALE SINGING: *Jontue*

ANNCR (VO): Come to find the beautiful fragrance of Jontue. Sensual . . . but not too far from innocence.

FEMALE SINGING: *Jontue*

(SFX: MUSIC CONTINUES)

ANNCR (VO): Jontue from Revlon. Wear it and be wonderful.

FEMALE SINGING: *Jontue*

368

VO: Welcome to the Timex Freeze Test. I'm going to freeze this Quartz Analog Timex in this liquid nitrogen at 320 degrees below.

How cold is it? Watch this carnation. Baby, that's cold.

Will our Timex Quartz Analog work? I knew it would.

Durability, beauty and great design aren't expensive.

Just rare.

So wear a Timex.

Because Timex makes technology beautiful.

How am I doing, John Cameron Swayze?

369 GOLD
ART DIRECTOR
Anthony Angotti
WRITER
Joe O'Neill
CLIENT
Club Med
DIRECTOR
Michael Seresin
PRODUCTION CO.
Brooks, Fulford,
Cramer, Seresin
AGENCY PRODUCER
Lorange Spenningsby
AGENCY
Ammirati & Puris

370
ART DIRECTOR
Anthony Angotti
WRITER
Joe O'Neill
CLIENT
Club Med
DIRECTOR
Michael Seresin
PRODUCTION CO.
Brooks, Fulford,
Cramer, Seresin
AGENCY PRODUCER
Lorange Spenningsby
AGENCY
Ammirati & Puris

371
ART DIRECTOR
Anthony Angotti
WRITER
Tom Thomas
CLIENT
BMW of North America
DIRECTOR
Henry Sandbank
PRODUCTION CO.
Sandbank Films
AGENCY PRODUCER
Lorange Spenningsby
AGENCY
Ammirati & Puris

372
ART DIRECTOR
Jim Fitts
WRITERS
Jon Goward
Michael Feinberg
CLIENT
New England Car Wash
Association
DIRECTOR
Marc Yale
PRODUCTION CO.
Cinema Graphics
AGENCY PRODUCER
Jim Fitts
AGENCY
ClarkeGowardCarr
&Fitts/ Boston

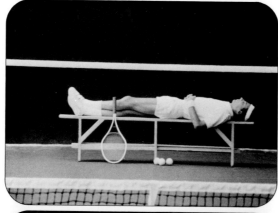

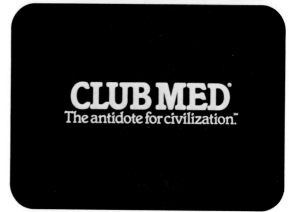

369 GOLD

ANNCR: At Club Med you can water ski...play tennis...snorkel...or sail...wind surf...or play volley ball...

At Club Med you can exercise everything. Including your right not to exercise anything.

SONG: *The Club Med vacation. The antidote for civilization.*

370

ANNCR: If a year of civilization has taken its toll, we recommend one week at Club Med. CLUB MED. Where there are no clocks, no phones. No reminders of everyday life at all. Where you'll be rejuvenated by great sports. Nourished on French cuisine. And the only difficulty you'll encounter will be leaving.

SONG: *The Club Med vacation. The antidote for civilization.*

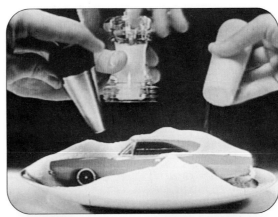

371

ANNCR: BMW presents the only form of interior decoration that ever made a luxury car perform better. Such 'decorations' as an engine driven by microprocessors with an electronic system that actually calculates when service is needed. And a suspension based on a design so advanced it has earned an international patent. The BMW 528e. The difference between advanced gimmickry and advanced technology.

372

VO: Everybody likes a little salt on what they eat. But do you know what salt likes to eat? Cars. Which is worth remembering. Because every winter, several million tons of very hungry salt gets dumped on the roads around here. So if you've been on the roads lately, get your car into a car wash. Before it gets eaten right out from under you.

373
ART DIRECTOR
Maurice Mahler

WRITER
Ted Littleford

CLIENT
Fotomat

DIRECTOR
Dick Loew

PRODUCTION CO.
Gomes Loew

AGENCY PRODUCER
Rob Ewing

AGENCY
Foote, Cone & Belding

374
ART DIRECTORS
Bob Tore
Tom Mabley

WRITER
Arlene Jaffe

CLIENT
IBM

DIRECTOR
Dick Loew

PRODUCTION CO.
Gomes Loew

AGENCY PRODUCER
Robert L. Dein

AGENCY
Lord, Geller, Federico,
Einstein

375
ART DIRECTOR
Rich Kimmel

WRITER
Jim Kochevar

CLIENT
The Eureka Company

DIRECTOR
Bob Kurtz

PRODUCTION CO.
Kurtz & Friends

AGENCY PRODUCER
Lee Lunardi

AGENCY
Young & Rubicam/Chicago

376
ART DIRECTOR
Steve McGuire

WRITER·
Jim Lange

CLIENT
Sands Hotel & Casino

DIRECTOR
Bob Hulme

PRODUCTION CO.
Paisley Productions

AGENCY PRODUCER
Jim Lange

AGENCY
Kalish & Rice/Phila.

373

GRANNY #1: My son's baby.

GRANNY #2: Such a nice little baby.
 My son's baby.

GRANNY #1: Such a big baby.

ANNCR: The Fotomat Custom Series print

GRANNY #2: My son's car.

GRANNY #1: Such a big car.

ANNCR: It's brighter, bolder.

GRANNY #1: Such a big house.

ANNCR: But best of all, they're bigger.
 They're brighter, bolder and best of all, bigger.

3RD LADY: My son's baby.

2ND LADY: Such a nice little baby.
 My son's baby.

3RD LADY: Oh such a big baby.

ANNCR: Get the extra-big Fotomat Custom
 Series Prints. And just for the holidays, get a like
 roll of Fotomat color print film *free.*

374

(MUSIC)

GARY MERRILL (VO): If you run a small business, profits
 can get squeezed when inventory doesn't match up
 with production. What you need is a tool for
 modern times...

 The IBM Personal Computer.

 Not only can it help you plan ahead, it'll balance
 your books and give you more time to make dough.
 And the cost?
 That's the icing on the cake.
 Your own IBM Personal Computer.
 Try it at a store near you.

375

WOMAN (VO): I had the dirtiest apartment in town.
I just didn't have room for a big vacuum cleaner.

So one day I brought home a new kind.

Could it get the hidden dirt?

Ha, the dirt didn't think so.
My cat didn't think so.

But this was the Mighty Mite... from Eureka.

(SFX: EUREKA!)

It was compact, but it had power.
Mighty Mite went everywhere the dirt was, and got it!

ANNCR (VO): Mighty Mite from Eureka. Gets dirt you can't see.

376

(MUSIC)

ANNCR (VO): When you see what's on the card at a lot of places in Atlantic City—it's pretty hit and miss—

(SFX: BELL DINGS.)

ANNCR (VO): And the chorus line's a little too far off Broadway—

But—it's not that way at the Sands.

377
ART DIRECTOR
Craig Joslin
WRITER
Peter Angelos
CLIENT
Seattle-First National Bank
DIRECTOR
Brian Gibson
PRODUCTION CO.
N. Lee Lacy
AGENCY PRODUCERS
Craig Joslin
Peter Angelos
AGENCY
McCann-Erickson/Seattle

378
ART DIRECTOR
Norm Bendell
WRITER
Tom Murphy
CLIENT
Yves St. Laurent
DIRECTORS
Marc Mayhew
Dan Kohn
PRODUCTION CO.
SPS Production
AGENCY PRODUCER
Dan Kohn
AGENCY
Bozell & Jacobs

379
ART DIRECTOR
Dave Baldwin
WRITER
Rob Charker
CLIENT
Jus-rol Ltd/Pommes
Noisettes
DIRECTOR
Graham Rose
PRODUCTION CO.
Rose-Hackney
Productions
AGENCY PRODUCER
Linda Gilbert
AGENCY
W.S. Crawfords Ltd/London

380
ART DIRECTOR
Bob Musachio
WRITER
Steve Katcher
CLIENT
Sharp
DIRECTOR
Frank Stiefel
PRODUCTION CO.
Michael Ulick
Productions
AGENCY PRODUCER
Nancy Braunstein
AGENCY
Rosenfeld, Sirowitz & Lawson

377

TV NEWS REPORTER: We're here with the spokesman of one of the world's largest financial firms following the announcement that Seattle First National Bank is offering a savings account with a rate of interest competitive with Money Market funds.

Your reaction, sir...

BULL: SILENT

REPORTER: Then—uh—you know that Seafirst's new Market Rate Savings are insured by the F.D.I.C...

BULL: SILENT

REPORTER: Then how do you respond to the claim that your Money Market fund just doesn't rate anymore?

BULL: SILENT

REPORTER: How long have you been in this field, anyway?

378

WOMAN: ...so it has come to this!

MAN: You have the manor house. The chalet in San Moritz.

WOMAN: I suppose you will want the paintings.

MAN: They're yours.

WOMAN: Such generosity! I assume you're keeping the cars.

MAN: Only the Bugatti. The Jaguar, the Rolls—all yours.

WOMAN: I am inconsolable.

MAN: Apparently.

WOMAN: But whatever will become of you?

MAN: Don't worry. I'll be just fine.

ANNCR (VO): Yves St. Laurent.
One of life's consolations.

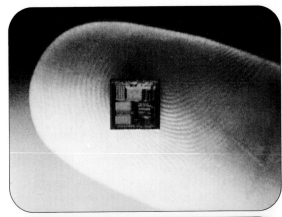

379

MAN: I've eaten potatoes, all my life. Chipped
potatoes, boiled, roast, even sautéd....

.... and quite frankly, I was bored with
potatoes....

.... then I tried Jus-Rol Pommes Noisettes....

.... vive la différence.

.... fluffy balls of mashed potato in a crispy coat.

.... I like them a lot.

MVO: Jus-Rol Pommes Noisettes.
Vive la différence.

380

(SFX: MUSIC UNDER THROUGHOUT.)

ANNCR (VO): When Sharp replaced 300,000 transis-
tors and diodes with this tiny chip, it opened a
whole new world of wonders.

Like taking a big copier and everything it can
do and making it into one of the smallest of any
paper copiers in the world.

Introducing the Sharp SF-750 Copier.

The Sharp SF-750, a very small, very big idea

...and where do big ideas like this come
from...?

From Sharp minds come Sharp Products.

381
ART DIRECTOR
Rob Lopes
WRITER
Patricia Malkin
CLIENT
Lifesavers
DIRECTOR
Mark Story
PRODUCTION CO.
Pfeifer-Story
AGENCY PRODUCER
Dominique Bigar
AGENCY
Dancer-Fitzgerald-Sample

382
ART DIRECTOR
Al Schmidt
WRITERS
Dave Fairman
Fred Wood
CLIENT
Ralston Purina
DIRECTOR
David Stern
PRODUCTION CO.
Associates & Toback
AGENCY PRODUCER
Bob Carney
AGENCY
Tatham-Laird & Kudner/
Chicago

383
ART DIRECTOR
Nancy Rice
WRITER
Tom McElligott
CLIENT
Armour/Gold 'N Plump
DIRECTOR
Jim Hinton
PRODUCTION CO.
Wilson-Griak
AGENCY PRODUCER
Judy Carter
AGENCY
Fallon, McElligot, Rice/Mpls.

384
ART DIRECTOR
Bill Berenter
WRITER
Martin Greenhouse
CLIENT
Knickerbocker Toy
Company
PRODUCTION CO.
Richard Williams Animation/
Los Angeles
AGENCY PRODUCER
Merle Bloom Associates
AGENCY
Berenter Greenhouse Elgort

381

MOTHER: My husband is about to eat a new candy.

(SFX: BONK!)

MOTHER: New super-fruity Bonkers. My son thought Bonkers was gum.

(SFX: BONK!)

MOTHER: He knows it's candy now. Chewy fruit candy with this extra-fruity inside. So super-fruity when you eat Bonkers fruit candy.

(SFX: BONK!)

ANNCR (VO): Bonkers bonks you out!

MOTHER: Some candy!

(SFX: BONK!)

ANNCR (VO): Artificially flavored.

382

ANNCR (VO): A Special Dinners Special Report:

Recent tests revealed cats...prefer the taste of Purina Special Dinners brand cat foot...3 to 1...

...over other leading dry cat foods.

Ah...wait a minute...Um...That's 3 to 1.

Its taste is preferred...*3* to 1. Because Special Dinners has something ordinary cat foods don't have...

a special taste that makes Special Dinners preferred 3 to 1.

We...just can't seem to find the one.

383

(SFX: ROOSTER CROWS)

ANNCR (VO): For years southern chickens have been trucked into Minnesota.

(MUSIC UNDER: "STOUT-HEARTED MEN")

ANNCR (VO): Now Gold'n Plump—the only chicken that's grown in Minnesota—declares war.

Presenting the Gold'n Plump Chicken Corps

...an elite flock dedicated to stopping the invasion of southern chickens...

...and to insuring that every store offers you Gold'n Plump chickens, the freshest chicken money can buy.

So go ahead Minnesota...eat well tonight. Gold'n Plump chickens are guarding your table.

384

RAGGEDY ANN: We Knickerbocker toys have raised Debby. But you grownups know, some Knickerbocker toys have raised entire families.

CURIOUS GEORGE: Last year when she fell it was me she ran to.

HOLLY HOBBIE: I helped her through her first day of school.

RAGGEDY ANN: You see, we Knickerbocker toys are her best friends. She loves us, and we—love her back.

VO: Knickerbocker. Toys that love you back.

385
ART DIRECTOR
Pete Coutroulis
WRITER
Lynne Kluger
CLIENT
Six Flags Magic Mountain
DIRECTOR
Don McPherson
PRODUCTION CO.
Eggers Films
AGENCY PRODUCER
Lynne Kluger
AGENCY
Della Femina, Travisano
& Partners/Los Angeles

386
ART DIRECTOR
Ken Grimshaw
WRITER
John Donnelly
CLIENT
San Domingo
DIRECTOR
Barry Myers
PRODUCTION CO.
Spots
AGENCY PRODUCER
Sandy Watson
AGENCY
KMP Partnership/London

387
ART DIRECTOR
Warren Greene
WRITER
Barry Udoff
CLIENT
No Salt
DIRECTOR
Phil Marco
PRODUCTION CO.
Phil Marco
Productions
AGENCY PRODUCER
Ivan Malomut
AGENCY
Cadwell Davis Partners

388
ART DIRECTOR
Frank Ceglia
WRITER
Roger Feuerman
CLIENT
Hallmark Cards
DIRECTOR
Robert Brooks
PRODUCTION CO.
Brooks, Fulford,
Cramer, Seresin
AGENCY PRODUCER
Mootsy Elliot
AGENCY
Young & Rubicam

385

ANNCR (VO): We asked members of the Twelve
    Hundred First...to demonstrate what it's like to
    ride new Free Fall at Magic Mountain.

SERGEANT: "OK men...drop your chutes."

(SFX: WIND AS DOOR OPENS.)

ANNCR (VO): Free Fall. We just take you to the top of
    a gigantic tower.

    Push you to the edge. And then drop you off.

    Without any parachute...wires...or cables...to
    slow you down.

    Free Fall.

    To experience it...you have to come to Six Flags
    Magic Mountain.

    Or see your Army recruiter.

386

SOLICITOR (READING): To my unfaithful young wife, I
    leave my faithful old Bentley.

    And my Chippendale chairs to my ass of a son.

    My San Domingo pale cream sherry I leave to
    Reynolds.

    We both know that the finest sherry comes
    from Spain. And only a truly British palate could
    fully appreciate it.

(SFX: SLAM)

RELATIVE: B-but, the estate!

SOLICITOR: That goes with the San Domingo.

(VO): San Domingo pale cream sherry from Gonzalez
    Byass.

387

ANNCR (VO): Are you a saltaholic?

Sure you are, because salt hides in most everything. Even where you don't expect it. Most Americans get 20 times the salt their bodies need. So why salt the salt? NoSalt flavors like salt without salt. Cook with NoSalt. Shake with NoSalt. Since there's so much salt in most everything, who needs more salt?

NoSalt. And shake the salt habit.

Ask for it in restaurants, too.

388

(MUSIC UNDER)

LISA: Miss Elliott, has he finished his tea yet?

MISS ELLIOTT: He should be just about done.

LISA: Thanks.

(MUSIC)

LISA SINGS (VO): *Oh, I knew it was your birthday, but you didn't know I knew. And I just wanted to find the right surprise for you.*

PROFESSOR: Good afternoon, Lisa.

LISA: Good afternoon Professor.

PROFESSOR: Are we prepared?

LISA: I think so.

PROFESSOR: Hm, let's see what Mr. Beethoven thinks.

(MUSIC)

LISA SINGS (VO): *So I'm giving you this Hallmark and I hope that you will see, what I'm giving you is a part of me.*

PROFESSOR: Thank you Lisa.

ANNCR (VO): Make someone's birthday special. Give a little of yourself. Give a Hallmark.

(MUSIC OUT)

389
ART DIRECTORS
Paul Singer
Ron Becker

WRITERS
Bob Hildt
Joe Tantillo

CLIENT
Fuji Photo Film

DIRECTOR
Murray Bruce

PRODUCTION CO.
Murray Bruce
Productions

AGENCY PRODUCER
Jean Muchmore

AGENCY
Geers Gross Advertising

390
ART DIRECTOR
Ted Shaine

WRITER
Diane Rothschild

CLIENT
Procter & Gamble/
Coast Soap

DIRECTOR
Bert Steinhauser

PRODUCTION CO.
Bert Steinhauser Productions

AGENCY PRODUCERS
Cheryl Nelson
Sheldon Levy

AGENCY
Doyle Dane Bernbach

391
ART DIRECTORS
Bud Shehab
Brian Gregg

WRITER
Dick Hazlett

CLIENT
Quasar

DIRECTOR
Bob Giraldi

PRODUCTION CO.
Giraldi Productions

AGENCY PRODUCER
Treva Bachand

AGENCY
Needham, Harper & Steers/
Chicago

392
ART DIRECTOR
Dean Stefanides

WRITER
Earl Carter

CLIENT
Nikon

DIRECTOR
Dennis Chalkin

PRODUCTION CO.
Dennis Chalkin
Productions

AGENCY PRODUCER
Gary Grossman

AGENCY
Scali, McCabe, Sloves

389

(MUSIC UP)

ANNCR : Watch closely. You're about to see something you've never seen before. Here comes Fuji Film with color pictures so true to life, it's a real breakthrough.
Fuji Film.
Fuji's advanced technology has developed a precise color balance.

The better the color balance, the truer the picture.

Consistantly brighter...clearer. With Fuji, seeing is believing.

So see for yourself.

Get Fuji Film.
And get the true picture.

Fuji. Official Film of the Los Angeles 1984 Olympics.

(MUSIC OUT)

390

(MUSIC THROUGHOUT.)

ANNCR: Some work makes you a little more tired than other work. That's why one thing waiting for every player in the NFL is a bar of Coast deodorant soap. Coast is made to revive you, and with its cool, stimulating scent and a thick, creamy lather that feels terrific on your skin, Coast refreshes you and rejuvenates you and picks you up in a way no other soap can.

And if Coast can help after a day like this, imagine how it can make you feel after a day in the office.

No tired is too tired for Coast.

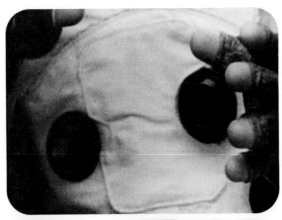

391

(SFX: TAPE: Chairman...)

CHAIRMAN: Call me when you get a Quasar.

WOMAN: Call us dear when you get a Quasar.

ANNCR (VO): For quality and dependability, shouldn't you have a Quasar?

SINGERS: *QUASAR*

392

VO: When the space shuttle took off, one of the few things on board that didn't have a backup system ...was a Nikon camera.

393
ART DIRECTOR
Howard Smith
WRITER
Mary Ann Zeeman
CLIENT
Maxell
DIRECTOR
Dick Loew
PRODUCTION CO.
Gomes Loew
AGENCY PRODUCERS
Richard Berke
Gary Grossman
AGENCY
Scali, McCabe, Sloves

394
ART DIRECTOR
Steve Montgomery
WRITER
Rodney Underwood
CLIENT
Nickelodeon-Warner Amex
DIRECTOR
Mark Story
PRODUCTION CO.
Sandbank Films
AGENCY PRODUCER
Ann O'Keefe
AGENCY
Scali, McCabe, Sloves

395
ART DIRECTOR
Sam Scali
WRITER
Michael Robertson
CLIENT
American Can Co.
DIRECTOR
Bill Hudson
PRODUCTION COS.
Bill Hudson Films
AGENCY PRODUCER
David Perry
AGENCY
Scali, McCabe, Sloves

396
ART DIRECTOR
Nancy Rosenbaum
WRITERS
Hal Friedman
Brian Sitts
Jim Patterson
CLIENT
Burger King
DIRECTORS
Jonathon Yarbrough
Steve Gluck
PRODUCTION COS.
Summerhouse Films
Grand Street Films
AGENCY PRODUCER
Edgar C. Kahn
AGENCY
J. Walter Thompson

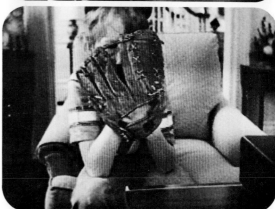

393

VO: If you play your video recordings a lot...

(SFX: VCR EJECT)

VO: you need a more durable tape.

(SFX: TAPE BEING REMOVED FROM SLEEVE.)

VO: Maxell HGX.

(SFX: LOADING TAPE)

MOTHER (VO): While you're away, Sonny, don't forget your exercises—one, two, one...

ANNCR (VO): With HGX you can play your recordings...one, two, one, two...over and over. And still get a great picture. One, two... Maxell HGX. The long term video tape. One, two. Maxell. It's worth it.

394

(SFX: GAME SHOW)

ANNCR (VO): Most of what kids see on T.V....

(SFX: SOAP OPERA)

ANNCR (VO): isn't really for them.

(SFX: SIT-COM)

ANNCR (VO): But now there's...Nickelodeon. Nickelodeon's the only cable T.V. station devoted totally to the interest of kids. We offer a wide variety of shows for kids...but they all have one thing in common. They're not recommended for mature audiences.

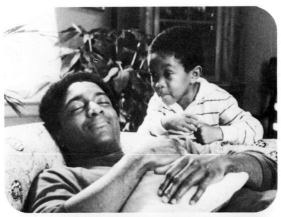

395

(SFX: KNOCK, KNOCK)

LITTLE GIRL 1: Can I use your bathroom? Susie said it's O.K.

(SFX: KNOCK, KNOCK)

LITTLE GIRL 2: Susie said I can use your bathroom, O.K.?

(SFX: KNOCK, KNOCK)

LITTLE GIRL 3: Susie said it's O.K. to use your bathroom.

SUSIE: Mom, we need more toilet paper.

MOM (VO): In the linen closet, Susie.

ANNCR (VO): Introducing Northern Soft Prints. Now you get more than softness. With our decorated rose print...you get a more attractive bathroom.

VO: Hi, Susie.

LITTLE GIRL 4 (VO): Susie sent me.

ANNCR (VO): New Northern Soft Prints.

396

BOY: There he is, lyin' on the couch when from nowhere, he's thinkin' about a great big juicy Whopper!

SINGER: *Flame-broiled Whopper*

BOY: But why should he care about a Whopper?

SINGER: *With cheese and tomato and onion—crispy lettuce, too.*

BOY: Fight it, Dad, fight it!

SINGERS: *Aren't you hungry?*
Aren't you hungry for Burger King now?

BOY: Got 'im again!

Consumer Television 30 Second Single

397
ART DIRECTORS
Greg Weinschenker
Deyna Vesey
WRITERS
Linda Kaplan
Lee Gardner
CLIENT
Toys "R" Us
DIRECTOR
Ron Dexter
PRODUCTION CO.
The Dxtr's
AGENCY PRODUCER
Meredith Wright
AGENCY
J. Walter Thompson

398
ART DIRECTOR
Larry Frey
WRITER
Gary Lande
CLIENT
Illinois Bell
DIRECTOR
Jim Wotring
PRODUCTION CO.
Wotring/Kuwalski
AGENCY PRODUCER
Hank Sabian
AGENCY
N.W. Ayer/Chicago

399
ART DIRECTOR
John Coll
WRITER
Bob Hoffman
CLIENT
KYUU Radio
DIRECTOR
Bob Eggers
PRODUCTION CO.
Eggers Films
AGENCY PRODUCER
Carol Tanner
AGENCY
Allen & Dorward/
San Francisco

400
ART DIRECTOR
John Coll
WRITER
Bob Hoffman
CLIENT
KYUU Radio
DIRECTOR
Bob Eggers
PRODUCTION CO.
Eggers Films
AGENCY PRODUCER
Carol Tanner
AGENCY
Allen & Dorward/
San Francisco

397

MAN SINGING: *I don't want to grow up I'm a Toys "R" Us kid.*

LITTLE BOY SINGING: *They got a million toys at Toys "R" Us that she can play with.*

MAN SINGING: *I don't want to grow up I'm a Toys "R" Us kid*

WOMAN SINGING: *They got the best for so much less you'll really flip your lid*

SINGERS: *From bikes to trains to video games it's the biggest toy store there is. Gee wiz!*

MAN SINGING: *I don't want to grow up cuz baby if I did*

WOMAN SINGING: *I couldn't be a Toys "R" Us kid*

LITTLE GIRL SINGING: *More games more toys oh boy!*

MAN SINGING: *I want to* (STARTS CLEARING THROAT)

SINGERS: *I want to be a Toys "R" Us kid.*

398

(MUSIC UNDER)

(SFX: FAUCET BREAKING)

HER: I'll call the plumber.

(MUSIC UP)

(SFX: CHANDELIER FALLING)

HER: I'll call the electrician.

VO: Maybe you can't fix everything, but if your Bell phone isn't working...

HIM: Does the other phone work?

HER: Yeah...

HIM: I'll fix it myself.

(SHE REACTS WITH HORROR)

VO: ...the only repair person you need is you. Just bring it to any Bell PhoneCenter. In most cases we'll replace it on the spot...

(HE EXCHANGES PHONE)

VO: ...and you'll have a phone that works again.

(SFX: DIAL TONE)

HER: You did fix it!

HIM: Of course!

VO: Do-it-yourself phone repair.

(SFX: HAMMERING, ALL PICTURES FALL OFF WALL.)

VO: Another handy idea from Illinois Bell.

399

MOM: Hello. My son John is the manager of KYUU. Well, if he doesn't make them the number one radio station—it could be his tush. So please listen to KYUU. (MUSIC UNDER) They play the nicest music by Fleetfoot Mike and the Doodie Brothers. You'll help my son John, I know you will.

VO: You can listen to KYUU. Or you can break a mother's heart.

400

(MUSIC UNDER)

MOM: You're watching television again. You're not listening to KYUU. I guess my John will never be number one. He'll probably move back with me. And he'll forget to feed my poor little Binky. And Binky will go to the hospital and I'll spend all my savings on him. But don't you worry. You're busy watching television.

VO: You can listen to 99.7 KYUU. Or you can break a mother's heart.

401
ART DIRECTOR
Peter Jones
WRITER
John Kyriakou
CLIENT
Greb Industries
DIRECTOR
Ian Leech
PRODUCTION CO.
The Partners
AGENCY PRODUCER
John Auriemma
AGENCY
J. Walter Thompson/Toronto

402
ART DIRECTOR
Steve Rustard
WRITERS
Mac Churchill
Jim Sanderson
CLIENT
Sea Galley Restaurants
DIRECTOR
Tom McNeil
PRODUCTION CO.
North Star
Productions
AGENCY PRODUCER
Robert La Chance
AGENCY
J. Walter Thompson/
San Francisco

403
ART DIRECTOR
Ted Duquette
WRITER
Ted Charron
CLIENT
New England Brown Egg Council
DIRECTOR
Sid Myers
PRODUCTION CO.
Griner/Cuesta
AGENCY PRODUCER
Beverly Monchun
AGENCY
Ingalls Associates/Boston

401

(SFX: THROUGHOUT)
ANNCR: The new Wilderness Boot from Kodiak.
Wilderness.
Built Kodiak tough.
With steel plates and steel toes.
Resists the cold and repels the wet.
It's just got to be the Wilderness Boot... from Kodiak.
MAN: Thanks for the walk.

402

SINGERS: *Who's got crab legs?*
  Who's got crab legs?
  Who's got crab legs?
  We've got crab legs! (Sea Galley!)
  We've got crab legs!
  We've got crab legs! (Sea Galley!)
  We've got Snow! (Snow! Snow!)
  King! (King! King!)
  Dungeness, too!
  Get your crab legs! (Sea Galley!)
  Get your crab legs! (Sea Galley!)
  We've got crab legs!
  So come get your crab legs—tonight!

403

MALE VO: Everyone likes fresh food...but how do
  you tell if the food you're buying is *really
  fresh?* It can be quite a problem. Especially
  when it comes to eggs. But thank goodness you
  live in New England. Because, in New England,
  eggs that come from local farms are brown...
  and that makes it very easy to tell if an egg is
  fresh. All you have to do is look at it.

JINGLE: *Brown eggs are local eggs, and local eggs
  are fresh.*

Consumer Television
30 Seconds Campaign

404
ART DIRECTOR
Lee Stewart
WRITER
Bill Teitelbaum
CLIENT
Wiss Snips
DIRECTOR
Henry Sandbank
PRODUCTION CO.
Sandbank Films
AGENCY PRODUCER
Bill Teitelbaum
AGENCY
Howard, Merrell & Boykin/
North Carolina

405
ART DIRECTOR
Dianne Campbell
WRITER
Beth McLure
CLIENT
AT&T Long Lines
DIRECTORS
Steve Horn
Dan Nichols
PRODUCTION COS.
Steve Horn Productions
Michael Daniel Productions
AGENCY PRODUCER
Gaston Braun
AGENCY
N.W. Ayer

406
ART DIRECTORS
Dave Davis
Nick Gisonde
WRITERS
Robert Tamburri
Jeane Bice
Charlie Breen
CLIENT
Miller Brewing /Lite Beer
DIRECTORS
Bob Giraldi
Steve Horn
PRODUCTION COS.
Giraldi Productions
Steve Horn Productions
AGENCY PRODUCERS
Marc Mayhew
Eric Steinhauser
AGENCY
Backer & Spielvogel

407
ART DIRECTOR
Joe Del Vecchio
WRITER
Peter Bregman
CLIENT
GTE
DIRECTORS
Mark Story
Jeff Mayo
PRODUCTION COS.
Pfeifer Story
Jeff Mayo Productions
AGENCY PRODUCERS
Stuart Raffel
Jim Callan
AGENCY
Doyle Dane Bernbach

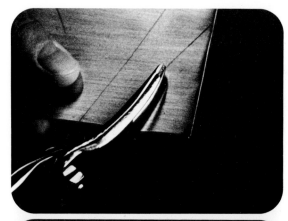

404

VO: Compared to ordinary snips, Wiss Metalmaster snips will give you twice as much leverage.

That means you can cut down to the tip of the blades: without leaving ragged edges, without overcutting, and without losing your control on the turns.

So now you can deal with sheet metal . . . as if you were cutting paper.

Wiss Metalmaster snips from Coopertools, the difference between work and workmanship.

405

BOY #1: Bet you're glad your brother finally went away to school.

BOY #2: Yeah.

BOY #1: You get his room, his bike, and everything. What a deal.

BOY #2: Yeah.

BOY #1: And just think . . . no one to call you Peeper anymore.

BOY #2: Yeah.

MOTHER: David, your brother's on the phone. He wants to talk to you!

BOY #2: Brian? For me? Oh boy!

BOY #2: Hi Brian!

OLDER BROTHER: Hey Peeper! How ya doin' kid?

MUSIC AND SINGERS: *Reach out, reach out and touch someone.*

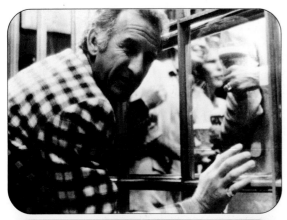

406

UECKER: Alright maybe I wasn't the greatest player of all time. But fans, they forgive and forget. Why, when I go in here they'll be buying me my favorite beer. Lite Beer from Miller.

MAN: Are you a-a, Bob Uecker?

BOB: Yeah, how ya doin'? These fans, I love 'em. They know us ex-big leaguers drink Lite because it's less filling and it tastes great. Well, can't keep the gang waitin'. Ugh-h. These fans (huh), are always jokin'.

ANNCR.: Lite Beer from Miller. Everything you always wanted in a beer. And less.

UECKER: Wow they're having a good time in there.

407

CATMAN: Gentlemen. We need to cut back to show a profit. Suggestions?

MAN 1: We could lay off 40% of the work force.

CATMAN: Too brutal...

(SFX: KABOOOM!!!)

MAN 2.: Uh...eliminate the executive cars and...

CATMAN: Excessive.

(SFX: WHOOOOOOOOSH!!!!)

CATMAN: How 'bout you, Phipps?

PHIPPS: Well, sir...we could *buy* a business phone system from General Telephone.

We'd get state-of-the-art digital equipment.

Reliable phone company service.

And, sir, with the benefits of ownership, we'd save a bundle in the long run.

CATMAN: Brilliant!!!!

And I'm not one to give out compliments.

PHIPPS: Heh. Heh...Sort of noticed, sir.

408

(DRAMATIC MUSIC)

vo: Since 1975 we changed a few things on the Rabbit.

We made it faster.

We made it more economical.

We made it more reliable.

Seven years and 15,000 changes later, we improved the way the Rabbit runs,

not the way it looks.

409

(MUSIC UNDER)

ANNCR (VO): Rather than compare personal computers ourselves,

we asked the computers which one was better on the basis of price and memory.

The Apple II preferred the Commodore 64.

Then we asked the IBM

and it picked the Commodore 64.

Then the Radio Shack chose

the Commodore 64.

That's what we like about our competition.

They're so honest.

The Commodore 64.

(MUSIC OUT)

410

ANNCR: Chemical Bank now offers... Rosenfeld
Luggage.
Sure it's made of heavy duty nylon, but it's
also... beautiful. And practical. And we're giving
it away. Invest $5,000 in one of Chemical's high
interest C.D.'s and a three-piece set of designer
luggage is yours. So come into Chemical Bank.
And claim your baggage. Certain C.D.'s require
larger minimum deposits. Additional information
about deposits, eligibility qualifications and
restrictions available at any branch. Substantial
interest penalties for early withdrawal. Member
FDIC. Offer may be withdrawn without notice.

411

ANNCR (VO): Over 55 million people in America
today work very hard at something besides their jobs.

And that's staying in shape.

If you're one of those people who struggles to stay
in shape, well, thanks to Calvin Klein, the virtues
have never been quite so evident.

Calvin Klein introduces Active Wear.

412
ART DIRECTOR
Barry Vetere
WRITER
Tom Mesner
CLIENT
Commodore
DIRECTOR
Mike Cuesta
PRODUCTION CO.
Griner/Cuesta
AGENCY PRODUCER
Bob Van Buren
AGENCY
Ally & Gargano

413 GOLD
ART DIRECTOR
Michael Tesch
WRITER
Patrick Kelly
CLIENT
Federal Express
DIRECTORS
Patrick Kelly
Joe Sedelmaier
PRODUCTION COS.
Kelly Pictures
Hampton Road Films
Sedelmaier Films
AGENCY PRODUCER
Maureen Kearns
AGENCY
Ally & Gargano

414 SILVER
ART DIRECTOR
George Euringer
WRITERS
Helayne Spivak
Tom Messner
CLIENT
MCI
DIRECTOR
Bob Giraldi
PRODUCTION CO.
Giraldi Productions
AGENCY PRODUCER
Jerry Haynes
AGENCY
Ally & Gargano

415
ART DIRECTORS
Roger Rowe
Jeff Young
Bob Jeffers
WRITERS
John Gruen
Mark Schneider
Brian Quinn
CLIENT
General Foods
DIRECTORS
Michael Seresin
Steve Horn
Bob Brooks
PRODUCTION COS.
Brooks, Fulford,
Cramer, Seresin
Steve Horn Productions
AGENCY PRODUCER
Sandra Breakstone
AGENCY
Ogilvy & Mather

412

MAN: Do do do do, hut hut hut... (CONT. UNDER ANNCR)

ANNCR (VO): There are those who worry that video game playing can become obsessive.
At Commodore, while we think that's a little extreme, increasing your game scores may not always increase your I.Q.

(MUSIC UNDER)
So Commodore's games come in a different package: A full-fledged computer, the VIC 20, that allows your mind to expand into the thousands of things a computer can do... In addition to playing games.

413 GOLD

GUY: I need that package of slides for a major presentation tomorrow at 10:30 a.m.

COMPETITOR: You got it!

GUY: Not noon, not 3:00, 10:30 a.m.

COMPETITOR: You got it!

GUY: Listen to me. No slides, no presentation.

COMPETITOR: You got it!

GUY: Well, where is it?

COMPETITOR: You'll get it!

(SFX: BARKING)

ANNCR (VO): Next time send it Federal Express.
Now Federal schedules delivery by 10:30 a.m.
So when we say you got it, you'll get it.

414 SILVER

(MUSIC UNDER)

MAN: Have you been talking to our son on long distance again?

WOMAN: (NODS AND WHIMPERS)

MAN: Did he tell you how much he loves you?

WOMAN: (NODS AND WHIMPERS)

MAN: Did he tell you how well he's doing in school?

WOMAN: (NODS AND WHIMPERS AND CRIES)

MAN: All those things are wonderful. What on earth are you crying for?

WOMAN: Did you see our long distance bill?

(MUSIC)

ANNCR (VO): If your long distance bills are too much, call MCI. Sure, reach out and touch someone. Just do it for a whole lot less.

415

SONG: *The day is gray there's not much doing.*
Nothing much seems worth pursuing
Time to get something brewin'
you and Maxwell House got the taste that's made
for sharin', so share a cup or two.
It don't take much to make a moment
Maxwell House and you.

GIRL: Hi.

SONG: *Get that "Good to the Last Drop" Feeling*

BOY: Hi.

GIRL: Coffee?

SONG: *With Maxwell House only Maxwell House gives you "Good*

BOY: That's good.

SONG: *to the Last Drop" Feeling*

BOY: Hey, can I take your picture?

GIRL: Really?

BOY: Yah. You look great.

SONG: *Maxwell House!*

Consumer Television 30 Second Campaign

416

ART DIRECTORS
Joe Toto
Al Ragin

WRITERS
Pam Cohen
Marcia Sarubin

CLIENT
Schlitz Brewing

DIRECTOR
Bob Giraldi

PRODUCTION CO.
Giraldi Productions

AGENCY PRODUCERS
Carmon Johnston
Richard Wysocki

AGENCY
Benton & Bowles

417

ART DIRECTOR
Bill Schwartz

WRITER
Chris Perry

CLIENT
Sentry Hardware

DIRECTOR
Herb Stott

PRODUCTION CO.
Spungbuggy

AGENCY PRODUCER
Chris Dieck

AGENCY
Meldrum & Fewsmith/Ohio

418

ART DIRECTOR
Anthony Angotti

WRITER
Joe O'Neill

CLIENT
Club Med

DIRECTOR
Michael Seresin

PRODUCTION CO.
Brooks, Fulford,
Cramer, Seresin

AGENCY PRODUCER
Lorange Spenningsby

AGENCY
Ammirati & Puris

419

ART DIRECTOR
Ron Travisano

WRITER
Jim Weller

CLIENT
WABC-TV

DIRECTOR
Steve Horn

PRODUCTION CO.
Steve Horn Productions

AGENCY PRODUCER
Vera Samama

AGENCY
Della Femina, Travisano
& Partners

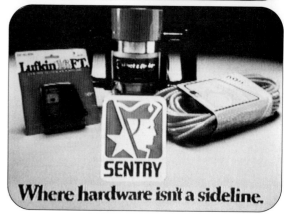

416

(MUSIC)

FOUR TOPS SINGING: *Tonight you're still a bachelor. Tomorrow's almost here. So while you're still a free man, let's bring on the beer...*

KOOL & THE GANG: Bull!

FOUR TOPS: Bull?

KOOL & THE GANG: *On this night to remember it's all clear. You deserve to celebrate with more taste than beer. The Bull's got a taste so big, so bold, so smooth, Let's all party with the Schlitz Malt Liquor Bull.*

ALL: *Don't say beer, say Bull.*

BACHELOR: Hey gang, how about another Bull?

(SFX: RUMBLING)

(SFX: CRASH)

ALL: No one does it like the Bull.

417

(MUSIC: LIGHT HUMOROUS TEMPO UNDER THROUGHOUT)

VO: Some stores offer a small selection of hardware ...and "advice" like this:

DISCOUNT SALESMAN: You need a washer.

DISCOUNT SALESMAN: How's this beauty?

VO: But Sentry Hardware offers thousands of products like... Carol 50 foot outdoor extension cords, $6.66. Black and Decker routers $52.44. Lufkin 16 foot unilok tapes $4.44 *plus advice* like this:

DEALER: You need a washer. How's this beauty?

VO: Sentry. Where hardware isn't a sideline.

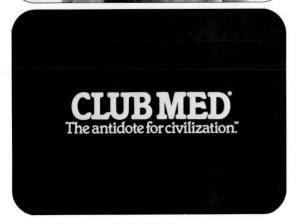

418

ANNCR: If a year of civilization has taken its toll, we recommend one week at Club Med. CLUB MED. Where there are no clocks, no phones. No reminders of everyday life at all. Where you'll be rejuvenated by great sports. Nourished on French cuisine. And the only difficulty you'll encounter will be leaving.

SONG: *The Club Med vacation. The antidote for civilization.*

419

VOICES: Good evening, here's the news. Good evening, here's the news.

ANNCR (VO): Today, television seems to be producing newscasters who all look and sound the same. But one news team has never lost its personal touch.

BILL: Gee, . . . you look kinda nice tonight.

ROGER: I do?

BILL: Yea, who dressed you?

ROGER: Funny.

ANNCR (VO): Because on Eyewitness News we're as different as the city we report to.

BILL: Rog—please don't forget to smile tonight.

ROGER: I *am* smiling.

420
ART DIRECTOR
Jerry Box
WRITER
Jim Copacino
CLIENT
Alaska Airlines
DIRECTOR
Joe Sedelmaier
PRODUCTION CO.
Sedelmaier Films
AGENCY PRODUCER
Virginia Pellegrino
AGENCY
Chiat/Day/Livingston-
Seattle

421
ART DIRECTOR
Frank Fristachi
WRITER
Neil Drossman
CLIENT
Airwick/Binaca Mouthwash
DIRECTOR
Jim Johnston
PRODUCTION CO.
Johnston Films
AGENCY PRODUCER
Rhoda Malamet
AGENCY
Drossman Yustein & Clowes

422
ART DIRECTOR
Jill Parsons
WRITERS
Ken Mullen
Phil Wiggins
CLIENT
Swift
DIRECTOR
Ross Cramer
PRODUCTION CO.
Brooks, Fulford
Cramer, Seresin
AGENCY PRODUCER
Jane Bearman
AGENCY
TBWA/London

423
ART DIRECTOR
John Burk
WRITER
Bill Evans
CLIENT
Prince Manufacturing
DIRECTOR
Henry Trettin
PRODUCTION CO.
N. Lee Lacy
AGENCY PRODUCER
Clare Hartman
AGENCY
Richardson Myers & Donofrio/
Baltimore

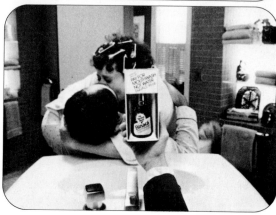

420

FLIGHT ATTENDANT: Munchie time!

PASSENGER: This is it?

ANNCR VO: Has your airline lost its taste for food?

PASSENGER: This is it?

PASSENGER: Evidently, this is it.

ANNCR (VO): Next trip try Alaska Airlines Gold Coast
Service.
It'll leave a good taste in your mouth.

421

VOICE (ANNOUNCERY): Introducing new Binaca mouthwash concentrate

GUY (SLEEPILY): Wha?

VO: Just fill the cup with water

MAN: Honey

VO: then squirt.

MAN: squirt

VO: New Binaca is concentrated

MAN: concentrated

VO: so you pay for mouthwash, not water

MAN: Ohhhh

VO: Wait. This little 2½ oz. bottle's a great value.
Makes 96 ounces

MAN: 96 ounces

VO: of minty fresh Binaca mouthwash.

MAN: Honey

VO: That's a lot of Binaca blaaaaaasssts.

(SFX: EXPLOSION)

MAN: Wow

WOMAN: Good morning, honey. Honey!

VO: Introducing new Binaca mouthwash
concentrate.

Prince. The powerful
new force in tennis.

422

(SFX: NATURAL THROUGHOUT)

PARSON: As you're Americans, we thought we'd offer you...steaks!...

FIRST AMERICAN CLERGYMAN: You bet!

PARSON (VO): Butterball Turkey breast steaks. What would the Pilgrim Fathers have made of them?

PARSON (LIVE): Being deep basted, you see, their goodness goes through and through.

SECOND AMERICAN CLERGYMAN: If they'da had steaks as juicy as these they'da nivver gotten aboard the Mayflower!

(SFX: GUFFAWS AND LAUGHTER.)

MVO: Turkey breast steaks from Butterball.

Juicy all the way to the parson's nose.

423

(MUSIC WITH VOICE OVER):

This is the Prince Player. Touring pro Vincent Van Patten. Winner over John McEnroe at a world super tennis tournament in Tokyo. Vince's natural quickness combined with the lightning-swift response of his Prince Graphite are key to one of the most stylish and aggressive games in pro tennis.

Prince.

Classic.

Pro.

Woodie.

Graphite.

The powerful new force in tennis.

424
ART DIRECTORS
Ron Travisano
Paul Basile

WRITER
Jerry Della Femina

CLIENT
WABC-TV

DIRECTOR
Gerry Cotts

PRODUCTION CO.
Metzner Productions

AGENCY PRODUCER
Joanne Diglio

AGENCY
Della Femina, Travisano
& Partners

425
ART DIRECTOR
Eric Hanson

WRITER
Bob Finley

CLIENT
Kay Bee Toy Stores

DIRECTOR
Jerry Collamer

PRODUCTION CO.
Team Productions

AGENCY PRODUCER
Bob Finley

AGENCY
Sachs, Finley/Los Angeles

426
ART DIRECTORS & WRITERS
Faith Popcorn
Stuart Pittman

CLIENT
Renfield Importers

DIRECTOR
Elbert Budin

PRODUCTION CO.
Ampersand

AGENCY PRODUCER
Joan Bennett

AGENCY
BrainReserve

427
ART DIRECTORS
Allan Beaver
Bob Phillips

WRITERS
Larry Plapler
Peri Frost

CLIENT
People Express

DIRECTOR
Mike Cuesta

PRODUCTION CO.
Griner/Cuesta

AGENCY PRODUCER
Rachel Novak

AGENCY
Levine, Huntley, Schmidt
& Beaver

424

ANNCR : What do you think of Tom Snyder?

ANNIE : I think he's a very nice man. (BARK) Easy
Sandy.

ANNCR : He's Tom Snyder.
He's on Eyewitness News.
Tonight at 11.

425

V.O.: Buy Kenner's Play Dough from a toy store that
won't play around with your dough. Kay Bee Toy
Stores.

 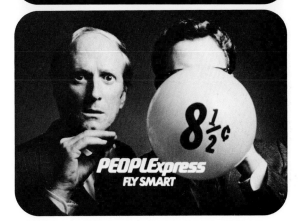

426

(MUSIC THROUGHOUT)
V.O.: Champagne of the connoisseur.

427

ANNCR: According to the government, it costs 20¢ a mile to drive your car. For an average of 8½¢ a mile you can fly on People Express Airlines.

**Consumer Television
10 Seconds Single**

428
ART DIRECTORS
Ron Travisano
Paul Basile
WRITER
Jerry Della Femina
CLIENT
WABC-TV
DIRECTOR
Gerry Cotts
PRODUCTION CO.
Metzner Productions
AGENCY PRODUCER
Joanne Diglio
AGENCY
Della Femina, Travisano
& Partners

429
ART DIRECTOR
Stan Block
WRITER
Frank DiGiacomo
CLIENT
WNBC Radio
DIRECTOR
Mark Story
PRODUCTION CO.
Pfeifer Story Productions
AGENCY PRODUCER
Linda Tesa
AGENCY
Della Femina, Travisano
& Partners

430
ART DIRECTOR
Dennis D'Amico
WRITER
Bob Montell
CLIENT
MCI
DIRECTOR
Henry Sandbank
PRODUCTION CO.
Sandbank Films
AGENCY PRODUCER
Jerry Haynes
AGENCY
Ally & Gargano

431
ART DIRECTOR
Jeff Roll
WRITER
Bill Hamilton
CLIENT
Wienerschnitzel
DIRECTOR
Jim Hinton
PRODUCTION CO.
Wilson-Griak
AGENCY PRODUCER
Morty Baran
AGENCY
Chiat/Day-Los Angeles

428

(VIOLIN MUSIC)

HENNY YOUNGMAN: Tom Snyder, if you had your life to live over again... Don't do it.

ANNCR: He's Tom Snyder.
He's on Eyewitness News.
Tonight at 11.

429

ANNCR (VO): Howard Stern returns to New York as afternoon D.J. on 66 WNBC.

WOMAN: Papa, Howard's coming home.

MAN: Not to this home.

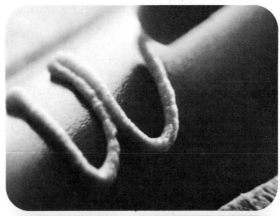

430

ANNCR (VO): Last year, Americans spent 36 billion on long distance.

Put your money into your pocket, instead of your phone.

Call MCI. The Nation's long distance phone company.

431

(MUSIC: ORIGINAL THROUGHOUT.)

SINGERS: *Wienerschnitzel, Wienerschnitzel, Weldon P. Wienerschnitzel Hot Dogs!*

432
ART DIRECTOR
Eric Hanson
WRITER
Bob Finley
CLIENT
Kay Bee Toy Stores
DIRECTOR
Jerry Collamer
PRODUCTION CO.
Team Productions
AGENCY PRODUCER
Bob Finley
AGENCY
Sachs, Finley/Los Angeles

433 GOLD
ART DIRECTOR
Michael Tesch
WRITER
Patrick Kelly
CLIENT
Federal Express
DIRECTOR
Patrick Kelly
PRODUCTION COS.
Hampton Road Films
Kelly Pictures
AGENCY PRODUCER
Maureen Kearns
AGENCY
Ally & Gargano

434
ART DIRECTOR
Amil Gargano
WRITER
Ron Berger
CLIENT
Calvin Klein
DIRECTOR
Adrian Lyne
PRODUCTION CO.
Jennie
AGENCY PRODUCER
Janine Marjollet
AGENCY
Ally & Gargano

435
ART DIRECTOR
Barbara Schubeck
WRITER
Jamie Seltzer
CLIENT
Georgia-Pacific Maisy
Daisy
DIRECTOR
Henry Sandbank
PRODUCTION CO.
Sandbank Films
AGENCY PRODUCER
Joe LaRosa
AGENCY
Altschiller, Reitzfeld,
Solin/NCK

432

VO: Toys are fun. Shopping for them should be too.
Kay Bee Toy Stores.

433 GOLD

(SFX: PAPER RUSTLING, SHAKING)

ANNCR (VO): You've got a lot riding on this letter.
And you going to hand it over to the Post
Office. Federal Express has an alternative.

434

ANNCR: Over 55 million Americans now struggle to stay in shape. For those who succeed, there's Calvin Klein's beautiful collection of Active Wear.

435

WOMAN: MD has 400 sheets per roll. About this much more than most other 2-plys.

If you don't think it's a lot . . . think of it when you're down to this.

436
ART DIRECTOR
Betsy Nathane
WRITER
Melissa Huffman
CLIENT
Wine World
DIRECTOR
Sid Avery
PRODUCTION CO.
Sid Avery & Associates
AGENCY PRODUCER
Marty Kleppel
AGENCY
keye/donna/pearlstein-
Beverly Hills

437
ART DIRECTOR
Dean Stefanides
WRITER
Steve Kasloff
CLIENT
Volvo
DIRECTOR
Rick Levine
PRODUCTION CO.
Levine/Pytka
AGENCY PRODUCER
Dane Johnson
AGENCY
Scali, McCabe, Sloves

438 SILVER
ART DIRECTOR
Dean Stefanides
WRITER
Earl Carter
CLIENT
Nikon
DIRECTOR
Dennis Chalkin
PRODUCTION CO.
Dennis Chalkin Productions
AGENCY PRODUCER
Gary Grossman
AGENCY
Scali, McCabe, Sloves

436

(SFX: SNIFFING BOUQUET)

ANNCR (VO): Is Beringer's new 1981 Chenin Blanc as delicious as last year's gold medal winner?

If you can tell them apart you've got a better nose than our wine-master.

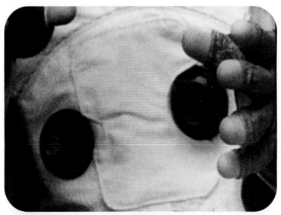

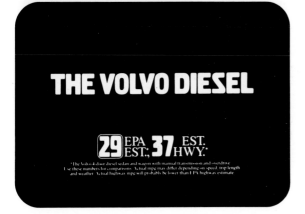

THE VOLVO DIESEL

29 EPA EST. **37** EST. HWY.*

*The Volvo 4-door diesel sedan and wagon with manual transmission and overdrive. Use these numbers for comparisons. Actual mpg may differ depending on speed, trip length and weather. Actual highway mpg will probably be lower than EPA highway estimate.

437

ANNCR (VO): Now there's even one *more* thing... that goes into a Volvo that lasts a long time. Announcing the Volvo Diesel.

438 SILVER

VO: When the space shuttle took off, one of the few things on board that didn't have a backup system... was a Nikon camera.

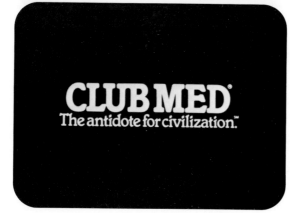

439
ANNCR: Club Med presents intensive tennis weeks.
Hours of expert lessons every day for players
whose game could use a little brushing up.

440
(MUSIC UNDER)

MOM: Listening to KYUU is one of those things you
as a person can do to help people who need you.
Take my son John, please.

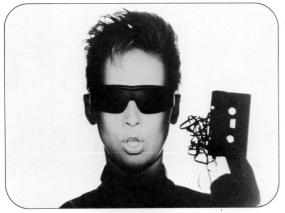

441

NEW WAVE WOMAN: New wave...shouldn't be recorded
    on punk tape.

ANNCR (VO): Maxell. It's worth it.

442

(MUSIC UNDER)

VO: If you're looking for challenge, our doors are
    wide open.

SUPER: U.S. ARMY. Be all you can be.

443 SILVER
ART DIRECTOR
George Euringer
WRITER
Helayne Spivak
CLIENT
MCI
DIRECTOR
Bob Giraldi
PRODUCTION CO.
Giraldi Productions
AGENCY PRODUCER
Jerry Haynes
AGENCY
Ally & Gargano

444
ART DIRECTOR
George Euringer
WRITER
Helayne Spivak
CLIENT
MCI
DIRECTOR
Bob Giraldi
PRODUCTION CO.
Giraldi Productions
AGENCY PRODUCER
Jerry Haynes
AGENCY
Ally & Gargano

445
ART DIRECTOR
Barry Vetere
WRITER
Tom Messner
CLIENT
Commodore
DIRECTOR
Mike Cuesta
PRODUCTION CO.
Griner/Cuesta
AGENCY PRODUCER
Bob Van Buren
AGENCY
Ally & Gargano

446 GOLD
ART DIRECTOR
George Euringer
WRITER
Tom Messner
CLIENT
MCI
DIRECTOR
Bob Giraldi
PRODUCTION CO.
Giraldi Productions
AGENCY PRODUCER
Jerry Haynes
AGENCY
Ally & Gargano

443 SILVER

(PHONE RINGS. A VERY SLEEPY WOMAN PICKS UP THE
　　PHONE)

MOM: Hullo?

DAVE: Mom? Surprise! It's Dave.

MOM: Dave?

DAVE: Your son. I'm sorry I woke you but the long
　　distance rates are cheapest after 11 p.m.

MOM: (SNORES)

DAVE: Mom? Put Dad on, Mom.

　　Dad? Dad? Mom?...

ANNCR (VO): To save 15 to 50% on long distance before
　　as well as after 11 p.m., call MCI.

　　And never reach out and wake someone again.

444

(SOUND OF PHONE RINGING. IT'S PICKED UP AND A VERY
　　SLEEPY VOICE SPEAKS):

LYN: Hullo?

HAROLD: Lyn? It's Harold. I'm calling long distance.

LYN: What time is it?

HAROLD: 2 a.m. your time, sleepy head!

LYN: 2 a.m.?

HAROLD: Oh, you wouldn't believe the money I save
　　by calling after 11 p.m.

LYN: Oh, really?

HAROLD: For sure.

LYN: I can save you even more money, Harold.

HAROLD: How, baby?

LYN: (CLICK AT RECEIVER IS HEARD)

ANNCR (VO): To save 15 to 50% on long distance before
　　as well as after 11 p.m., call MCI.

　　And stop talking in someone else's sleep.

445

MAN: Do do do do, hut hut hut... (CONT. UNDER ANNCR)

ANNCR (VO): There are those who worry that video game playing can become obsessive.
At Commodore, while we think that's a little extreme, increasing your game scores may not always increase your I.Q.

(MUSIC UNDER)
So Commodore's games come in a different package: A full-fledged computer, the VIC 20, that allows your mind to expand into the thousands of things a computer can do... In addition to playing games.

446 GOLD

(MUSIC UNDER)

MAN: Have you been talking to our son on long distance again?

WOMAN: (NODS AND WHIMPERS)

MAN: Did he tell you how much he loves you?

WOMAN: (NODS AND WHIMPERS)

MAN: Did he tell you how well he's doing in school?

WOMAN: (NODS AND WHIMPERS AND CRIES)

MAN: All those things are wonderful. What on earth are you crying for?

WOMAN: Did you see our long distance bill?

(MUSIC)

ANNCR (VO): If your long distance bills are too much, call MCI. Sure, reach out and touch someone. Just do it for a whole lot less.

447
ART DIRECTOR
Larry Leblang
WRITER
Mel Richman
CLIENT
Ryder Truck Rental
DIRECTOR
Henry Holtzman
PRODUCTION CO.
N. Lee Lacy
AGENCY PRODUCER
Nancie Brown
AGENCY
Mike Sloan Advertising/
Miami

448 GOLD
ART DIRECTOR
Dave Davis
WRITER
Bob Meury
CLIENT
Sony Corporation-
Betamax Components
DIRECTOR
Gary Princz
PRODUCTION CO.
EUE Productions
AGENCY PRODUCERS
Lois Rice
Bruce Giuriceo
AGENCY
Backer & Spielvogel

449 SILVER
ART DIRECTOR
Roy Grace
WRITER
Irwin Warren
CLIENT
Volkswagen
DIRECTOR
Henry Sandbank
PRODUCTION CO.
Sandbank Films
AGENCY PRODUCER
Bob Samuel
AGENCY
Doyle Dane Bernbach

450
ART DIRECTOR
Charles Baker
WRITER
Tim Crowther
CLIENT
Toyota Corona
DIRECTOR
Ross Nichols
PRODUCTION CO.
Ross Nichols Productions
AGENCY PRODUCER
Maureen Esse
AGENCY
D'Arcy McManus & Masius
P/L- Australia

447

MAN: Right now, you can rent any size gasoline-
powered truck in Ryder's fleet for one low daily
rate, plus the variable mileage charge.

Want a nice little truck?

That's the daily rate.

How about a little bigger?

Same rate.

Want one way out to here?

Still the same.

When Ryder rents trucks at this price, we
almost hate to let them go.

VO: Ryder. $29.95 a day for the best truck money
can rent.

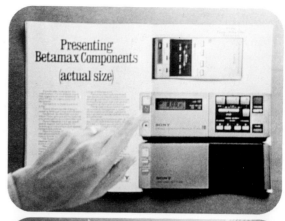

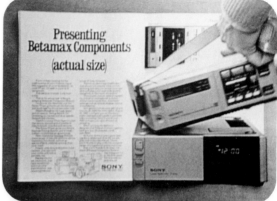

448 GOLD

ANNCR: Have you seen the latest ad for Sony
Betamax Components? There they are. Actual
size.

I can't believe it. They look so real. Oh. They are
real! This is terrific.

And look. A wireless remote control that does
just about everything. Let's see. Umm. Reverse,
whoh...whoh. And forward. In almost any
speed you want. Boy, that was fast. Umm, I'd
better put it back.

And Betamax Components are so compact and
lightweight, you can take the recorder anywhere
to shoot your own movies. This could be my big
chance!

Let's see. What else is there to play with. Oh, a
coupon. Oh, there's the Sony Trinicon Color
Camera. It gives you instant replay right
through the eyepiece...There's even an offer for
free tapes. Mmm...I think I'll keep the
coupon.

The Sony Betamax Component System.

You know what?

I think I'll keep the whole thing.

449 SILVER

(DRAMATIC MUSIC)

vo: Since 1975 we changed a few things on the Rabbit.

We made it faster.

We made it more economical.

We made it more reliable.

Seven years and 15,000 changes later, we improved the way the Rabbit runs,

not the way it looks.

450

(SOUND: 100% OPEN COUNTRY AMBIENCE. JUST THE HINT OF A WHISTLING BREEZE.)

(SFX: 100%. CORONA PULLS UP...ENGINE IS SWITCHED OFF...DOOR OPENS AND SHUTS...FOOTSTEPS AWAY.)

MALE VO (VERY UNDERSTATED): If all the Toyota Coronas sold in Australia were parked end to end...they'd reach from Melbourne...to Sydney.

That's a quarter of a million Coronas.

And a quarter of a million people who've chosen Corona for its reliability...comfort...and all-round good value.

A quarter of a million. That's a lot of Coronas.

But then, the Corona is a lot of car.

(SFX: 100%, FOOTSTEPS.)

(SFX: PARKING TICKET BEING TORN OFF AND SLAPPED ON.

Television Technique
Best Spokesperson
60 or 30 Seconds
Single

451
ART DIRECTOR
Dick Lemmon
WRITER
Jan Zechman
CLIENT
WKQX Radio
DIRECTOR
Tim Newman
PRODUCTION CO.
Jenkins/Covington/Newman
AGENCY PRODUCER
Liz Wedlan
AGENCY
Zechman & Associates/Chicago

Television Technique
Best Brand Image
60 or 30 Seconds
Single

452
ART DIRECTOR
Roy Tuck
WRITER
George Watts
CLIENT
Jamaica Tourist Board
DIRECTOR
Ed Barnett
PRODUCTION CO.
Johnston Films
AGENCY PRODUCER
Scott Kulok
AGENCY
Young & Rubicam

453
ART DIRECTOR
Barry Vetere
WRITER
Tom Messner
CLIENT
Commodore
DIRECTOR
Mike Cuesta
PRODUCTION CO.
Griner/Cuesta
AGENCY PRODUCER
Bob Van Buren
AGENCY
Ally & Gargano

454 SILVER
ART DIRECTORS
Mark Nussbaum
Bob Lenz
WRITER
Barry Lisee
CLIENT
Miller Brewing/High Life
DIRECTOR
Joe Hanwright
PRODUCTION CO.
Larkin Productions
AGENCY PRODUCER
Barry Lisee
AGENCY
Backer & Spielvogel

451

(ROCKERS: EACH LINE IS DELIVERED BY A DIFFERENT PUNK, ALTERNATING IN A RANDOM SEQUENCE.)

SCRATCH: We'd like to tell you about a really stupid radio station.

SIMON: Q101.

L.A.: They say the "Q" stands for quality music.

DENISE: What a laugh.

L.A.: They don't play "The Dead Boys"

DENISE: "The Flesh Eaters"

SIMON: "The Germs"

SCRATCH: All you get is Fleetwood Mac.

DENISE: Fogelberg.

L.A.: Best of the 60's.

SIMON: James Taylor.

DENISE: The Beatles.

SCRATCH: The Eagles.

L.A.: Nothing.

ANNCR: Q101. The Q is for quality music.

SIMON: They give you "Let's Lynch the Landlord"?

SCRATCH: Never.

452

SINGER: *Come back to Jamaica*

RUNNER: Come run on a ribbon of white sand.

SINGER: *What's old is what's new*

HOSTESS: Come sip blue mountain air.

SINGER: *We want you to join us*

BOAT CAPTAIN: Come ride our gentle tradewinds.

SINGER: *We made it for you*

PRIEST: Come share our happiness

SINGER: *So make it Jamaica*

WAITER: Come take tea by the sea.

SINGER: *Make it your own*

WOMAN #1: Come daydream in a private cove.

SINGER: *Make it Jamaica*

MAN: Come glide through enchanted evenings

SINGER: *Your new island home*

WOMAN #2: Come share the incomparable variety that brought Noel Coward home to Jamaica year after year. Come, make it Jamaica again. And again.

SINGER: *Make it Jamaica, your new island home.*

453

(MUSIC UNDER)

ANNCR (VO): Rather than compare personal computers ourselves,

we asked the computers which one was better on the basis of price and memory.

The Apple II preferred the Commodore 64.

Then we asked the IBM

and it picked the Commodore 64.

Then the Radio Shack chose

the Commodore 64.

That's what we like about our competition.

Theyre so honest.

The Commodore 64.

(MUSIC OUT)

454 SILVER

(MUSIC UNDER)

(VO): 'Round here, well I guess we take work about as serious as anybody else. But I'll tell you somethin' boys, come sundown ain't nobody more serious about havin' a good time.

(MUSIC IN): *Welcome to Miller Time. It's all yours, and it's all mine. Bring your thirsty self right here, you've got the time we've got the beer for what you had in mind. Welcome to Miller Time.*

(VO): The best beer for the best time of the day. Miller High Life.

(MUSIC): *Bring your thirsty self right here, you've got the time, we've got the beer for what you have in mind. Oh-oh; Welcome, you know you're welcome, welcome, everybody's welcome. Welcome to Miller Time. Yours and mine.*

455
ART DIRECTOR
Tony DeGregorio
WRITER
Ken Schulman
CLIENT
Sony
DIRECTOR
Bob Gaffney
PRODUCTION CO.
Bob Gaffney Productions
AGENCY PRODUCER
Dick Standridge
AGENCY
McCann-Erickson

456
ART DIRECTOR
Barry Vetere
WRITER
Tom Messner
CLIENT
Commodore
DIRECTOR
Mike Cuesta
PRODUCTION CO.
Griner/Cuesta
AGENCY PRODUCER
Bob Van Buren
AGENCY
Ally & Gargano

457
ART DIRECTOR
Joseph Puhy
WRITER
Mark Schneider
CLIENT
Lincoln-Mercury
DIRECTOR
Nick Lewin
PRODUCTION CO.
Jennie
AGENCY PRODUCER
Joseph Puhy
AGENCY
Young & Rubicam

458 GOLD
ART DIRECTOR
George Euringer
WRITER
Tom Messner
CLIENT
MCI
DIRECTOR
Bob Giraldi
PRODUCTION CO.
Giraldi Productions
AGENCY PRODUCER
Jerry Haynes
AGENCY
Ally & Gargano

455

ANNCR (VO): Paulatuk, the Arctic Circle
The winters can be ten months long and fifty degrees below.
So people stay home and watch a lot of TV.
Maybe that's why the Tatkiak family chose the only TV to win an Emmy for its beautiful picture.
The Sony Trinitron.
But maybe the Tatkiaks chose a Sony because the nearest TV repairman is two-hundred and fifty miles away.

456

(SFX: GAME)

ANNCR (VO): This kid just got a video game for Christmas. He can look forward to years of fun trying to reach 18,000,000.

(MUSIC UNDER)

This kid just got a Commodore VIC 20 home computer.

He can look forward to learning basic computer language, doing his own programs, and playing some games along the way.

And maybe even inventing his own games.

Oh, a final argument for the VIC 20.

Someday, both kids will be looking for a job.

(MUSIC OUT)

457

(MUSIC UNDER)

ANNCR (VO): Your perception of the American automobile is about to change.

(MUSIC)

For Mercury is redefining the future of the American car. Mercury is redefining the shape...

(MUSIC)

the handling...

(MUSIC)

the power...

(MUSIC)

the ride...

(MUSIC)

the performance... Mercury is redefining the quality and reshaping your view of the American automobile. Look and see what an American car can be.

Look to Mercury. The substance shows.

458 GOLD

(MUSIC UNDER)

MAN: Have you been talking to our son on long distance again?

WOMAN: (NODS AND WHIMPERS)

MAN: Did he tell you how much he loves you?

WOMAN: (NODS AND WHIMPERS)

MAN: Did he tell you how well he's doing in school?

WOMAN: (NODS AND WHIMPERS AND CRIES)

MAN: All those things are wonderful. What on earth are you crying for?

WOMAN: Did you see our long distance bill?

(MUSIC)

ANNCR (VO): If your long distance bills are too much, call MCI. Sure, reach out and touch someone. Just do it for a whole lot less.

**Television Technique
Best Brand Image
60 or 30 Seconds
Single**

459
ART DIRECTOR
Sal Sinare
WRITERS
Robert Black
Don Hadley
CLIENT
Alaska Tourism
DIRECTOR
Robert Abel
PRODUCTION CO.
Robert Abel
& Associates
AGENCY PRODUCER
Steve Neely
AGENCY
Foote, Cone & Belding/
Honig–San Francisco

460
ART DIRECTOR
Chuck Davidson
WRITER
Deanne Torbert Dunning
CLIENT
Piaget Polo Watches
DIRECTOR
Klaus Lucka
PRODUCTION CO.
Klaus Lucka Productions
AGENCY PRODUCER
Chuck Davidson
AGENCY
Harry Viola Advertising

461
ART DIRECTOR
Pedro Marin-Guzman
WRITERS
Dick Greenlan
Greg Alder
CLIENT
SRA
DIRECTOR
Bob Kersey
PRODUCTION CO.
Urban Bioscope
AGENCY PRODUCER
Ivan Robinson
AGENCY
Phillips, Horne, Greenlaw/
Australia

459

MAN: I guess I've wanted to go to Alaska since I was
an eight-year-old boy listening to my father talk
about it.

(MUSIC UP FULL)

SINGER: *Alaska is a story that my father told*
Of swift rivers running with salmon and gold.

Alaska is the feeling that won't let me be.

Alaska is the great land calling down to me.

Alaska.

Alaska is a river running wide and deep.

Sparkling with memories that are mine to keep.

Alaska is so many things I have never known.

Alaska is the great land calling me home.

(MUSIC BECOMES QUIET.)

MAN: I went to Alaska last year and I discovered an
interesting thing. That eight-year-old boy is
still alive.

SINGER: (SOFTLY) *Alaskaaaaaa.*

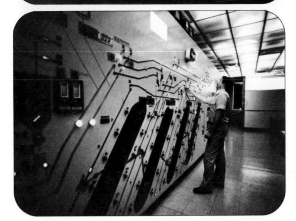

460

vo: Hand carved in Switzerland
Solid 18 carat gold
Water resistant quartz
The Piaget Polo day/date
The ultimate sports watch

461

(ELECTRONIC MUSIC THROUGHOUT)

ANNCR: If you have to send anything, anywhere, send it by train.

At the State Rail Authority you'll find the biggest freight service in Australia, with a 2,000 train network of computer-controlled schedules.

You'll find we serve the world's most modern coal facility at Port Waratah.

You'll find an overnight, interstate container service.

And a new parcel service that can speed across town or across the state at less cost than any other system.

At the State Rail Authority, we're not just building new trains, we're building a whole new railway.

462
ART DIRECTOR
Pedro Marin-Guzman
WRITER
Greg Alder
CLIENT
SRA
DIRECTOR
Bob Kersey
PRODUCTION CO.
Urban Bioscope
AGENCY PRODUCER
Ivan Robinson
AGENCY
Phillips, Horne, Greenlaw/
Australia

463
ART DIRECTOR
Bill Bate
WRITERS
Ian Mackrill
Peter Witcombe
CLIENT
Oasis Industries/
Schweppes Lemonade
DIRECTOR
Roy Thomas
PRODUCTION CO.
Ad-Film Ltd.
AGENCY PRODUCER
Ian Mackrill
AGENCY
Gray Scott Inch
Advertising Ltd./New Zealand

464
ART DIRECTOR
Chris Reeves
WRITER
Helen Lewis
CLIENT
Thomas Hardy & Sons
DIRECTOR
Tony Williams
PRODUCTION CO.
Marmalade Films
AGENCY PRODUCER
Helen Lewis
AGENCY
Leo Burnett Pty. Ltd./
Australia

462

(ELECTRONIC MUSIC THROUGHOUT)

ANNCR: If you take a train to work you'll find we've been to work on the trains.

You'll find electronic signalling that's more efficient.

Stations that have been rejuvenated. Parking stations that are free.

New tracks that can handle more trains.

New trains that are more comfortable.

And new computers that help them run on time.

Take a train, and you'll find what thousands of new passengers have already found.

At the State Rail Authority, we're not just building new trains, we're building a whole new railway.

463

BUTLER: A drink, Madam?

PENELOPE KEITH: Ah yes, Barringer. A long drink this evening, please.

BUTLER: Could I recommend a Classic Dry Lemonade on ice?

P.K.: That's a mixer, Barringer!

BUTLER: That's Schwepping, Madam.

P.K.: Schwepping?

BUTLER: Schwepping is Classic Dry Lemonade in a tall glass.

Ah Madam...everyone these days drinks Classic Dry Lemonade long.

P.K.: Everyone!

Well it's *far* too good for them.

464

WOMAN: Jonathon! I always thought his name was John, didn't I, John?

(SHE FADES UNDER)

VO: National boring dinner party championship's bronze medallist.

MAN: It's my first effort at, y'know, building a fence...

VO: silver medallist...

MAN: (CONTD) It's very... sturdy, isn't it Mother?

(SFX: SNORES)

VO: and here's the gold medallist, and grand champion.

VO: At this dinner party however, Hardy's Old Castle Riesling was served, so it simply wasn't in the contest.

Hardy's Old Castle Riesling.

Always enjoyable,

Never boring!

465 GOLD
ART DIRECTORS & WRITERS
Steve Diamant
Rick Boyko

CLIENT
Handgun Control

DIRECTOR
Cosimo

PRODUCTION CO.
Cosimo Productions

AGENCY PRODUCERS
Steve Diamant
Rick Boyko

466
ART DIRECTOR
Julie Brumfield

WRITER
Ira Sitomer

CLIENT
United Negro College Fund

DIRECTOR
John Danza

PRODUCTION CO.
Birbrower/Danza

AGENCY PRODUCER
Ted Storb

AGENCY
Young & Rubicam

467
ART DIRECTOR
Lou Colletti

WRITER
Lee Garfinkel

CLIENT
Anti-Graffiti

DIRECTOR
Bob Giraldi

PRODUCTION CO.
Giraldi Productions

AGENCY PRODUCER
Rachel Novak

AGENCY
Levine, Huntley, Schmidt
& Beaver

465 GOLD

ANNCR (VO): In Japan last year, 48 people lost their lives to handguns...

ANNCR (VO): In Great Britain...8.

ANNCR (VO): In Canada 52.

ANNCR (VO): And in the United States...10,728.

ANNCR (VO): God bless America

466

(SFX: TRUCK STOPPING)

(MUSIC UNDER)

MAN: Ready lift.

ANNCR (VO): Sometimes you have to use your muscles while you are learning to use your mind. This part-time gardener is a full time college student. He attends one of the forty-two private predominantly Black Colleges and Universities of The United Negro College Fund. He's working because it's the only way he can afford college. He wants an education too much to give up.

When you support the fund, you help keep his tuition down, so with this part-time job, he can continue his education.

MAN: Leon.

ANNCR (VO): And when he graduates he can make his own contribution to society.

Help a college student help himself.

MAN: Hey, do a good job on that exam you hear!

ANNCR (VO): Support the United Negro College Fund. The mind is a terrible thing to waste.

467

PACO: Music is part of our lives.

RAY: It represents our culture, our tradition, our beauty.

EDDIE: What's on these walls is not part of that beauty and culture.

CELIA: (IN SPANISH) Writing on the walls is not prestigious. Please do not write on the walls.

JOE FRAZIER: We got where we are today by wrecking other fighters.

MARVIS FRAZIER: That's right pop, not by wrecking our city's walls.

MIKE NEWLIN: Look at this junk. Graffiti doesn't make your life better. It just makes your neighborhood look worse.

Hey, make your mark in society. Not on society.

**Public Service
Television Single**

468
ART DIRECTOR
Bruce Dundore
WRITER
Fred Siegel
CLIENT
NY City Department
of Sanitation
DIRECTOR
Bert Steinhauser
PRODUCTION CO.
Bert Steinhauser Productions
AGENCY PRODUCER
Sandy Bachom
AGENCY
Backer & Spielvogel

469
ART DIRECTOR
Lou Colletti
WRITER
Lee Garfinkel
CLIENT
Anti-Graffiti
DIRECTOR
Bob Giraldi
PRODUCTION CO.
Giraldi Productions
AGENCY PRODUCER
Rachel Novak
AGENCY
Levine, Huntley, Schmidt
& Beaver

470 SILVER
ART DIRECTOR
Gary Alfredson
WRITERS
Mabon Childs
John Dymun
CLIENT
PA Committee for Effective
Justice
DIRECTOR
John Pytka
PRODUCTION CO.
Joseph Pytka Productions
AGENCY
Ketchum Advertising/
Pittsburgh

471
ART DIRECTOR
Ron Spataro
WRITER
Joe Baraban
CLIENT
Lung Association
DIRECTOR
Joe Baraban
PRODUCTION CO.
Joe Baraban
AGENCY PRODUCER
Ron Spataro
AGENCY
Bozell & Jacobs of Houston

468

(SFX: TRAIN.)

(SFX: TRAIN COMES TO A HALT.)

(SFX: TRAIN STARTS UP AGAIN.)

ANNCR (VO): Garbage. You don't have to put up with
it anymore. New York, let's clean up New York.

469

(SFX: SUBWAY OR STREET)

GENE: My name is Gene Anthony Ray. You know me
as Leroy from "Fame." When I was growing up
in Harlem I really wanted to be a dancer. I
knew it was going to be tough. But I had talent
and it would have been stupid to waste it.

That's why I can't believe it when I see kids
wasting their talent messing up walls with
graffiti. If you want to make something out of
your life, you can. You just have to use your
talent the smart way.

'Cause believe me, fame is seeing your name up
in lights. *Not* seeing it sprayed on the subway.

ANNCR: Make your mark in society. Not on society.

This message brought to you by the Mayor's Task
Force on Graffiti.

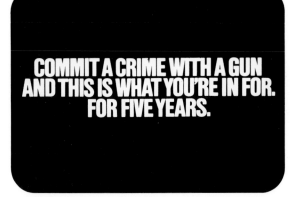

470 SILVER

INMATE #1: Have you ever heard a tough guy cry? Yeah, I hear 'em crying here every night.

VO: Pennsylvania has a new law.

INMATE #2: Steel, concrete, cold, hatred, bitterness. This is every single day.

VO: From now on, a crime with a gun means you're in for five years.

INMATE #3: Imagine being in a cell, 5 ft. by 8 ft., with a guy you don't even like.

VO: No deals. No parole, no exceptions.

INMATE #4: There are times in here when you become so desperate you want to call out to someone, you want to talk to someone, but there is nobody who cares.

VO: Five years is a ton of time.

INMATE #5: Sometimes you wake up in the night-time and you will scream. That's how bad it is in here. This is a hard situation. You don't want to come in here.

VO: Commit a crime with a gun and this is what you're in for.

(SFX: CELL DOOR SLAMS.)

VO: For five years.

471

(SFX: MUFFLED SOUND OF ADULT'S HACKING COUGH HEARD FROM BEHIND DOOR OF PARENTS' BEDROOM.)

(SFX: MUFFLED COUGHING CONTINUES AS CONCERNED LITTLE GIRL COMES DOWN HALLWAY.)

(SFX: AS LITTLE GIRL OPENS DOOR TO PARENTS' BEDROOM, LOUDER UNMUFFLED COUGHING IS HEARD.)

GIRL: Is daddy going to be all right?

ANNCR (VO): No.

Public Service
Television Single

472
ART DIRECTOR
Jim Fitts
WRITERS
Jon Goward
Michael Feinberg
CLIENT
American Red Cross
DIRECTOR
Jim Fitts
PRODUCTION CO.
Barbara Swallow Productions
AGENCY PRODUCER
Jim Fitts
AGENCY
ClarkeGowardCarr & Fitts/Boston

473
ART DIRECTORS
Abby Dix
Dick Willis
WRITER
Jeff Bremser
CLIENT
Butterfield Youth Services
DIRECTOR
Dick Willis
PRODUCTION CO.
DIX & Associates
AGENCY PRODUCER
Abby Dix
AGENCY
DIX & Associates/Kansas City

Public Service
Television Campaign

474 GOLD
ART DIRECTOR
Gary Alfredson
WRITERS
Mabon Childs
John Dymun
CLIENT
PA Committee for Effective
Justice
DIRECTOR
John Pytka
PRODUCTION CO.
Joseph Pytka Productions
AGENCY
Ketchum Advertising/
Pittsburgh

472

(SFX: HEARTBEAT GRADUALLY SLOWING DOWN)

The adult human body contains from 4 to 6 quarts of blood. If you lose just one quart rapidly, you have minutes to replace it. However, if enough people haven't been giving blood, finding it may be extremely difficult. Because unfortunately, we at the Red Cross can only give what we get.

(SFX: HEARTBEAT STOPS)

The Red Cross. We're out for blood.

473

MAN IN CAR: Get out of here. Go on, get out of here. I said get out of here, now. NOW!

MALE (VO): America's throw-away society includes its children. Believe it or not, thousands of kids are discarded every year—abandoned like so much worthless trash.

At Butterfield Youth Services, we exist for one reason: To help the kids nobody wants. And we can only stay in existence with your help. Write or call for information. Butterfield Youth Services, Marshall, Missouri. Help us give these kids a chance. Fade out music.

474 GOLD

INMATE #1: What is prison like? It...It hurts...prison hurts.

(SFX: CELL DOOR SLAMS.)

475

ANNCR: Bill Emrich, who's mentally retarded, lives in a supervised group home. But, during the day, he works on a county road crew, putting up highway guide posts. Posts that will help keep Bill, and his neighbors, safe. Being retarded never stopped anyone from being a good neighbor.

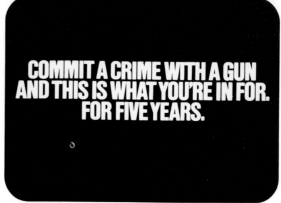

476 SILVER

INMATE #1: Have you ever heard a tough guy cry? Yeah, I hear 'em crying here every night.

VO: Pennsylvania has a new law.

INMATE #2: Steel, concrete, cold, hatred, bitterness. This is every single day.

VO: From now on, a crime with a gun means you're in for five years.

INMATE #3: Imagine being in a cell, 5 ft. by 8 ft., with a guy you don't even like.

VO: No deals. No parole, no exceptions.

INMATE #4: There are times in here when you become so desperate you want to call out to someone, you want to talk to someone, but there is nobody who cares.

VO: Five years is a ton of time.

INMATE #5: Sometimes you wake up in the night-time and you will scream. That's how bad it is in here. This is a hard situation. You don't want to come in here.

VO: Commit a crime with a gun and this is what you're in for.

(SFX: CELL DOOR SLAMS.)

VO: For five years.

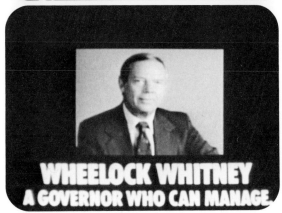

WHEELOCK WHITNEY
A GOVERNOR WHO CAN MANAGE.

Polling Place →

WHITNEY
A GOVERNOR
WHO CAN MANAGE.

477

ANNCR (VO): Most politicians these days don't seem to be able to give you a clear vision of the future.

Whether it's the economy, taxes or unemployment...

...the answers seem to get more and more blurred.

In fact, sometimes it almost seems as if they don't *want* you to see.

On November 2nd, you can begin to get the clear, focused answers you deserve about Minnesota's future.

Vote for Wheelock Whitney...a Governor who can manage.

478

ANNCR (VO): A lot of your friends and neighbors are taking trips out of Minnesota...

...following the companies who were forced to take trips out of Minnesota because of taxes...and move to states where business and full employment are encouraged by government. There's one way to stop all these trips out of state...

...on September 14th take a short trip to your polling booth and vote for Wheelock Whitney...a Governor who can manage.

479

SENATOR ORRIN HATCH (VO): Our future in this country depends upon the education of our children. I see in our young people more desire to learn, more desire to progress, and more desire to be involved. We have exceptional young people today.

ANNCR: America has turned some sort of corner in the last two years. Almost without knowing it, the Seventies became the Eighties, and with it, a new Administration, a new majority in the U.S. Senate, a new conservative style of thinking... a new kind of leadership: Senator Orrin Hatch.

ATTORNEY GENERAL SMITH: The Amendment to Section Two is just bad legislation. I yield not an inch to Senator Kennedy...

SENATOR TED KENNEDY: Do you want to explain it then Mr. General?

ATTORNEY GENERAL: No, I don't think this is the time or the place to do that.

KENNEDY: Well, if you're going to say that I have misstated...

SENATOR HATCH: Mr. Kennedy...

KENNEDY: Excuse me Mr. Chairman, but...

HATCH: Mr. Kennedy, let him answer the question and you'll be able to ask any questions you want.

KENNEDY: He's said that I have misstated...

HATCH: You've just accused the Administration of some things that are inaccurate, he says. Now let him finish showing you how inaccurate they are.

KENNEDY: All right.

SENATOR HATCH (VO): It's a lot what I thought it would be, but it's also so much more. I never dreamed of the difficulties of being a Senator. I never dreamed of the times that you have to stand up and how difficult it is sometimes to stand up, because sometimes, you're just not sure. Nobody can have all of the answers, and I certainly don't claim to have them. Being a Senator is a very difficult thing, but it's also a very rewarding thing. You feel like you're really helping the people in your State. I believe in what I'm doing or I wouldn't do it. I believe in the future of my children, and I'm going to insure for all children, including my own, that there's a future, like there was for me.

ANNCR: Senator Orrin Hatch.

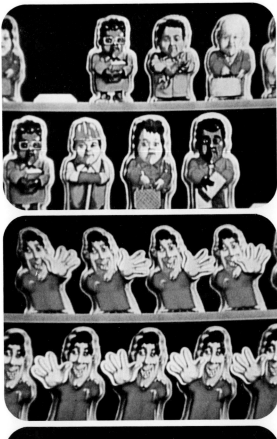

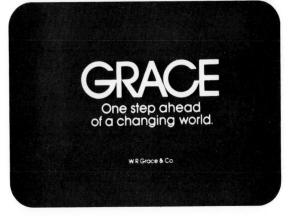

GRACE
One step ahead
of a changing world.

W R Grace & Co

480

(SFX: SHOOTING GALLERY)

ANNCR (VO): In the past four years unemployment in Minnesota has more than doubled from 72,000 to over 148,000...teachers, office workers, miners, executives, factory workers...in fact, just about the only Minnesotans who haven't been affected by unemployment...are...politicians. What Minnesota doesn't need is more promises. What we do need is more answers. Wheelock Whitney...a Governor who can manage.

481

VO: This is the product of an unproductive economy. Our economy.

We once thought it just couldn't happen here. But from the early '60s to the late '70s, America's growth in productivity decreased by 85 percent.

Investment growth in factories and equipment dropped by 75 percent.

And hidden in those statistics are countless losses: Lost jobs, lost incomes, lost dreams.

At W. R. Grace, we consider the loss of any American industry a death in the family.

And even though our interests are worldwide, our first responsibility is to revive productivity at home.

Start with your own job. If you see a better way to do it, do it.

The drive and dreams that first built America's factories are needed now to re-open them. And each of us holds the key.

At W. R. Grace, we want all of us to stay one step ahead of a changing world.

6

Index

Index

Production Companies

Agencies

Clients

WE MAKE VERY MAGNETIC TAPE.

Exceptional tape attracts exceptional customers. People who'll pay a little more for quality and keep coming back for it.

For example, Maxell audio tape is so good it brings in customers who buy over 40% more cassettes in a year than the average cassette buyer.

And according to research, Maxell has a more loyal following than any other tape. So much so that 2 out of every 3 people who walk out of your store with one of our cassettes planned on doing it before they even came through your door.

So maybe you should stock up on Maxell, and see how magnetic a magnetic tape can be.

maxell
IT'S WORTH IT.